THE CELTS

FRANK DELANEY

by the same author

James Joyce's Odyssey
Betjeman Country

THE CELTS

FRANK DELANEY

Little, Brown and Company

Boston   Toronto

First U.S. Edition

First published in Great Britain 1986 by
BBC Publications and Hodder & Stoughton Ltd.

Library of Congress Cataloging-in-Publication Data

Delaney, Frank, 1942–
  The Celts.

  1. Celts.   I. Title.
D70. D38   1987   909'.04916   87–16853
ISBN 0–316–17993–0

PRINTED IN THE UNITED STATES OF AMERICA

For my dear friend, Susan Collier

ILLUSTRATIONS

PICTURE ACKNOWLEDGMENTS

Pages 20–21 Dr J. Biel, Landesdenkmalamt, Baden-Württemberg; 27 Hallstatt Museum: 33 (top),
39, 42 (top) Mansell Collection; 42 (bottom) Courtesy of the Trustees of the British Museum; 43
Mansell Collection; 47 Bulloz; 57 Mansell Collection; 65 Eric Lessing/Magnum, from The John
Hillelson Agency (Naturhistorisches Museum, Vienna); 66 Eric Lessing/Magnum, from The John
Hillelson Agency (Hallstatt Museum); 67, 68 Eric Lessing/Magnum, from The John Hillelson Agency
(Naturhistorisches Museum, Vienna); 69 Dr J. Biel, Landesdenkmalamt, Baden-Württemberg; 70
Eric Lessing/Magnum, from The John Hillelson Agency (Württembergisches Landesmuseum,
Stuttgart); 71 (top) Dr J. Biel, Landesdenkmalamt, Baden-Württemberg; 71 (bottom) Eric Lessing/
Magnum, from The John Hillelson Agency (Württembergisches Landesmuseum, Stuttgart);
72 Eric Lessing/Magnum, from The John Hillelson Agency; 73 Lauros-Giraudon (Musée des
Antiquités Nationales, Saint Germain en Laye); 74 Werner Forman Archive; 75, 76, 77 Aerofilms
Ltd; 78 (top) Werner Forman Archive; 78 (bottom) Brian Brake, from The John Hillelson Agency;
79 (top) Giraudon (Museo Capitolino, Rome); 79 (Bottom) David Richardson; 80 Musei Capitolini,
Rome (Barbara Malter); 89 (top) BBC Hulton Picture Library; 89 (centre) Mansell Collection; 89
(bottom) Musée des Beaux-Arts, Beaune; 93 BBC Hulton Picture Library; 113 Eric Lessing/
Magnum, from The John Hillelson Agency (British Museum); 114 Eric Lessing/Magnum, from
The John Hillelson Agency (Salzburger Museum Carolino Augusteum, Salzburg); 115 Eric Les-
sing/Magnum, from The John Hillelson Agency (British Museum); 116 Historisches Museum, Bern,
photo S. Rebsamen; 117 Werner Forman Archive (British Museum); 118 Eric Lessing/Magnum,
from The John Hillelson Agency (Museum Novo Mesto, Slovenia, Yugoslavia); 119 (top) Württembergisches Landesmuseum, Stuttgart; 119 (bottom) Eric Lessing/Magnum, from The John
Hillelson Agency (Museum für Vor- und Frühgeschichte, Saarbrücken); 120 Werner Forman
Archive (National Museum of Ireland, Dublin); 122 (top) Werner Forman Archive (Musée Archéologique de Breteuil, Oise); 122 (bottom), 123 (left) Courtesy of The Trustees of the British
Museum; 123 (right) Werner Forman Archive (British Museum); 124 Courtesy of The Trustees of
the British Museum; 125 (left) Eric Lessing/Magnum, from The John Hillelson Agency (British
Museum); 125 (right) Courtesy of The Trustees of the British Museum; 126 (top left) Bulloz (Musée
des Antiquités Nationales, Saint Germain en Laye); 126 (top right); Giraudon (Musée des Antiquités
Nationales, Saint Germain en Laye); 126 (bottom left) Documentation Photographique de la
Réunion des Musées Nationaux (Musée des Antiquités Nationales, Saint Germain en Laye); 126
(bottom right) Courtesy of The Trustees of the National Museums of Scotland; 127 (left) Eric
Lessing/Magnum, from The John Hillelson Agency (Naturhistorisches Museum, Vienna); 127 (right)
Werner Forman Archive (British Museum); 128 Courtesy of the Trustees of the British Museum;
131 (left) Hallstatt Museum; 131 (right) Prähistorisches Abteilung, Naturhistorisches Museum,
Vienna; 148, 149 BBC Hulton Picture Library; 161 (top) Eric Lessing/Magnum, from The John

Hillelson Agency (Naturhistorisches Museum, Vienna); 161 (bottom) Documentation Photographique de la Réunion des Musées Nationaux (Musée des Antiquités Nationales. Saint Germain en Laye); 162 Eric Lessing/Magnum, from The John Hillelson Agency (Museum Joanneum, Graz); 163 Eric Lessing/Magnum, from The John Hillelson Agency (Musée Archéologique, Dijon); 164 Documentation Photographique de la Réunion des Musées Nationaux (Musée des Antiquités Nationales, Saint Germain en Laye); 165, 166 Werner Forman Archive (National Museum, Copenhagen); 167 Eric Lessing/Magnum, from The John Hillelson Agency (National Museum, Copenhagen); 168 Eric Lessing/Magnum, from The John Hillelson Agency (Musée Borely, Marseille); 169 Eric Lessing/Magnum, from The John Hillelson Agency (Musée Borely, Marseille); 170 (top and bottom) and 171 (The Book of Kells, f34r, f29r and f28v) The Board of Trinity College, Dublin; 172 and 173 (The Lindisfarne Gospels, Cotton MS Nero D. iv, f26v and f139) The British Library Board; 174 National Museum of Ireland, Dublin; 175 Belzeaux-Zodiaque (National Museum of Ireland, Dublin); 176 National Museum of Ireland, Dublin; 183 Welsh Arts Council; 183 Welsh Folk Museum, Cardiff; 190 Courtesy of 'Punch'; 191 BBC Hulton Picture Library; 196 Marc Riboud, from The John Hillelson Agency; 197 (top) Aberdeen City Libraries; 197 (bottom) National Museums of Scotland; 210 National Galleries of Scotland, Edinburgh; 211, 220 Mansell Collection 221 Michel Philippot/Sygma, from The John Hillelson Agency.

THE TEXT

The author and publishers are grateful for permission to quote from the following:
Oxford University Press for *The Tain* by Thomas Kinsella and *Early Irish Lyrics* by Gerard Murphy; Penguin for S:A. Handford's translation of Caesar's *The Conquest of Gaul* and *Selected Poems* by Dafydd ap Gwilym translated by Rachel Bromwich; Macmillan, London and Basingstoke, for poems by W.B. Yeats from *Collected Poems* and *A Vision*, and from *Later Poems 1972–1982* by R.S. Thomas; Faber & Faber for *The White Goddess* by Robert Graves; A.D. Peters and Company for Frank O'Connor's translation of *The Midnight Court* by Brian Merriman; the Royal Irish Academy for *The Celtic Ethnography of Posidonius* by J.J. Tierney; David Higham Associates for 'The force that drives the green fuse through the flower' by Dylan Thomas from *The Poems* published by Dent; and Canongate Publishing for *Springtide and Neaptide – Selected Poems, 1932–72* by Sorley MacLean.

AUTHOR'S ACKNOWLEDGMENTS

This book originated alongside a series of television programmes for BBC2 in London. Six fifty-five-minute documentaries, with a short introductory feature, were filmed in several international locations across Europe from Hungary to Western Ireland, and in North America, in a co-production which included FR 3 in Rennes and the national television network of Austria. To the following people involved in the making of the series I wish to express my thanks.

David Richardson, Producer and Director, filmed the programmes and contributed valuably and extensively to the editorial process. His clear and constructive direction, his visualisation of the subject matter, his wish to break new ground, provided stimulus and influences which greatly aided the writing task. He also proved to be a valuable editor of ideas, and for these and other gifts – his commitment, his overall clearheadedness, his rigorousness, his capacity to attend to detail – I am enormously grateful.

Tony MacAuley, a Senior Producer with the BBC in Northern Ireland, contributed similar support, especially in the fleshing-out of the original idea, in the consideration of music and other aspects of Celtic culture – and he remained tactful, inventive, wise and thoughtful. I am deeply thankful to him for help above and beyond the call of duty.

Cindy Watson researched the series and provided valuable references, introduced expert interviewees and possibilities, offered suggestions to the production team which proved fruitful and interesting as well as authoritative. The production office in Glasgow, under the aegis of Executive Producer, Gordon Menzies, was administered by Joan Townend, Production Assistant on most locations to David Richardson – in which capacities she arranged travel and facilities: her opposite number in Belfast, Maeve Armstrong, was equally effective on the Irish locations, and in Scotland and North America. To them I owe much gratitude: likewise to Glenda James, Assistant Producer, and Richard Lewis, Executive Producer for BBC Wales.

The principal cameramen on the series were Douglas Campbell in Scotland and Russ Walker in Wales; to them and their crews, including sound recordist, Mike Donald, and lighting engineer, Graham Hopkins, I wish to offer my sincere appreciation. At all times their efforts made a taxing schedule easier to work through and their professional competence and cooperation were exemplary, especially when there seemed an excess of water or mud or smoke in the proceedings. I wish further to thank Brian Wenham, Director of Television Broadcasting at the BBC and Graeme MacDonald, Controller of BBC2, for their encouragement, advice and assistance when needed – and to Patrick Chalmers, Controller, BBC Scotland.

In the writing of this book I received immense support from my editor, Ion Trewin, Editorial Director of Hodder & Stoughton: not for the first time did his advice and sympathy prove enabling, especially at times of great pressure. Eric Major, Managing Director of Hodder & Stoughton, was similarly supportive, and I am further grateful – and yet again – to my agents, Michael Shaw and Sue Freathy at Curtis Brown. Sarah Smith, Head of the Illustrations Department at BBC Publications, supplied remarkable cooperation, with photographs culled from a wide and varied range of sources, and all accomplished with great speed and good humour, and I am grateful, too, to Tony Kingsford at BBC Publications for his part in the editorial process.

When the project began – and all through filming – I had occasion to refer to a number of authorities whose names may already appear in their rightful place among the authors listed in the select bibliography, but I would particularly like to single out and thank the following people, (even if, in some cases, their works have already been mentioned): the consultants to the television series, Professor William Gillies at Edinburgh, Professor Proinsias MacCana at the Institute of Advanced Studies in Dublin, Professor Kenneth O. Morgan at the Queens College in Oxford, Dr Richard White, Director of Gwynnedd Archaeological Trust at the University of Bangor in North Wales. My particular thanks go to Professor Charles Thomas at the University of Exeter for thoughtful help, support and guidance in the early stages of the project and at intervals throughout, and for his hospitality and that of his wife, Jessica Mann. Professor Barry Cunliffe at Oxford, Dr Maire de Paor and Dr Liam de Paor in Dublin, Dr Peter Reynolds at Butser in Hampshire, Dr Anne Ross in Southampton, Dr Jean le Dhu in Brittany, Dr Gwynfor Evans in Wales, Dr Bryan MacMahon in County Kerry, Mr Ulick O'Connor in Dublin and Dr Jorg Biel in Stuttgart all made contributions by way of advice or interview which greatly assisted my work.

Finally I must record my appreciation of the work of my secretary Sheila Jordan, in respect of whom the word 'painstaking' is particularly appropriate. Her care and attention, her extra research assistance, her overall command of detail relating to both television series and book, added an extra dimension of support without which such a long and demanding project would have proved much more difficult, perhaps impossible.

CONTENTS

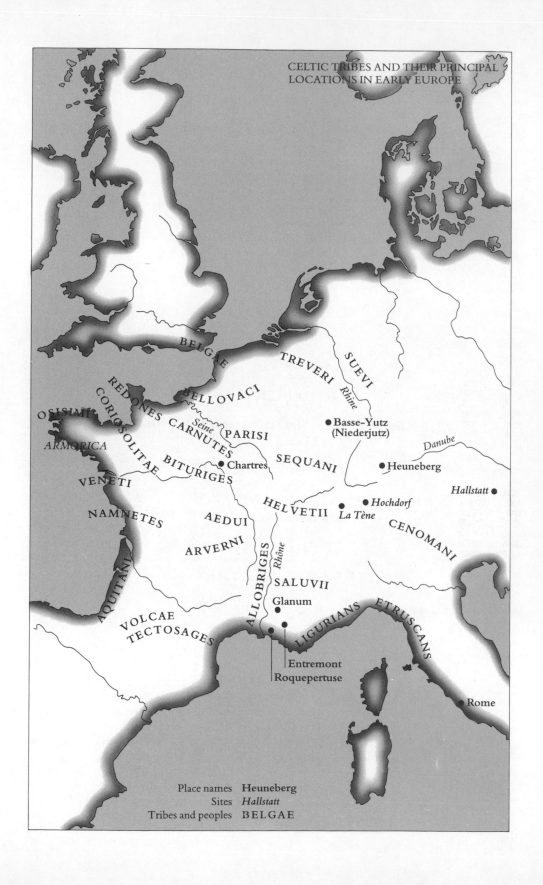

CELTIC TRIBES AND THEIR PRINCIPAL
LOCATIONS IN EARLY EUROPE

Rhine

Seine

BELGAE

TREVERI SUEVI

BELLOVACI

REDONES

CORIOSOLITAE

CARNUTES

PARISI

SEQUANI

Danube

OSISIMI

ARMORICA

BITURIGES

Chartres

Heuneberg

Hallstatt

VENETI

AEDUI

HELVETII

Hochdorf

NAMNETES

ARVERNI

La Tène

CENOMANI

AQUITANI

ALLOBRIGES

Rhône

SALUVII

Glanum

VOLCAE
TECTOSAGES

LIGURIANS

ETRUSCANS

Entremont
Roquepertuse

Rome

Basse–Yutz
(Niederjutz)

Place names   **Heuneberg**
Sites   *Hallstatt*
Tribes and peoples   BELGAE

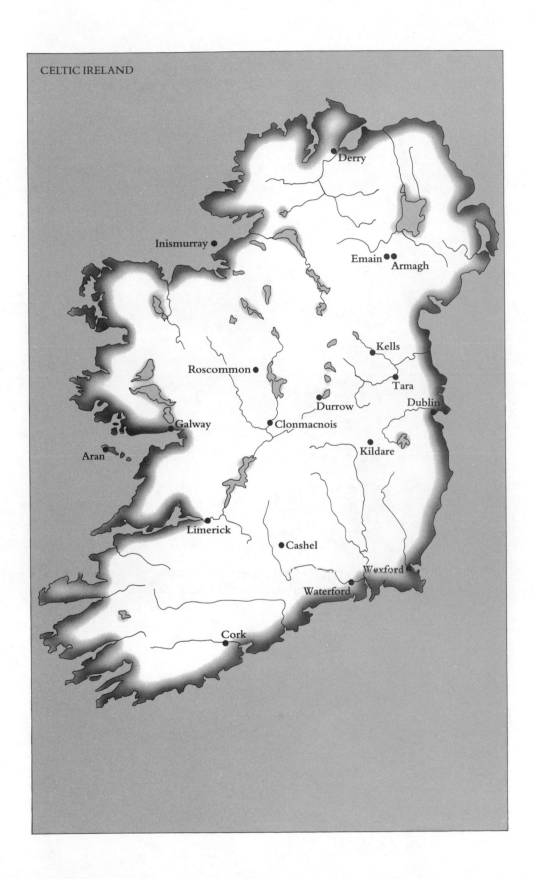

CELTIC IRELAND

Derry

Inismurray

Emain Armagh

Kells

Roscommon

Tara

Durrow Dublin

Galway Clonmacnois

Aran Kildare

Limerick

Cashel

Wexford

Waterford

Cork

THE 1ST CENTURY BC: CELTIC BRITAIN
AND NORTHERN GAUL

SKYE

TAEZALI

CALEDONES

VENICONES

● Mons Graupius

DAMNONII

● Edinburgh

Glasgow ●

● Lindisfarne

SELGOVAE

······ Hadrian's Wall

BRIGANTES

● Whitby

ISLE OF MAN

PARISI

ANGLESEY

● Beaumaris

● Caernarvon

DECEANGLI

CORITANI

ICENI

Aberystwyth ●

ORDOVICES

TRINOVANTES

DYFED

CATUVELLAUNI

● Colchester

SILURES

St Albans ●

London ●

CANTII

● Canterbury

ATREBATES

DUMNONII

DUROTRIGES

Tintagel ●

BELGAE

BELLOVACI

REDONES

PARISI

OSISIMI

INTRODUCTION

Roots. Ancestral, or folk, or race memory. Genetic recollections created centuries before we were born, by those tribes and seeds we sprang from. Whose unnameable moods and feelings we carry around. Whose inexplicable pulses – felt but not understood – we enjoy.

Such random thoughts – untrained, even dangerous – follow the very word 'Celt'. Of all the people on Europe's mass, do the Celts inspire, at first sight, the quickest imagination – and the least discrimination? The word 'Celtic' excites immediately, automatically, a host of images: memories of gold and music, of bards, princes and Druids, of fighting, talking and horsemanship – or pictures of thatched cottages, round towers, harps, high crosses, rocky coasts and shawls. A cliché is a phrase worn smooth by rubbing.

When I was invited some years ago by the BBC to consider writing and presenting a series of television programmes about the Celts, the original, tentative proposal suggested six half-hours of music and song, somewhat light-hearted, generous. As the idea expanded, and more co-producers came to the table, it became apparent to all concerned that the Celts advanced a case for more suitable treatment: mere kilts and *ceilidhes* could not begin to tell the tale. The enormous body of scholarly material, and the brilliant, jewelled antiquities bore sincere witness to a people whose identity had become diffuse and confused. Yet the same surprisingly simple question cropped up again and again: who were the Celts?

If the question had to be asked, it had to be answered. General knowledge agreed that the Celts originated somewhere in Europe, perhaps the Eastern bloc, perhaps even further east; that they now live on the West Atlantic seaboard, Ireland and Brittany, in the Highlands and islands of Scotland, in Wales, and more fragmentarily in Cornwall and on the Isle of Man; and that they might even have contributed in some way to the gypsy population of Britain. Aha! Did this mean they derived – like the word 'Gypsy' – from Egypt? But what about the physical descriptions – the Irish and Scots, tall, fair-skinned and fair-haired, and the Welsh, small and dark, stocky and a little swarthy? More clichéd impressions came out to play. The Celts went naked and shouting into battle. And such famous hospitality. They practised polygamy. And all those gorgeous brooches and chalices.

Many other civilisations also summon wonder: the Incas, the Egyptians, the Chinese, the Minoans, the Mayans. How did the Celts differ from any such post-primitive, prehistoric people in a temperate climate, who made the same giant leap from food-hunting to food-production? And alongside other fabulous civilisations, did the Celts also carve hieroglyphics; or predict by auguries; or raise massive and mysterious stone structures; or dwell in strange, citied forests? Clearly the most important task must be to separate the fact from the legendary impression. Not the simplest mission: the Irish, for instance, teach as history the existence of an ancestral people who cast spells and made magic, the race of Dana, a goddess.

The academic and archaeological sources reveal that at the height of their civilisation the people called 'Celts' wrote down nothing of themselves, no European literature in the classical sense of the Greeks or Romans. Western literacy had hardly begun when the Celtic civilisation reached its first great early plateau, six centuries before Christ: the literary fiction that is history scarcely affected them. Consequently, until two great archaeological discoveries were made in the nineteenth century, one in Austria, one in Switzerland, the Celts had occupied a less than satisfactory place in academic scholarship.

But when the main access to a people is through what they made rather than what they wrote, they become more real – closer, warmer. They become simple, profound: contact with them is direct, as sincere as the shape of the pot they threw, or the colour of the gold they spun, or the rub of the wool they wove. Thereby – a pleasing irony – the record of prehistory proves more reliable than history.

The filming of the BBC television series took place, east to west, from Hungary to Boston, through Austria, Germany, Switzerland, France, England, Scotland, Wales, Ireland, Nova Scotia. We sought tangible evidence – a carving near Lake Balaton outside Budapest; linguistic evidence – a Gaelic-speaking woman in Cape Breton; cultural evidence – museums in pretty Alpine towns, or dusty French provincial municipal buildings; imaginative evidence – the Iron Age reconstructions at Butser Farm in Hampshire in the lush South of England, the village by the reeds of Craggaunowen in County Clare in Western Ireland. All in order to ask again and again: who were the Celts? And now a new question began to materialise: what, if any, connection can, or may be made with the 'Celtic fringe' of Ireland, Scotland, Wales, Brittany, Isle of Man, Cornwall?

At the height of their development, the Celts constituted an archetypal European people: tribal, familial, hierarchical, agricultural. They were a brilliant people, of the oral tradition. A superstitious people, who actively sought deeper beliefs. A practical people, but producing penetrating intellectual concepts. Not a political people, although they enjoyed many sophisticated legal structures. They did not achieve or desire a cohesive political nationhood, although their motivation, the unity of the tribe, might have been the perfect political model. Nor were they an imperial people, although they colonised many lands, and in some cases left a dominant cultural imprint for ever. And did their wonderful gifts of craftsmanship and metal working name them? Say the etymologists, 'Selt – prehistoric instrument with chisel edge.'

They appreciated beauty and eroticism and they wedded the practical to the exquisite. In their art they proceeded from the geometric patterns of the primitive tribe to the abstract expression of their civilisation. They exercised a philosophy which saw truth as a diamond, many-faceted and precious. And thereby they celebrated one quality of life vital to them – personal, spiritual freedom. But they also cut off people's heads, offered human sacrifice, burnt men, women, children and animals alive *en masse* in enormous wicker effigies.

The past keeps changing. Even if presented in a dispassionate manner, in a 'correct' academic style, history – whatever it pretends – has never been pure record. In dealing with a subject such as the Celts and their civilisation, tradition – long more the ally of opinion than of truth – also has to be taken into account. Therefore, certain facts have to be accepted more than emphasised: for instance, Celts must have existed before the date of the artefacts discovered by the Austrian archaeologists at Hallstatt (described in Chapter 1). Hallstatt represents the first academic checkpoint, the earliest verifiable date at which the Celts could be apprehended.

In the writing of this book I have amplified somewhat on the television series, and made the important addition of four Celtic legends. All – so familiar to me since childhood – have been chosen from Ireland's cycles of mythologies. Their presence is designed to convey, in translations of the Celts' own words, some of the mysticism, power and moral duplicities which generated their lustrous but vague image.

And, in harmony with the Celts' own inclination towards paradox, I am left with two feelings – frustration and excitement. Frustration because they outwit any attempt to encapsulate them: in any selection from such a multitude of facts there will always remain the fundamental point, the gleaming detail, the essential argument, which should have been included.

My excitement stems from the sense of wonder which they inspire, spirits in a well, giants sleeping within a cave – a magic not at all dimmed by the sober power of those cultural gifts which they bequeathed.

Frank Delaney
London, Summer, 1986

I

BEGINNINGS

The village of Hochdorf sits in rich farmland a few kilometres from the edge of the Black Forest in Southern Germany. One day in 1968 Dr Jorg Biel, an archaeologist with the State Service of Antiquities of Baden-Württemberg in Stuttgart, twenty kilometres away to the north-west, received a telephone call from Renate Liebfried, a teacher and a hobby archaeologist in Hochdorf. She had previously made useful discoveries and now she had come across a site of possible interest. Dr Biel paid her due attention, though on this occasion they agreed that the site she was reporting seemed less than engrossing. But then she mentioned 'an unusual rise' in another field: the ploughs, she said, kept striking big and unexpected rocks.

Ten years passed before Dr Biel got around to investigating Hochdorf, and even then, he admits, only because Frau Liebfried telephoned her insistence from time to time. The site was a tumulus, a burial mound of the Celts.

The farmer granted permission, the mayor of Hochdorf gave his blessing, Dr Biel sank a trench. His previous experience of the many princely burials which had been discovered in the Baden-Württemberg region indicated that such graves were typically encircled by stone ramparts. He and his digging team began to strike banded rows of shaped boulders, of a type foreign to these fields. Next, the early tunings-up of excitement began to hum. In the rubble small bronze objects appeared, decorated pendants, a disc – not in themselves of major importance but they did suggest that the grave had never been robbed or vandalised.

The excavation soon began to establish that this ritual tomb consisted of two great compartments. Many centuries past, the oak-beamed walling and roofing had collapsed under the weight of fifty protective tons of stone. The tumulus had stood eight metres high, with the inner room, the actual burial chamber, measuring some twenty square metres. Here the people of prehistoric Hochdorf buried a Celtic chieftain who merited a great mausoleum. He lay on a bronze, high-backed couch embossed with ritual dancing figures and horses pulling a cart. The bier rested upon eight metal statues of women: each one a hand-high buxom unicyclist, on her wheel of bronze or iron, the couch's casters. Dr Biel's fibre analysis revealed, embedded in the bronze, horsehair, hemp, wool, and the fur of badgers, on which the dead prince had reposed. No trace of human hair, which suggested that in the months between death and the construction of the memorial grave the body had been preserved – in a vat of honey or, more likely given the absence of any human hair, salt. And flowers; the traces of pollen from the chemical analysis identified

The grave of the chieftain at Hochdorf. One of the most lavish Celtic burial chambers ever uncovered, the grave goods display connections with other European civilisations, and perhaps from further afield. The size and lavishness of the burial suggest that the body had been preserved for some time in order to build the chamber, and to make the gold artefacts with which he was bedecked.

Opposite, top: Dr Jorg Biel, the archaeologist based in Stuttgart who uncovered the Hochdorf tomb, and who directed the excavations and analysis.

Opposite, left: The Hochdorf 'dig' in progress: the archaeological importance took on greater significance once it became clear that, unusually, the grave had never been looted or vandalised.

local blooms of late summer, early autumn. The year, the archaeologists said, around 550 BC, and the man who died, this Celtic prince of Hochdorf, forty years old.

Taller, at six feet, than his contemporaries, a big man in every sense, and as his subjects garlanded him with flowers, they likewise dressed him in fine robes of Chinese silk, richly embroidered. At his head they placed a hat made of birch-bark, smaller than a coolie's but of the same shape. Touch it and shiver: from what exotic trade did it come? His grave goods included iron nail-clippers, a wooden comb and some fish-hooks. Above all, he was decked out with gold; traces of the smithwork were found, suggesting that the gold had been specially fashioned at the graveside. Around his neck he wore a gold band, as broad as the spread of a hand. Gold brooches fastened his cloaks; he wore a gold armlet, corded, patterned, indented. In his wide leather belt, inset with a gentle gold band, he wore an exquisite gold dagger, beautifully figured, tapered and burnished. And on his feet a pair of shoes embellished with stripes of gold but, whether in haste or celebration, his mourners had placed each shoe on the wrong foot.

In the outer chamber, Dr Biel found the remains of a cart, a sturdy, four-wheeled waggon made of ash and elm and maple, elaborately plated, on strongly crafted iron-bound wheels, festooned with bronze chains and figurines. They had piled it high with the necessities of after-life, bowls, plates, platters – and knives for hunting and slaughtering. The funerary hangings on the walls, sumptuous textiles, disintegrated when presented to the air. In one corner stood a bronze cauldron which still held the sediment of four hundred litres of fermented honey-mead, extracted from the pollen of a hundred and twenty-five different plants. The cauldron had been made by Greek slaves in a colony in the south of Italy, a gift, perhaps, from another tribal leader or purchased from a trader. The handles included three lions, originally identical, mass-produced. Evidently one of the lions had suffered damage and the replacement fashioned by a Celtic craftsman contains more imagination, humour. Nearby, on the walls of the tomb, hung a row of ornamented drinking-horns. One, five litres large, held a mighty draught for the prince himself, the eight others for his favourite companions.

And do we dream? Dr Biel sat on this closed, exhausted tumulus on a warm summer day and talked laconically of his discovery. Aerial reconnaissance and scientific photography have suggested to him that beneath the clay of these surrounding wide farms lie many other similar Celtic graves.

Factually, the grave at Hochdorf corroborates existing evidence, and constitutes a fortunate and comprehensive collection, a meeting-point of much that was already both known and felt. Hochdorf provides a convenient summary of other European Celtic finds initiated a century earlier by antiquarians in Austria and Switzerland, and whose significance generations of scientists continue to piece together as the expanding archaeological definition of the Celts.

In addition Dr Biel's discovery reinforces both the scholarship and the popular myth – Hochdorf confirms prosperous grandeur and legendary aura in the Celtic civilisation. The prince came from a sophisticated and successful society, identified, described and called 'Keltoi' by the Greeks and Romans. This vivid tribal people populated many parts of Europe for the seven centuries before Christ, living on hills, cultivating river valleys, the Elbe, the Danube, the Rhine.

Initially – and fundamentally – Hochdorf and similar funeral displays, greater or smaller, identify Celts all over Europe. When they buried their dead they equipped them for a long voyage: the grander the deceased, the richer the grave goods. And Hochdorf stimulates an enquiry consistent in all discussion of the Celtic imagination and in the popular connotations of the word 'Celt' – where does the fact end, where does the myth begin, which is which?

A French definition says that 'prehistory stops with the first written document' – by which principle the Celts qualify as a prehistoric people. Like any civilisation, they emerged rather than arrived; they developed over centuries rather than sprang forth with one bound. Humanity, a work-in-progress, can never satisfactorily be halted at one beginning point. Their individual trappings, those qualities, habits and manners which cause a culture and civilisation eventually to be recognised and named, adhered to the Celts naturally, in the slow turning of the centuries. They differed not in the possession of common characteristics in behaviour or survival, but in selection and emphasis, in management and distribution.

With the recession of the Ice Age, Europe grew temperate, and gradually became populated by small scattered hunting communities, nomads, who pursued the herds through the seasons. Next, they mastered the knowledge of food production, and settled down to farming, mainly along those rivers which they and their forefathers had followed. Movement spread – through the continent and the centuries. Indo-European warriors, masterful on horseback, pushed across the steppes of Eurasia, through Bohemia, through what is now Czechoslovakia and the plains of Hungary. Other immigrants came up from Persia, from Asia Minor, from the fringes of 'the Most Ancient East'. New settlers raised stock and improved the rudimentary farming. By 4500 BC, competent farmers developed in the extreme west of mainland Europe, as far as Holland, emulating the strong agriculture, root crops, cereals, fruits, herbs, animal husbandry, which had created new economies in Greece and Bulgaria and Minoan Crete five thousand years before. By 3000 BC farmers stabilised the territories of France and Britain. Two thousand years before Christ, Europe's population comprised variegated peoples whose major ancestral travels had begun to trickle to an end, settlers who brought with them particular traits and styles – and their instinctive remembrance of the magic of mysterious peoples in their innate legends, their unconscious ancestral forces.

Archaeology is a new science: deprecators question whether it ought to be considered merely a craft. Advocates point to the speed at which archaeology has matured in the couple of hundred years since the inspired guesses of well-meaning but relatively unscientific antiquarians, and since then, by leaps and bounds in the four decades since the introduction of more precise scientific dating (by radiocarbon 14) in 1949. But without the archaeologists, the Celts might well have remained in the glowing grip of the literary or oral romantics.

The pathway of archaeological discovery which leads from primal gloom, through the shadows of post-Ice Age Europe, to the gold of Hochdorf winds long and complex – and copiously documented. It stretches from the Balkans to the pastures of Ireland, and spans hundreds of centuries, thousands of doctorates, strewn with inklings and proofs so numerous that only the major connections can be mentioned here (and debate will always bubble about which choice is ever most apposite).

The archaeological traces have been, and continue to be, painstakingly put together from records of finds all over Europe. The principal, acknowledged points of contact remain as signposts along the Celtic way. Scholars have established the major thrust of Celtic existence sufficiently to permit profound debate on finer points. Archaeology's value becomes ever clearer – summarised by the eminent British archaeologist Mortimer Wheeler who once insisted that he was 'not digging up things, but digging up people'.

Begin with the Neolithic people, accepting that the Stone Age spans from 3400 BC to 1600 BC. Living on their pastures in Central and Northern Europe, they had developed, according to the marriage between their needs and abilities, a stone axe mounted on – not tied to – a handle, for which a hole had been fashioned in the stone axe-head. By the year 2500 BC, itinerant people on the move from the south Russian Steppes to the Rhine valley, to Belgium and Holland, had improved upon this implement, and had the habit of burying examples of it, finely-wrought, in the graves of their warriors. From about 1500 BC, the stone began to give way to a metal shaft-hole axe, of bronze or copper. Such a weapon had previously existed, widespread, in the Balkans, and further east and north in the Caucasus, where the inhabitants had developed their skills and comforts ahead of the new nomadic Europeans.

Parallel with the evolution of the axe from stone to metal ran the emergence of a particular type of pot, a domestic vessel, which had been ornamented distinctively by pressing rows of cords into the pre-baked clay. By 3000 BC in regions north of the Black Sea, families used this corded ware. By 2500 BC, people who used both the Cord-Ware pot and the Shaft-Hole axe had populated the major river valleys of Europe, the Rhine and the Danube. But at the same time as these developments, another influence drifted in from a different direction, with again, a domestic pot as the hallmark. From the south of Spain, and from the coastal strip of North Africa, came the Bell-Beaker people, between 2500 and 2000 BC. Their vessels, beautifully made, red in colour, were characterised by a unique bell-shape. These have been excavated in Neolithic graves from Portugal to Scotland, in French and Spanish caves.

In such fusion and overlapping were the Celts born? In Prague, Czechoslovakia, a Bell-Beaker was found, extensively patterned with corded marks; in Wiltshire in England an almost identical vessel: both have been dated to about 2000 BC, by which time the plethora of small, variegated nomadic groups who constituted the early Europeans had burgeoned, stabilised and expanded into larger, more monolithic cultures.

And with a pleasing symbolism, the characteristic most commonly employed to identify the emergence of these more homogeneous people came not from their living but their dying – the rites of burial. As the wilderness of Europe after the Ice Age became more predictably habitable, farming settled down, improving the methods of cultivation, or giving way to trade where the land proved uneconomic. Metalworking advanced: new methods of manufacture, of casting and shaping, led to new tools and weapons, more effective and more durable, enabling ever more land to be won. These accomplished Europeans – the ones in whom we shall become interested - rose to their highest standards in Southern Germany in the Danube valley, in Austria and Bavaria, by lakes in Switzerland.

Fifteen hundred years before Christ, many Europeans habitually buried their dead, singly or communally, in barrows; fashioned mounds of earth, sometimes in small groupings, sometimes in large cemeteries. These mounds were found in Southern Germany, in Burgundy, in Bohemia, in Switzerland, along the Danube, in Belgium, in Britain. Their creators became known – named by the archaeologists – as the Tumulus People. In Poland, Silesia, Saxony and, again, Bohemia, another burial rite came to be observed: mourners cremated their dead, placed the burnt bones in urns and buried them in wide cemeteries – the Urnfield Culture.

Significantly, these burials included grave goods, ordinary, human, domestic objects, the affectionately-held mundane possessions of a body. One major presence among such details conveys in shape, form and usage, the spirit and the timelessness, the wide connections of the Celts' development. Between two and three thousand years before Christ, a barrow grave in Southern Russia contained a silver vase with a picture of a horse. In 1750 BC, a horse received a celebrated burial in Egypt. Between two thousand and a thousand years before Christ, in the middle Volga region of Russia, two horses were interred in a barrow wearing the ornate bone-made cheek-pieces of their bridles. Fourteen hundred, thirteen hundred, twelve hundred years before Christ, from Greece to Scandinavia, the horse appeared on rock carvings, in burial chambers, as ornaments on grave goods, accompanied by a waggon or a chariot.

Driving through Europe, on long roads in Germany, beneath scenic Austrian foothills, in lush mid-France, in time-warped Hungarian plains, the contours of the land – given the nature and curiosity of my journey – take on pungent significance. Beneath what slope might I find a shaft-hole axe? That curious terraced hill – a barrow grave, an Urnfield cemetery? The pot on a cottage windowsill in Hungary – are those cord-marks? And underneath all this clay, as if seeing a cross-section illustration of the earth in a child's storybook or the *National Geographic Magazine*, do I see the bones of horses, laid and splayed, in final hobbled splendour?

By the year 800 BC the prehistoric smoke begins to disperse. The picture (to play upon words) hardens – with the use of iron. The first firm, materially-based, extensive classification of the Celts began as a result of the local and amateur enterprise of one man, an ordinary citizen, neither a scholar nor an archaeologist.

Georg Ramsauer lived in the village of Hallstatt, a baroque and pretty place, an Austrian chocolate box, which claims to be 4500 years old. It sits by a lake in the area called the Salzkammergut – 'the place of good salt', regional capital,

Salzburg, the salt town. The salt from these mountains preserved the food of old Europe. Crucial to the local economy, 'the kitchen's gold' became the agent which breathed new and respected life into the cultural identity of the Celts. They mined the salt at Hallstatt more than two and a half thousand years ago. (Other prehistoric salt-mining sites, from Czechoslovakia to the eastern coast of England, also generated immense trade. France, then Gaul, gained a substantial reputation among the Romans for its salted food products.)

In 1846, Ramsauer, the Director of the Hallstatt State Mine, had his imagination fired by the stories of his workers' ancestry. Before his time, the body of a prehistoric miner had been found, fully intact in the salt. A local row even blew up as to whether the body – undoubtedly of a pagan – should receive Christian burial. And from time to time, other bits and pieces turned up in the salt corridors. But on the hill above the village, a few metres away from the tree-line, just above the terminus, today, of the funicular railway, Ramsauer discovered, in several curious grassy mounds, a huge prehistoric cemetery. It contained up to two and a half thousand graves – and he, with scrupulous care, investigated, between 1846 and 1862, almost a thousand of them. Then, the Academy of Sciences in Vienna, hearing of Ramsauer's huge zeal and marvellous discoveries, sent a team of investigators to Hallstatt. They arrived in 1876, thirty years after Georg Ramsauer's original scrutinies, and began an exhaustive investigation of the interior of the salt mine. From their finds they not only pieced together a picture of prehistoric life in this seemingly remote lakeside village, but the cumulative effect of their – and Ramsauer's – work provided the very first technical definition of the Celts. Intercepted at this specific period, within Europe after 800 BC, this iron-using people, the Celts, were identified and described by the term 'The Hallstatt Culture'. Such terminology stands in line with one of archaeology's most succinct and renowned definitions: 'We find certain types of remains – pots, implements, burial rites, house forms – constantly recurring together. Such a complex of regularly associated traces we shall term "a cultural group" or "a culture". We assume that such a complex is the material expression of what today would be called a people.'

Prehistoric Hallstatt traded salt – with effective commercial results – to the south as far as Italy, to the north as far as Bohemia. To begin with, the Viennese antiquarians summarised the mining activities from what they found (digging up people again). The museum at Hallstatt contains the well-preserved evidence – a leather hat, fragments of clothing, gloves for sliding down the wooden struts of the mineshaft, leather shoes, a hod of timber and leather to take the salt to the collection point within the mountain. Traces of human faeces were found, and the remains of food, of beans, apples and cherries, barley and wooden spoons and dishes, shards of pottery.

Even more significantly, disparities between the finds in the salt mines and the cemeteries above suggested a class structure – with the miners who slaved in the bowels of the Austrian mountains as the worker bees of a well-to-do society living off the salt's profits. Hallstatt, the first cohesive discovery of the Celts' past, clarified, altered the colour of, the ancient map of Europe. Before these discoveries of Iron Age life, the word 'civilisation' meant, in European terms, Greek or

Left: Georg Ramsauer, Director of the State Salt Mines at Hallstatt, Austria. His amateur interest in the forebears of his miners led to the detailed discovery and analysis of the cemetery on the hillside at Hallstatt, and thereby introduced one of the major definitions of the early Celtic civilisation – Hallstatt Culture.

The finds at Hallstatt aroused great interest among European antiquarians, and notable figures in the world of archaeology, such as the Duchess of Mecklenburg, were still conducting extensive investigations half a century after Georg Ramsauer's first discoveries.

In 1876, archaeologists from the Academy of Sciences in Vienna came to the salt mines at Hallstatt. Their investigations threw more detailed light – diet, food, clothing, working implements – on the early inhabitants, whom they dated to approximately seven centuries BC.

Roman, largely. Generations of antiquarians had depended almost entirely upon classical writings whose evidence was their final authority. They never granted comparable importance or value to material from any other culture, especially a non-literary barbarian one. But now 'the glory that was Greece, the grandeur that was Rome' had a proven tangible rival – the opulence, and clear structure of the Celtic civilisation.

The grave goods – predominantly iron-made – from the cemetery above and around the Hallstatt mines, indicated a sophisticated and hierarchical society. These people, superb ironworkers, owned and buried beautifully-decorated vessels, ornamented weaponry and horse trappings, all of a standard much advanced upon that recorded from earlier Europe, reflecting a decisive and recognisable social structure, which, as it developed, could be found in the society of the chieftain at Hochdorf.

The date usually ascribed to the Hallstatt artefacts begins at approximately 770 BC. As the remains of both the miners and the mine-owners were assessed, the nineteenth century antiquarian investigators remembered their texts – the words, sometimes geographically inaccurate, of the old historians. Cosmopolitan influence flourished on the swords, the daggers, the vessels found at Hallstatt. The Greeks, Romans and Etruscans had, after all, described trade with a distinctive people who lived in Central European regions, people called 'Keltoi' – in the words of one historian 'the first of the prehistoric peoples north of the Alps whose names were known to the Greek and Roman world, for they shared certain common features, including some linguistic affinity'. The prehistoric man who had crawled as a nomad across Europe, along a pathway signposted by battle-axes, corded-ware pottery and bell-shaped beakers, tumulus and urn burials, who lavishly and distinctively decorated his well-crafted implements, had, so to speak, arrived. European antiquarians recognised this major stage of human culture; at the very least, the Bronze Age had been left behind.

The Hallstatt Culture reflects the Celts in their state of development between the beginning of the ninth century BC and the middle of the seventh century BC – an iron-using, farming, trading people with fixed patterns of habitation and society. Further archaeological definition began to refine the Hallstatt Culture internally so that discoveries elsewhere in Europe – of agreed Celtic origin – could be defined as belonging on the same point of development as the Celts who had dwelt in Hallstatt. In Britain and Ireland, for example, objects have been found which, although dated to, say, 400 BC, have nonetheless been described as Hallstatt, because their sophistication (or comparative lack of it) had only advanced as far as the primary Hallstatt date, i.e., beginning after 800 BC.

On mainland Europe, however, the Celtic pathway's next signpost – the spiritual, intellectual, social development of the Celts as a people, as a civilisation – is indicated by yet another find, made at the same time as Georg Ramsauer was digging up his ancient miners, but some years ahead of the Viennese antiquarians' arrival in Hallstatt.

A few kilometres outside Neuchâtel in Switzerland stands La Tene – an undistinguished area, now a drab caravan site, a part-time village of holiday chalets. A modern canal runs nearby and beneath the concrete of this holiday amenity flows the ancient River Thielle which once fed Lake Neuchâtel overground. In 1858, the waters at the eastern end – where the river flung an arm into the lake – sank to an unusually low level, and suddenly timbers appeared, blackened, waterlogged spars. The remains of a bridge? A jetty? Ribs from the body of time? In the mud beside the timbers archaeologists from Zurich found such a profusion of objects, of such beauty and sophistication, that the second great period of Celtic civilisation was declared. The name 'La Tene' (in translation, sweet paradox, 'The Shallows') became the next, major scholarly cognisance of the Celts. Where Hallstatt Culture constituted the first academically measurable moment, the civilisation's further refinement came in La Tene Culture. Initial speculation considered La Tene as some kind of massive votive offering place, some sacrificial location. But, eventually, the find in the waters seemed too concentrated, too exquisite, too large: subsequent examination continues to suggest a wealthy settlement which one day had to be fled in a hurry – a huge flood, perhaps, or some other act of the gods? Substantial and ongoing excavations at nearby Champrevetres confirm busy and continuous life by the lake at Neuchâtel for hundreds of centuries. La Tene Culture, however, intercepts the Celts during their rapid and remarkable burgeoning – root to flower in two hundred years.

The terms 'Hallstatt' and 'La Tene' became the standard archaeological short-hand for recording the growth, the civilising of Celts. Both definitions no longer refer merely to the geography of the two discoveries: rather they measure periods of time, spans of the Celtic civilisation anywhere, and thereafter catalogued according to the style of the artefacts found in those two major discoveries. Thus, in the broadest terms, Hallstatt stretched from between 800 BC and 700 BC to between 600 BC and 500 BC and La Tene Culture denotes a period which took over from Hallstatt Culture. Early La Tene Culture refers to the Celts between 600 BC and 500 BC; middle La Tene between 300 BC and 100 BC; late La Tene the dwindling time, when the Romans had begun to suffocate the Celts. If Hallstatt Culture may be seen as survival and breakthrough from basic comfort to the nucleus of civilisation, the Celts of La Tene Culture luxuriated, shone, swaggered, thought, expressed themselves. The word 'Hallstatt' came to denote an iron-using people who fitted the descriptions in the old verbal, written and trading histories, the descriptions of people called 'Keltoi', who were found to have such distinguishing customs as elaborate burials, or ornamented metalworking. La Tene meant more lavish burials, more advanced decoration on swords, helmets, brooches, more cosmopolitan influence.

La Tene Culture lifts the Celts from being just another of the myriad European tribally-originated peoples who made an impact in the days before literacy. La Tene spirit establishes the Celts as a real 'civilisation'. The Celts of the Hallstatt Culture produced strong, vigorous work, in which the ornamentation of a helmet or a sword, though primary, rose a notch above the primitive. The excitement issued from strength rather than delicacy. La Tene Culture, though, bequeathed some of antiquity's most gorgeous pieces of decorative art. Wildlife themes pushed into the realms of the abstract and fantastic. A tendril of a plant teased into itself, then spun outwards until it became pattern, a whorl, a whole inner world, leaping, coiling, dancing. And afterwards it strayed into other forms, not just the back of a mirror, not just the decoration of a pot – but into designs and images which eventually epitomised and perpetuated the legend of the Celts. When the oral tradition eventually received literary attention, the descendants of those early ironworkers ornamented their manuscripts similarly but even more lavishly.

La Tene Culture finds the Celts amongst wealth and glory and possession and expression. They had mobility, style, trade, power. They had given themselves definition; they had acquired a considerable presence; and they had, for their elegance and heroism, earned respect, an assured people. The prince at Hochdorf – whose period of existence spanned the bridge between the heavier expression of the Hallstatt Culture and the finer glories of La Tene – possessed status within his society, as did his Celtic counterparts in France, Austria, Switzerland, Belgium. The way of the Celts within that period, the five hundred years or so before Christ, fixed them in the popular imagination – mythological in their splendour, glorious in their gold and jewels, mysterious in the tracery of their ornamentation, opulent in the evidence of their possessions.

And the term 'La Tene' defines the essential vision of the Celts and their civilisation, marks their major cultural presence in Europe, when their attitude, personality, style, came of age. Through La Tene, Europe saw them as important, powerful and fascinating. Their spread across the continent, their multifarious presence, made them a force to be reckoned with. From their deep background in Eastern Europe, from intensive population of the German and Austrian river valleys, they spread westward. Graves in Western France, hillforts in the Low Countries, cultural emblems in England and Ireland, have all testified, under the archaeologist's trowel, to the Celts' irresistible influence.

By the time of the Celts' *annus mirabilis*, around the second century before Christ, the classical writers had begun to find this non-literate people more and more worthy of note.

Next to Iberia [wrote Strabo] Celtica lies to the east, extending as far as the River Rhine. Its northern side is washed by the whole length of the British Channel, for the whole length of the island of Britain is parallel and lies over against the whole of Celtica ... Its eastern side is bounded by the River Rhine whose stream runs parallel to the Pyrenees. On the south side it is bounded in part by the Alps, that is, the part beginning at the Rhine, and in part by the Mediterranean ... in which area are the notable cities of Marseilles and Narbonne ...

The geography of the first century BC, especially in a Greek writer's perceptions of Western Europe, may have been out of true in terms of precision – but not in impression. Strabo registered the Celts as a major and widespread European entity. Their wide proliferation derived, in part, from the original, post-primeval natural expansion of a people or culture. Centuries later they spread from their original European homelands in a series of famous and distressing migrations.

Often they set forth from a position of failing strength. The princely families of the Danube and Rhine valleys had established themselves in their hillfort fastnesses as rulers who farmed, and who had also opened up trade routes with the Italians, the Etruscans, the Greeks. Four centuries before Christ, economic deprivation grew rife; the pressure on such Celtic kingdoms often stemmed from dangerous overpopulation. One king in Central France weighed down with 'the burdensome excess of people', despatched for ever two of his nephews with 'as many followers as they thought would guarantee their competence to overpower any hostile armies they might meet'. (One nephew travelled to Southern Germany, another to Italy – he marched through the Alps, down the valley of the River Po and founded Milan.)

On many of these roamings the Celts struck terror into Europe; their very appearance generated fearsome legend. According to Diodorus Siculus, a first century BC historian from Sicily, who published his work in Rome:

On their heads they wear bronze helmets which possess large projecting figures lending the appearance of enormous stature to the wearer; in some cases horns form one piece with the helmet, while in other cases it is relief figures of foreparts of birds or quadrupeds. Their trumpets again are of a peculiar barbaric kind; they blow into them and produce a harsh sound which suits the tumult of war. Some have iron breastplates of chain mail while others fight naked, and for them the breastplate given by nature suffices.

Highly mobile and fast, these militant waggon trains of lethal raiders respected nothing. Circa 390 BC, tribes from Gaul sacked Rome, entered the Senate and pulled the Senators' beards. In 335 BC Alexander the Great received in a delegation a Celtic tribe from the Adriatic. In 279 BC, a tribe eventually called Galatians, who settled in Asia Minor (to be addressed three hundred years later by St Paul) raided Greece and pillaged that most sacred of places, Delphi. (Does some irony therefore arise, however well-founded factually, in history's vision of the Celts, especially in their latter-day incarnation, as an oppressed and colonised people?)

Tall in stature and their flesh is very moist and white, while their hair is not only naturally blond, but they also use artificial means to increase this quality of colour ... Some shave off the beard, while others cultivate a short beard; the nobles shave the cheeks, but let the moustache grow freely so that it covers the mouth. And so when they are eating, the moustache becomes entangled in the food, and when they are drinking, the drink passes, as it were, through a sort of strainer. When dining they all sit not on chairs, but on the earth, strewing beneath them the skins of wolves or dogs. At their meals they are served by their youngest grown-up children, both boys and girls. Beside them are hearths blazing with fire, with cauldrons and spits containing large pieces of meat. Brave warriors they honour with the finest portions of the meat ...

Exotic and unusual, as different as gypsies – the Celts exuded a flavour unlike anything known in Mediterranean Europe. They also sounded peculiar: linguistics conjecture that their reputation as 'barbarian' may have derived onoma-topoeically – the Celts 'babbled'. Certainly their habits and behaviour patterns gave offence to the more fastidious Romans and Greeks, such as the Stoic, Posidonius, and his diligent plagiarist, Strabo.

To the frankness and high-spiritedness of their temperament must be added traits of childish boastfulness and love of decoration. They wear ornaments of gold, torques on their necks, and bracelets on their arms and wrists, while people of high rank wear dyed garments besprinkled with gold. It is this vanity which makes them so unbearable in victory and so completely downcast in defeat. They ... let their hair grow long and wear baggy trousers; instead of the ordinary tunics they wear divided tunics with sleeves, reaching down as far as the private parts and the buttocks ...

Their arms correspond in size with their physique; a long sword fastened on the right side, and a long shield, and spears of like dimension, and the madaris, which is a kind of javelin. Some also use bows and slings. There is a wooden weapon ... which is thrown by hand and not by means of a strap, with a range far greater than that of an arrow and which they mostly use for bird-hunting as well as in battle. Even to the present day [Strabo lived circa 60 BC to AD 20; Posidonius, a century earlier] most people sleep on the ground and dine seated on a litter of straw. They have large quantities of food together with milk and all kinds of meat, especially fresh and salt pork. Their pigs are allowed to run wild and are noted for their height, and pugnacity and swiftness. It is dangerous for a stranger to approach them, and also for a wolf. Their houses are large and circular, built of planks and wickerwork, the roof being a dome of heavy thatch.

Since they left no self-generated literary reportage, their remains and artefacts provide the strongest picture of Celtic daily life. Frequently they settled amid great scenic beauty but for more than just aesthetic reasons – for the fish in the lake, the deer and timber in the woods, the rich loam for the crops. Their houses mirror the way they developed – into a solid and respectable society, whose structures, though basic, were sound, secure, capacious, whose social faith was placed in the extended family. Whether rectangular or circular, their dwellings either stood alone in isolated places or as part of a group in a fortified location. All domestic activity centred upon the fire; directly overhead a hole in the roof was cut with ingenuity – though the smoke escaped the rain did not come through. The men became warriors, hunters, farmers: the women cooked from cauldrons hanging upon crossbeams. They handmilled their own flour for their version of bread. They wove their own cloth from the fleece of their own sheep (they raised a breed which was capable of being plucked, rather than needing to be shorn). They made their own garments (including trousers with loops on them, to stop them drifting up the legs while on horseback). The typical family, as reported by contemporary observers, seemed unenquiringly and spontaneously hospitable and loquacious, much given to entertainment and argument.

They invite strangers to their banquets, and only after the meal do they ask who they are and of what they stand in need. At dinner they are wont to be moved by chance remarks to wordy disputes, and, after a challenge, to fight in single combat, regarding their lives as naught ... they frequently exaggerate with the aim of extolling themselves and diminishing the status of others. They are boasters and threateners and given to bombastic self-dramatisation, and yet they are quick of mind and with good natural ability for learning. They also have lyric poets whom they call 'Bards'. They sing to the accompaniment of instruments resembling lyres, sometimes a eulogy, and sometimes a satire. They have also certain philosophers and theologians who are treated with special honour, whom they call 'Druids'.

The typical Celts of popular imagination today derive from their style within that period of 500 years BC. In such structures lay their evolution and civilising. La Tene Culture also signifies a clear social pattern: they possessed enough autonomy and confidence to display their society lavishly. That extravagant personality and spirit which bred the luxurious ornamentation found an expression which ranged wider than those most popular visual connotations of the word 'Celtic', the famous torcs and fasteners and bracelets.

The whole race ... is madly fond of war, high-spirited and quick to battle, but otherwise straightforward and not of evil character. And so when they are stirred up they assemble in their bands for

A silver denarius struck in Rome, 40BC, showing the head of Vercingetorix – who was paraded through the streets as part of Caesar's triumphal displays.

Vercingetorix surrenders to Caesar after the defeat of the Celts at the Battle of Alesia, 52 BC. When defeat became apparent, Vercingetorix said to his fellow chieftains, 'I must accept my fate, I am at your disposal. You may make a gesture of reparation to the Romans either by killing me yourselves or surrendering me to Caesar.' Caesar, in his account of the Gallic wars, describes how Vercingetorix then came to him and surrendered, but since we only have Caesar's description, there is no reason to believe that his account was any less florid and romantic than this nineteenth-century engraver's depiction of the event.

battle, quite openly and without forethought, so that they are easily handled by those who desire to outwit them; for at any time or place and on whatever pretext you stir them up, you have them ready to face danger, even if they have nothing on their side but their own strength and courage ... Their strength depends both on their mighty bodies, and on their numbers ...

Supported in their grandeur by such terrifying reputation, the Celts occupied a proud and vivid place in mainland Europe – lushness in their civilisation, gold and flowers, and enough war and song and brutal savagery and imagination to fuel ten thousand legends. But however brilliant their presence, however admirable their farming skill, however exotic their artistic expression, they never managed to present themselves as one, organised nation. They remained a series of tribes, powerful and large families, rich and secure and experienced in warfare from defending their territories and possessions against their own Celtic neighbours or wandering marauders, always a wide and loose collective, composed of individual chieftains who would bow the knee to no single over-all leader. This posture numbered their days, and when finally they did unite, to defend tribal Gaul against Rome's war machine, it was too late.

The Mediterranean south knew about the Celts, feared them. In 59 BC Julius Caesar achieved the consulship in Rome, elected in a triumvirate with Pompey and Crassus. Caesar had already made a military reputation in Spain, now he sought new lands to conquer. He thought initially of moving towards Northern Italy and then swinging east to Dalmatia – with Yugoslavia as his eventual goal. But the governor of Transalpine or Narbonese Gaul died and opportunistic Caesar had the province assigned to him. With adroit timing: when his year of consulship drew to an end he began to fear arrest for the acts of corruption and violence he had committed in office. At the same time, the Helvetii, a Celtic tribe who had been driven out of their German homes into Switzerland, decided to migrate *en masse* across France to seek settlements on the Atlantic coast. The Romans found this migration threatening to such sway as they already had begun to establish in Gaul, so Caesar set off north with a newly-raised army and attacked the Helvetii beside the River Arroux at Armecy, where he slaughtered great numbers of them and dispatched the remainder back to Switzerland. Back in Rome praise resounded. Within the year, in 58 BC, he deliberately sought a confrontation with the fierce Aedui under their king Ariovistus, traditionally a Roman ally. Notwithstanding, Caesar engaged and defeated him on the plain of Alsace – thereby reversing the alliance in the interests of his own military success and imperial reputation. He routed the Belgae, too, who, according to Caesar's own account, were

descended from tribes which long ago came across the Rhine from Germany, and settled in that part of Gaul on account of its fertility, expelling the former inhabitants. The Belgae, they said, were the only people who, half a century earlier, when all the rest of Gaul was overrun by the Teutoni and the Cimbri, prevented the invaders from entering their territory – the recollection of which made them assume an air of much importance, and pride themselves on their military power.

'*Cum esset Caesar in citeriore Gallia [in hibernis]*': the Belgae gathered an army of 300,000 men 'when Caesar was in hither Gaul in winter quarters' – but he raised two new legions, bringing his total up to eight, by which time the Belgic tribes had begun to fall apart and offered almost no resistance. Only a tribe called the Nervii remained unvanquished and after a vicious see-saw battle on the River Sambre in 57 BC Caesar conquered them too. In 56 BC, Normandy and Aquitaine suffered successful expeditions by Caesar's generals: he himself even threw a bridge across the Rhine to subdue Germanic tribesmen. In 55 BC the Venetii from Brittany rebelled as a protest against the anticipated invasion of Britain by Caesar: for their pains they were slaughtered in Quiberon Bay. He then mounted his first raid on Britain, did not get the entirely propitious weather he wished for, had several ships damaged and was obliged to return to Gaul after eighteen days.

The profile of the Celts during Caesar's campaign reflects disunity leading to decline. From their original occupation of most of Central Europe and Bohemia, they had migrated in part and piecemeal, hopefully or peacefully. In this fashion they built Celtic settlements afresh, or, as in Gaul, augmented the ancient, existing Celtic presence. Across Europe the old order had begun to change. Gaul itself was experiencing dire problems, politically and militarily. The internal proliferation of tribes, most by now identifiably Celtic whatever their point of origin, had begun to disagree violently, while at the same time invaders from Northern Europe, and the Romans from the south, contributed to the country's instability. Various tribal kings sought either terms or alliance with the Romans, in order to protect their way of life, their riches, from other marauders. All failed – in one way and another. Enter Vercingetorix – 'the super warrior king', the son of a nobleman from the Auvergne, described by Caesar as *summae diligentiae*, a man 'of massive energy', a fearless warrior, and he, like many other Celtic kings in France, refused to consider any course other than opposition to Rome. Vercingetorix imposed, bullied and politicked until he had raised a huge army, drawn from tribes all over France, but in particular the central and northern regions. His guerrilla raids severely damaged and hampered Caesar's legions, inflicted several defeats. But the final conflict came in 52 BC, at the battle of Alesia in central France. To this hilltop Vercingetorix had repaired to lick his wounds after a surprise routing of his much-vaunted cavalry. Caesar surrounded Alesia: Vercingetorix sent for reinforcements. To cope with the threat both from within the town and the eventual attack from arriving reinforcements, Caesar built fortifications, pits studded with holes containing pointed stakes, a high smooth wall defended with spikes and surmounted by watchtowers every hundred metres. In twenty-eight days he built twenty-two kilometres of these ramparts.

The enemy knew that he was coming [wrote Caesar of himself] by the scarlet cloak which he always wore in action to mark his identity; and when they saw the cavalry squadrons and cohorts following him down the slopes, which were plainly visible from the heights on which they stood, they joined battle. Both sides raised a cheer, which was answered by the men on the rampart and all along the entrenchments. The Romans dropped their spears and fought on with their swords. Suddenly the Gauls saw the cavalry in their rear and fresh cohorts coming up in front. They broke and fled, but found their retreat cut off by the cavalry and were mown down. Sedullus, chieftain and commander of the Lemovices, was killed. Vercassivellaunus was taken prisoner in the rout, seventy-four standards were brought into Caesar, and only a few men of all the large army got back unhurt to their camp. When the Gauls in the town saw their countrymen being slaughtered in flight, they gave up hope and recalled their troops . . .

On the following morning, Vercingetorix spoke to his shattered countrymen. 'I did not undertake this war for private ends, but in the cause of national liberty.' And he gave them a choice – they could kill him themselves, or surrender him to the conqueror. They chose surrender – and their leader, in true Celtic tradition, put on his finest robes, went forth to Caesar's tent and laid down his sword at Caesar's feet. For six years the Romans kept Vercingetorix prisoner. On Caesar's triumphant return they paraded the Celt like an exotic animal through Rome and then strangled him. In 1865 a great statue was raised in his honour at Alesia: Napoleon III found Celtic zeal exciting.

In the centuries that followed Vercingetorix's defeat, the decline continued. Celtic raids across Europe, their reputation for terrifying combat tactics, their guerrilla-type colonising activities, their unusual, already legendary imprint upon European culture – all of these faded. The arrival of literacy, the incursions of organised armies, the advance of Christianity would erode further their ancient and self-sufficient character. The long, effacing process of assimilation had begun. The Keltoi receded into the general mass of European peoples, their colour and light dimmed. Chieftains who once gleamed with power, such as the man with the golden shoes at Hochdorf, found their stature, their wealth, their beliefs threatened, subdued. Even though other Celts persisted, in mainland pockets and on the isles to the west of Europe, the Roman conquest of Gaul heralded the beginning of the end of major Celtic European distinction. The extent to which any Celtic spirit could survive had become dependent upon how far the trumpets of Rome and the Western Empire would echo. Across the English Channel they could already be heard.

2

NATIONS

Few statues inhabit such appropriate locations: straining against the black, rigid bronze, Boudicca seems to threaten the Houses of Parliament at Westminster as she once assailed the institutions of the Roman Empire in Britain. The third century AD historian, Cassius Dio Cocceianus wrote:

She was enormous of frame, terrifying of mien, and with a rough, shrill voice. A great mass of bright red hair fell down to her knees: she wore a huge twisted torc of gold, and a tunic of many colours, over which was a thick mantle held by a brooch. When she grasped a spear, it was to strike fear into all who observed her.

Boudicca, the widow of Prasutagus, King of the Iceni, one of the leading tribes of East Anglia, bore no son, and when Prasutagus died he left half of his wealth to his two daughters, and the other half to Nero and the Roman Empire. This obeisant gesture characterised the 'client-king' relationship with the Emperor, who gave, therefore, his protection to the client-king's family in the event of bereavement.

Regrettably, the Roman officials carried out the necessary inventory of Prasutagus's wealth arrogantly, and gave offence to the widow and her people. Insensitively intent as ever upon colonisation, the Romans refused to honour Boudicca's position as ruler of her late husband's kindgom and they reduced the status of the Iceni territory, absorbing it into the Empire at the level of a mere 'civitas', a regional unit of administration. When Boudicca objected, the Romans flogged her, raped her two daughters. The Iceni, still powerful and already incensed at the punishing taxes of the Empire, rose in anger and gathered strength with the support of a neighbouring tribe, the powerful Trinovantes, whose land had also been confiscated. In her chariot, at great speed, with terrifying panache and little discipline, Boudicca went to war. (Incidentally, her more usual name of Boadicea has been attributed to a medieval scribe's error.)

Boudicca's rebellion broke out in AD 60 – ferociously. After a siege of only two days, she and her warriors sacked Colchester, the old Celtic centre in the east of England which the Romans had capitalised. Colchester was unwalled, it had no protection, no Roman legion available within a hundred miles; an eventual, hasty military rescue attempt dispersed in confusion *en route*. Virtually all the Roman inhabitants of Colchester, children too, died in the slaughter. The great temple, a wonder of the Roman world and hateful to the Celts, became a pyre.

In London (Londinium) her supporters got out of hand and by way of giving offerings of victory to the gods of war, skewered some of the Roman women lengthwise. St Albans in Hertfordshire (Verulamium), a Celtic settlement in alliance with Rome, also fell to Boudicca's fury. Finally, near Lichfield, the Fourteenth and the Twentieth Legions under the brilliant commander, Suetonius Paullinus, with fewer troops but precise and effective organisation, broke Boudicca's rebellion. Rather than be humiliated in likely and ignominious death at the hands of the enemy, the mighty Celtic warrior queen took poison. Her rebellion, brief, fierce and doomed, became a Vercingetorix-like metaphor for the decline of the Celts. An army mirrors the society from which it is drawn. The disparate Celts never could organise: their resistance to invasion and colonisation never achieved success. Their attitudinal individuality precluded nationality; they never attained that same depth of political and military unity which had enabled Rome to become a cohesive Empire. The story of the Celts' decline becomes a tale of utter colonisation, of being subsumed by other cultures, Romans, Saxons, Vikings, Normans; a story of erosion, of retreat and diminution, of winnowing, assimilation and retiral. Further and further back they retreated on promontories and islands, Atlantic Celtic ghettoes, out of reach and, where possible, inaccessible.

Before the Romans came to the South of England the fort of Camulos, the war god, possessed stature, a large Celtic tribal settlement (where the inhabitants' diet included – according to the archaeologists – copious quantities of shellfish). An extensive 'dig' made it possible, briefly in 1985, to see anew the tessellated Roman streets of Camulôdunum, as it became. Now that Colchester's uncaring town authority has permitted a shopping mall to be built on the site, the mosaic pavings have disappeared. Gone too are the wide black stripes and marks clearly visible along cross-sections of the excavations – proof of Boudicca's holocaust.

Colchester led – and typified – Rome's domination of the Celts, consolidated by the defeat of Vercingetorix in Gaul, and symbolised in Britain by the crushing of Boudicca (although her revolt attracted no more than local tribal support). During the period between 55 BC, when Rome in the person of Julius Caesar first invaded Britain, and AD 43, the year in which the realistic and effective conquest of the island was begun by Claudius, the fortunes of Camulodunum changed in line with the changing face of Britain.

By AD 10, Cunobelinus, 'King of the Britons', had established himself in a rich and prosperous rulership at Colchester. (His name meant 'the hound of the god of war': as Cymbeline, he leads the *dramatis personae* in Shakespeare's eponymous play.) His monarchy had Roman undertones: his coinage depicted a prancing horse surmounting letters from Cunobelinus's name, and on the obverse, an ear of corn symbolising the agriculture of his kingdom. Later coins even called him '*Rex*'. Before and during Cunobelinus's time, Colchester's considerable defensive proportions encompassed widespread areas of ground enclosed and fortified by a series of earthwork dykes, and took account of natural protection such as marshland and estuary. Cunobelinus died around AD 40, the Romans landed in Kent three years later, and Claudius himself, shambling, twitching, slobbering Claudius, marched into Colchester accompanied by elephants, having defeated on the Medway *en route*, Caractacus, the son of the late Cunobelinus.

BOADICEA HARANGUING HER TROOPS.

Boadicea (more correctly Boudicca), who attracted as much misrepresentation when she was alive as she did at the height of the Celtic romantic movement. She mounted the most ferocious revolt against the Romans in Britain. Smaller, more organised armies defeated her – but not before she had cut a bloody swathe across south-east England, the only Celtic leader to do so.

Claudius, sitting in court for sixteen days, set the tone for the manner in which Rome would subdue and rule the British Celts. He received the submission of several kings and granted their tribes Roman citizenship and friendship. (Boudicca's husband received this 'honour'.) The 'client-kings' were expected to collude publicly with the Roman Empire by guaranteeing not to revolt against it and by affording it protection against the other rebellious, or as yet unsubdued, Celtic tribes. In reward, these newly-Romanised Celtic chieftains – especially in the south and south-east – were patronised and entertained by the Roman officials, given status and titles: encouraged, they wore Roman dress, gained access to the lifestyle of the conquerors and otherwise faded into the Imperial culture. They appeared at local celebrations, went to the theatre, the temple, the baths: gradually Roman customs supplanted many Celtic traditions. Camulodunum became a colony for soldiers retired from the various Roman campaigns, *Colonia Claudia Victricensis*, distinguished like other such colonies by fine public buildings – above all a temple, dedicated, after his death probably, to Claudius, by then a god. The temple's presence and symbolism made it the target for Boudicca's fury.

Before the Roman conquest, the British Celts broadly resembled those of mainland Europe. Britain had received Celts for several centuries, first in small tribal bands, and later in the major migrations suggested in the description by Julius Caesar of 'Belgic immigrants who came to plunder and make war'. At the time of Caesar's abortive first landings in 55 BC, the island of Britain, including Scotland and Wales, contained many Celtic tribes, probably as much as two-thirds of the population. A large concentration of Celts dwelt along the south and south-west coasts; other intensively-populated Celtic communities inhabited lands along the Bristol Channel, in East Anglia, northern Wales, Cumbria and Northumbria.

The population is exceedingly large [wrote Caesar], the ground densely studded with dwellings, closely resembling those of the Gauls, and a great number of cattle. For money they use either bronze, or gold coins, or iron ingots of fixed weights. Tin is found inland, and small quantities of iron near the coast; the copper they use is imported. As in Gaul there is timber of every sort, except beech and fir. Hares, fowl and geese they do not think it lawful to eat, but rear them for pleasure and amusement. The climate is more temperate than in Gaul, the cold being less severe. The island has a triangular shape, with one side facing Gaul. One corner of this side, on the coast of Kent, is the landing-place for nearly all the ships from Gaul, and it points east; the lower corner points south. The length of this side is about 475 miles. Another side faces west, towards Spain; in this direction is Ireland, which is believed to be half the size of Britain, and lies at the same distance from it as Gaul. Midway across there is an island called Mona, and it is believed that there are also a number of smaller islands, in which according to some writers there is a month of perpetual darkness at the winter solstice. Our enquiries on this subject were always fruitless, but we found by accurate measurements with a water-clock that the nights are shorter than on the continent.

Would that all of Caesar's geography had been so diligently checked. He perpetuated the error of the ancient Romans who thought that the coast of France stretched in one line from Pyrenean Spain to the Hook of Holland, that Britain lay along it, and that Ireland, being west of Britain was off the coast of Spain, and the whole, therefore, could become an easily-won annexe of the Empire. Further, other contemporary writers have given the name of 'Mona' not to the Isle of Man, but to Anglesey in North Wales.

By far the most civilised inhabitants are those living in Kent, which area is all maritime, whose behaviour differs little from that of the Gauls. Most of the tribes in the interior do not grow corn but live on milk and meat, and their garments are skins. All the Britons dye their bodies with woad, which achieves a blue colour, and shave the whole of their bodies except the head and the upper lip. Wives are shared between groups of ten or twelve men, especially between brothers and between fathers and sons; but the offspring of these unions are counted as the children of the man with whom a particular virgin had first cohabited.

How Caesar invites ambivalence. Is such information about their cohabitation no more than the lore a conqueror likes to hear about the barbarians he is about to civilise? (You have to be wary of Caesar, too. Throughout *De Bello Gallico*, when Caesar praises an enemy highly you know victory will follow. As with Vercingetorix, where the implication is clear: it requires *diligentia summissima* to conquer a man described as *summae diligentiae*.)

Where the Celtic generations in Britain settled in strength they fortified. The invading Romans had to contend with a series of ramparted hillforts which were both habitat and defence. The hillfort commanded a vantage point over the nearby countryside, ideally with a clear view for three hundred and sixty degrees. Around the outside, earth from the digging of a great ditch had been piled into one or more ramparts – depending upon the style of the tribe, the availability of other materials or the steepness of the hill. This rampart was often further protected by the erection of a wall with timbering – Caesar from his French experience called it the *murus Gallicus*.

In Britain the excavations of such hillforts, such as Maiden Castle in Dorset, stand as archaeologically-verified monuments to the Celts who experienced the Roman occupation. Some of the forts assumed legendary status – Cadbury Castle in Somerset, the Camelot of the Round Table. Others developed from natural citadels, such as Castle Rock at Dumbarton on the River Clyde, the kingly capital of Strathclyde, and 'Fortress of all the Britons' – and further to the east of Scotland two castles, Stirling and Edinburgh. (The name 'Edinburgh', corrupted *via* 'Edwinesburgh', derives from the original 'Dun Aedynn' or 'Dinas Eidynn', the fort of a tribe who gave their name to the Celtic epic poem called 'The Gododdin' – and to Dunedin in New Zealand.)

Despite Caesar's major thrust in July of 54 BC, the British Celts remained substantially independent. In political terms, the main success of Caesar's invasion lay in having drawn attention to the possibilities of annexing Britain, and in having at least paved some of the way for any other ambitious Roman. And even though Caesar won popular credit for the invasion of Britain, several contemporary observers make it clear that they did not believe his activities had effectively colonised Britain. After Caesar, and after Claudius's initiative over eighty years later, the Romans campaigned by continuing to hurl legions against those local rulers whom they could not persuade into client-kingship or other bureaucratic submission. Up and down through Britain successive governors campaigned to subdue the Celts.

In AD 77, Gnaeus Iulius Agricola, aged thirty-eight, arrived. He had served under Suetonius Paullinus twenty years earlier and was remarkable enough to

Right: The bronze head of a statue of Claudius, now in the British Museum, found in 1907 on a river-bed in Suffolk.

Far right: Julius Caesar – a marble bust in the Louvre. Caesar's landings on the south coast in 55 and 54 BC gave him the popular reputation as the Roman conqueror of Britain. In effect he achieved little other than establishing the principle that Britain could be annexed.

Above: Of all the figures in Celtic lore, few have subsequently been dealt as much nonsense as the Druid. In reality, the Druid possessed power born of magical practice, arcane knowledge and the conduct of worship. The barbarous sacrifices which the Druids conducted shocked even the ungentle Romans.

have been made governor of Aquitaine, where he enhanced his reputation for fair dealing, energy, enterprise and military competence. England had largely succumbed to the Roman legions by then, and with the collusion of the client-kings, acted as the granary of Rome – as Julius Caesar had always intended. Agricola dealt with the troublesome Welsh – according to some historical sources – by annihilating the Ordovices, a tribe in North Wales. And when the Brigantes displayed a tendency to forget their allegiance to Rome, they were subdued too – and within a year of Agricola's arrival. A year later found the Empire consolidating in the northern regions of England, and thereafter, north of the Forth and Clyde rivers and deep into Scotland. By AD 80, most of the Lowlands of Scotland, and several coastal areas in the far north of England and the Borders seemed under Agricola's military thumb. Only the far Highlands were left – the legendarily ferocious Caledonii up in the north-west of Scotland. Roman military strength again carried the day – at Mons Graupius, tentatively set by scholars as the hill of Bennachie, in Garioch near the town of Inverurie, some twenty miles from Aberdeen. With the subsequent establishment of garrisons most of Scotland, like Wales, was now – however restlessly and rebelliously – as much a Roman dominion (in Roman theory anyway) as the rest of Britain. The building of Hadrian's Wall finally reflected the Western Empire's unease, and the need for fortification against both the Celts and the Picts – who bore at least some elemental similarities with the Celts. Some of them spoke a Celtic language; their name came from a Roman nickname meaning 'the painted ones': like the Celts they tattooed themselves. Speculation persists that their primary European origins may have been geographically close to those of the Celts.

In AD 82, during the campaign in Scotland, Agricola took a decision at the Mull of Kintyre not to cross the eleven miles into Ireland. The historian, Tacitus (who five years earlier had married Agricola's daughter), nonetheless reported the Roman governor's opinion: 'Frequently I have heard Agricola say that Ireland could be invaded and overcome by one legion and auxiliaries of moderate number.'

We have had to depend – due to the Celts' illiteracy – upon the Romans for the first extensive, factual, written picture of Celtic Britain (truly, if more ironically than usual, a case of history being written by the winners). We have to abide by the uncontradicted justifications and vanities of Julius Caesar, and by the reports from the writers and historians of the Empire who, though often ameliorated by subtle cynicism, were, frankly, camp followers like Tacitus. Despite the best scepticisms of historical scholarship and interpretation, it has taken archaeology to redress the balance, and to give us a picture of pre-Roman Celtic Britain.

Prehistorians suggest a culture lasting up to two thousand years, embracing Neolithic man, who migrated to Britain via North-eastern France. From about 1300 BC, the shapes of what would become the Iron Age began to appear in British society – the lone farm or group of farms, the clearing of forests, the cultivation of wide areas of pasture, the safe home on a hilltop for a family that had extended from settler to settlement.

The Bronze Age brought improved facilities. In the estuary of the River Thames archaeologists have discovered swords compatible with the weaponry of the Urnfield people from the Middle Rhineland regions. Even though, as has been argued, they may have belonged to travellers or raiders or traders, they do establish a connection between mainland Europe and Britain in the middle of the first millennium before Christ. Successive visitors derived from the same European prehistory, and progressively from the same cultural root and flower, the Hallstatt and La Tene Cultures. They developed along the same lines, from the smaller tribal grouping to the ever-increasing extended family structure until a localised, or petty kingship was arrived at – by which time land had been seized and an aristocracy arising from the family had been established. They too grew gleaming and powerful.

Following the simplest chronological pathway, the earliest Celts in Britain migrated from France in the days of the spreading Urnfield Culture, identified subsequently by their distinctive Bronze Age artefacts. By 700 BC, larger immigrations had begun, whose agricultural and burial rite traces have been found in the chalky coastlands of the south. Progressively, warriors bearing long bronze and iron weapons, identified as typical of Hallstatt Culture, penetrated the inland regions. From the early part of the fifth century BC, stronger and more numerous invaders arrived from France and the Low Countries and stamped their identity heavily upon the inhabitants. Many of these may have come from a tribe or larger grouping of people called the Pretani, in whose name lies the root of the word 'Britain'. An ancient writer, Pytheas of Massilia, whose work is now lost but was taken up by later scribes, mentioned what he called 'the Pretanic Islands'.

In the last days of Celtic freedom, the pre-Roman political structure of Britain mirrored, to a large degree, that which the Romans had overthrown in Gaul. These British Celts operated similar systems of kinship and tribal rule. They depended upon agriculture; they indulged in warfare; they accomplished beautiful metalwork and art; their society had a developed and recognisable structure. A Celtic alliance, which included trade, spanned the English Channel, even if it never exploited the full political potential it possessed.

The Roman occupation of Britain set about bringing to an end the Celtic civilisation in England. The Celts beyond the frontiers in Scotland and in Wales, using the wild terrain to fullest advantage, always restless, raised rebellion after rebellion, but in England the *Pax Romana* took over as the military administration gave way to an official civil service: civilians drawn from both the immigrant Roman officials and the native Romanised Celts governed the land.

The cultural erosion proceeded, too. As the Romans dealt in wine, their vessels suggested new forms to the Celtic potters. And Britain began to urbanise. With the building of the system of *civitates*, towns were constructed by the simple expedient of granting land to groups of legionaries who then settled in a designated area and turned it into a town. More usually, existing sites, villages or settlements were chosen and a network of such Roman towns soon spread across England – Winchester, Cirencester, Gloucester, Lincoln, Exeter. A garrison element appeared in the planning: many of the most Romanised towns in England were established in, or close to, regions still populated by lively Celtic tribes who had been there since the beginning of the Iron Age.

Inland in Provence, the winds of summer sometimes reach gale force, hot and noisy, a Provençal *mistral*. Driving from Orange, the road to the small town of Saint Rémy-de-Provence points so straight that only the Romans could have built it: through the town, a few more kilometres, to Glanum, the grey-white rubble of an ancient Roman town. All over the Roman Empire such traces linger. Have they but recently left? Turned off the water, gathered up the children, taken official papers and departed, summoned back to Rome?

For some centuries during the colonisation of Britain, urgent business at home, civil wars, internal strife, decadence and moral corruption had damaged the Roman Empire from within. From without, hordes, largely Germanic, Ostrogoths, Visigoths, Vandals, repeatedly broke through the Empire's frontiers, sundered her states. In Gaul entire regions required re-conquering as leaders revolted. In England, as usurper followed usurper, each uprising more savage and effective, the system of rule and the semblance of peace began to fall apart. Inevitably, all argosies were abandoned: all Romans abroad officially recalled.

The ghost town of Glanum evokes this termination of the Roman Empire. Through the blocks and pillars, through the arches and fallen walls the hot wind whistles. In the ruins, Rome may still be perceived, order and construction and regularity and system and power. The Roman Empire, seen in the rocks of Glanum, seems like an efficient eagle who alighted, marauded, fed awhile: came, saw, conquered – and left.

Invaders, like nature, abhor a vacuum. As Rome departed others moved in. If islands exist to be invaded, Britain offered proof. The Celts themselves – and their forerunners – had colonised the island; then the Romans: now came the new tide which neither the Romans nor their hybrid Romano-Celts, nor the active and fierce vestiges of the old, constantly-rebelling Celtic tribes could entirely stem.

East Anglia – the very name makes the point: look out from Lowestoft across these flattened seas and visualise the next inundation: the Angles and the Saxons and the Jutes. The Romans employed them – and Frisians, Franks, Alamanni – as mercenary legionnaires in Britain. From earlier occasional incursions, fighters and their families settled along the eastern shoreline. Boatloads of these Germanic tribes arrived anew, hardly one continuous army but sufficient in number to cause substantial disturbance to those Britons who had seized local and regional power after the Roman province collapsed. Such governmental unity as Rome had fashioned in England was threatened and faltering, and would disappear. Britons had re-emerged, individually or in groups of petty states and these Anglo-Saxons were the common enemy. Anglo-Saxon Britain, with diluted, fading Celtic influence and still-fresh Roman presence, moved onward and became Angleland, England.

Across the Irish Sea in Ireland, any disturbance of tranquillity during the period of Roman Britain, from 55 BC to circa AD 410, was self-induced. The freedom

The Roman triumphal arch at Orange in Provence, a *colonia*, where veterans of the European campaigns were rewarded with homes in a town excelling in ease, recreation and comfort.

from Rome meant that Ireland continued to develop as a Celtic country – if, in fact, the Irish were Celts? And if so, from what date and location? Even by the scholars' own admission the early Irish texts contain many fine examples of the inventive mind at work.

From the extensive linguistic, traditional and (comparatively incomplete) archaeological evidence there can be no doubt that Ireland answers the definition 'Celtic'. The difficulty arises in determining when, and by what manner of man, was the island made Celtic? The suggestions range from the mythic and mystic, such as the lost city of Atlantis, and any other kind of geographical Grail, to the poetic, such as the Book of Invasions, which says that the first arrivals in Ireland were relatives of Noah, fifty-one women and three men, who failed to gain entry into the Ark and sailed to Ireland:

> Fleeing from threatened flood, they sailed,
> Seeking the fair island, without serpent or claw;
> From the deck of their hasty barque watched
> The soft edge of Ireland nearward draw.

The men in this hasty barque failed to survive. One died of an embrace, one was buried in a stone heap, 'riot of mind, all passion spent' and one 'fled from the ferocious women lest he, too, by love be rent'. Other opinion – sometimes academic and as often refuted as stated – holds that the Celts of Ireland sprang from an aristocratic warrior group who left Galicia in Northern Spain, and whose colonising had as thorough an effect upon Ireland as the Roman conquest had upon Britain.

Firmer ground may be trod when discussing the nature of Irish society during the Roman period in Britain, i.e., just before the coming of Christianity to Ireland, commonly dated to AD 432, the arrival of Patrick. Bronze Age peoples had already populated the island when, circa 500 BC, travellers arrived whom archaeology has identified (according to Hallstatt Culture) as having stemmed from the lower Rhine regions. Via Scotland they came into Antrim, with frequent incursions from nearby Britain. In the next few centuries, scabbards, bronze horns and ornamented horse-trappings in La Tene style appeared in Ireland. Whether journeymen smiths made these for wealthy chieftains, or whether they belonged to a new wave of Celtic immigrants from Britain or Gaul (of La Tene Culture) still arouses archaeological debate. Furthermore, refugees from the Roman conquests, first of Gaul, then of Britain, must have found Ireland. In any event, by the first century BC a Celtic society of some depth and richness had gained ground.

The images of ancient Ireland come from epic poetry and cycles of legend. The picture the scribes painted was idyllic – comely princesses, bubbling clear streams and wide sweet rivers, golden vales, trees bowed down with fruit and singing birds, mighty rulers, justice and love, sweet music, cloth-of-gold, flowers, peace, a land flowing with milk and honey. One text described the idealised king, around whom the society revolved:

He was the finest king in Ireland before the belief [i.e. Christianity – this was a monkish, post-Christian text] and he worked the land for a mere two weeks of the springtime, yet it gave forth its crop of grain three times a year. Cuckoos sang from their perches between the horns of the kine;

every branch bore a hundred bunches of nuts and there were a hundred nuts in every bunch ... the calves matured into milking cows before their time ... one ounce of silver brought the purchase of twelve honey dishes and twelve bushels of corn. Ireland was a paradise where the flowers were filled with honey.

Many of the scribes, almost exclusively monks, copied out the legends of the oral tradition, albeit with only as much fidelity as their Christian censoriousness would permit. Literacy in Ireland dates realistically only from the fifth and sixth centuries AD, therefore the writers transcribed tales which the Romans would have heard had they invaded, and which, however exaggerated, even if derived from folk memory, have some basis in fact.

Archaeology now begins to support the epic impressions. Eamhain Mhacha, Navan Fort, near the city of Armagh, in Northern Ireland, stands in time as one of the most famous of all legendary places, the seat of great kings, the council chamber of powerful Druids. To Eamhain Mhacha, Setanta, the young Cuchu-lainn, set out, bearing with him his hurley stick and ball, made of silver and gold. In order to make his journey less tedious he would strike the ball with the hurley and throw the hurley after the ball, striking the ball in mid-air and carrying it further. Then he would fling his javelin, strike the hurley in mid-air, which would then strike the ball in mid-air and all travel further still. By dint of fleetness Setanta then caught them all before they touched the ground.

At Eamhain Mhacha archaeologists have unearthed the remains of the famous court, a place where tribute was given and received: the skull of one exotic gift, a Barbary ape, dated to the fifth century BC. From a small lake nearby several ceremonial trumpets emerged. And the excavated skull of a hound creates greater mythic speculation. When the boy Setanta resided in Eamhain Mhacha he was attacked by a mastiff of the smith Cualann. The boy defended himself by driving the ball with his hurley down the dog's savage throat and killing him. When the smith complained that he now would have no hound, Setanta said he would take the hound's place as a defender of the smith's valuable property and that is how his name changed from Setanta to Cu Chulainn, 'the hound of Cualann'.

Such mighty earthworks on Eamhain Mhacha: huge, extensive outer and inner ditches which must have taken years to construct. From any point of this circular rampart many miles of the wide and fertile countryside may be surveyed. It was a place both of residence and of worship. On one side stood a settlement of circular houses and at the centre of the fort the native Celts constructed a vast round temple, the roof-tree as high as twenty metres. It may have taken as long as ten years to build, and then on one appointed day, circa 100 BC, the entire edifice was deliberately burned to the ground. Nobody knows the reasons: to mourn the death of a loved king, or, on the instructions of the Druids, to propitiate a god in the interest of a good harvest, or to gain a victory against oncoming tribes?

The relationship between Ireland and Roman Britain comprised trading and raiding. Discoveries of Mediterranean pottery, Roman brooches and coins, prove the trade. The raids led to a sublime irony: their own militancy caused the first erosion of the Irish Celts. According to the schoolroom legend, a raiding party carried back with them and enslaved as a pig-herd the son of a Roman official.

The boy spent six years in captivity, then on his bare mountainside heard voices from Heaven telling him conveniently that a ship on which he could escape sat at anchor two hundred miles away. He found himself in Gaul and after many trials made his way back to his own family in Britain. A few more voices called out, he entered the Christian priesthood and responded to the heavenly visions urging him to evangelise Ireland. His name – Patrick.

An ignorant and humourless man whose enslavement presumably interrupted his education, Patrick left behind biographical details in slender writings of his own – in Latin but expressed colloquially without any thought for the rectitude of written Latin syntax. He reveals most in his *Confessio*, a rough-hewn and slender sort of *Apologia pro Vita Sua* which begins:

I, Patrick, a most untutored sinner and the lowest of all the faithful and the most despicable in the eyes of many, am the son of Calpurnius, a deacon who was the son of Potitus a priest, from the village of Bannaventa Berniae, who had an estate near it, where I was taken prisoner. At that time I was about sixteen years of age, I had no knowledge of the true God and I was borne away into captivity in Ireland with thousands of people ...

When Patrick arrived in Ireland the mainstream Celtic cultures of Alpine Europe had long begun to wane. He spoke a Celtic language, still the vernacular in Britain, and he found in Ireland a society 'tribal, rural, hierarchical and familiar'. The key to his mission lay in dealing with the petty kings. So dependent was the society upon the family, the kinship structure, that the king had more than temporal influence – he possessed sacred connotations, influenced the spirituality and moral-ity of his tribe with his power to officiate at worship, with his central role in all religious expression and with his court of warriors, jurists and Druids. Patrick successfully converted many of these kings – the people followed suit.

Patrick's conversions satisfied, or, with cunning appropriateness, became adapted to the Celtic appetite for legend. At Cashel, that proud and mysterious rock rising from the plains of Tipperary, sat the over-king who claimed sovereignty in the southern half of Ireland. At the king's baptism, Patrick accidentally put his pointed crozier through the king's foot. The king never cried out; Patrick saw the blood and, filled with remorse, asked the king why he had not protested. The king replied that he thought it was all part of the ceremony. The rock itself, in which was later built a church with strong Romanesque and Celtic influences, attracts another Patrician legend. Further to the north stands a gap-toothed mountain, egregious in the plain, called the Devil's Bit. Local legend says that Satan, pursued by Patrick and finding the mountain in his way, bit a large chunk out of it and raced on. When he found the lump of rock too heavy he dropped it at Cashel. A few miles away to the west, on the hill of Kilfeakle, Patrick lost a tooth and founded a church: Kilfeakle – *cill* – a church; *fiacail* – a tooth.

From the records kept nearest his time it appears that Patrick bears responsibility for the first batch of Catholic saints in Ireland:

... all bishops, distinguished and holy and full of the Holy Ghost, three hundred and fifty in number, all founders of churches. They had one head, Christ himself, and one leader, Patrick. They had one Mass, one liturgy, one tonsure from ear to ear. They celebrated one Easter, on the fourteenth moon after the spring equinox ... they did not reject the service and association of women because they were founded on the rock called Christ, and therefore they did not need to fear the heat of temptation ...

The conversion of Ireland, easily accomplished if Patrick and subsequent monks are to be believed, wrought profound changes upon the Celtic way of life. Patrick and his Latin prayers gained for Roman culture a toehold in Ireland, diluting the power of the Celtic expression. Christianity also brought the establishment of the monastery, with connotations of the extended family in religion, and power to obtain and maintain property. By the sixth century AD these changes had begun to seep through Ireland. In their last bastion the Celts of Western Europe thus began to lose the balance of power. Except in one notable arena – the Celtic art forms, where Christianity brought about a revival, a Golden Age, notably in the illuminations of the great manuscripts. In the Book of Kells, the Book of Durrow, the Lindisfarne Gospels, the monastic scribes wrote down, in brilliantly decorated form, the gospels and the other versions of the word of God. Clearly influenced by Hallstatt and (especially) La Tene Cultures at their most glorious, from these illuminations arise many of the immediate visual connotations of the word 'Celtic' today, the vivid, coloured whorling of a main capital letter, or a passage from the scripture decorated with loving care. Other artistic expression in ornamented sacred vessels or elaborate metalworked reliquaries also sprang from the monasteries, who either made or commissioned such work as an extension of worship. Thus, at the very point of dilution the Celtic civilisation produced its last – and perhaps greatest – flowering.

Drive north of Glasgow and out to the west, into Argyllshire, along the shores of long thin lakes. Not far inland from Jura, and near Loch Fyne, rises a rock-pile in the little vale of the River Add – Dunadd, on whose summit stands a flat rock with a weathered 'footprint': only a man whose foot fitted could become king of Scotland.

In the centuries directly after the birth of Christ, Dunadd flourished, one of the most powerful and important fortresses in Alba, as the country was then known. From Dalriada in County Antrim, a few miles away in Ireland, came the Scotii, whose name eventually attached to the entire country. These Scots set up a rulership called the Dalriada, of which Dunadd was the centre, and the west of Scotland thus became an Irish colony. The ensuing centuries of cross-fertilisation between the Irish and the Scots led to a virtual merging of the Scots and Irish Gaelic dialects. Further down along the west coast of Britain similar incursions occurred on a regular basis, sometimes colonising, sometimes trading, sometimes cultural. In Pembroke, South Wales, the territory of Dyfed was subdued and ruled by Irish invaders, as, to the north, likewise, the Isle of Man.

This colonisation wrought a further development – the forceful expansion of Christianity in Scotland and the North of England. In Britain, Columba of Iona became one of the most powerful figures in religious politics. In 563 he left Ireland after political difficulty – war and politics too often superseded his taste for worship – and with the divine model of twelve disciples he founded a monastery on the island of Iona off the west coast of Scotland. Unchanging in his instincts, Columba made Iona the spiritual seat of the Dalriada government, as well as the base from which the evangelisation of Pictish Scotland emanated. Eighty years later, as a result of the power of Iona, another monastery, Lindisfarne in the North Sea, was established by monks of Iona's community by virtue of a direct request from the King of Northumbria who had taken refuge among them.

The rapid and huge expansion of the Christian Church in the North of England, derived via Ireland and Iona, came into some conflict with the church in the South of England whose evangelists had been reaching northwards. The monk, Augustine, had arrived at Canterbury in 597, at Pope Gregory's request, specifically charged with the complete conversion of all the English, and may have experienced a twinge of envy, therefore, at the intensity of the religion already practised in the north. But Augustine had begun to insist upon the most up-to-date liturgical calendar issuing from Rome. The Irish Church, which influenced the North of England so heavily, had been out of direct touch with Rome for over a hundred years, and was celebrating its feasts on different days. The southern English evangelists, on behalf of Rome, attempted to bring the northerners into line, but the Irish Church sought to establish the facts for itself, and sent a mission to Rome. Once they ascertained the accuracy of the southerners' claims, the Irish immediately conformed to Rome's calendar. A split then happened, because even though the Irish Church concurred, the Church in the North of England did not, and when the King of Northumbria married a woman from Kent he found that he and his wife celebrated Easter on a different date. In order to resolve this absurd situation he called a meeting at Whitby in Yorkshire. The Roman calendar carried the day but the monks of Lindisfarne would not conform. The abbot and several of his brothers left the monastery. All liturgical disputes notwithstanding, Iona and Lindisfarne had established themselves as cornerstones in the foundation of a Gaelic Scotland.

As the Roman Empire receded, one of the most novel migrations in all of Celtic tradition had begun. From southern and eastern Wales, and especially from Cornwall, large numbers of settlers moved to Brittany. In Julius Caesar's time, the Venetii, whom he subdued in fierce fighting in 56 BC, dominated many peninsulas in Brittany. But even under Rome the Celtic cultures had never dwindled. By adding the migrations of the Welsh and Cornish to the other tribes who already dwelt there, the region may be regarded as twice Celtic.

The connections already existed between South Wales and Brittany; exchanges if not downright migrations had recurred over the centuries. New, and greater in this planned and deliberate colonisation, to judge from the linguistic evidence, was the Cornish element. Transactions in tin, mined extensively in Cornwall and transported to the shores of Brittany for overland trading throughout Europe, may explain the intensive Cornish awareness of the region called Armorica, which stretched from northern Brittany into Normandy. Undoubtedly, too, both the Welsh and the Cornish fled the Irish raiders who constantly attacked and colonised large stretches of the west coast of southern Britain. A further theory suggests that many of the settlers came from the ranks of mercenary soldiery, drafted in by the failing Roman Empire in Gaul to keep the marauders from Saxony, or the Franks, at bay.

The migration constitutes something of a historical phenomenon. The departing people came from a wide area of the south-west of Britain. The Celtic tribes of Devon, the area now represented by land directly east of the River Tamar, vacated vast areas of the county and the flight from the land of southern Wales also became extensive and constant.

The colonisation contained little unwillingness on either side. Settlers and incumbents reached calm agreement: many of the immigrants even maintained the homesteads they had left in Britain. The language of Armorica, which had included Gaulish Celtic and the Latin of Rome, received a great injection of dialects from Cornwall. The newly-established territory of Brittany divided into three kingdoms, Dumnonia, Bro Erech and, in the south and south-west, Cornouaille – Cornwall. In any development thenceforth, Armorica, now Brittany (referred to by Roman scribes as *Britannia Minor*) reverted in many ways to the tribal and social attitudes of the pre-Roman Celts of Gaul. Echoes rang out evoking the earliest Celts – in the interior of the region huge forests remained uncleared; romantically, the spirit of the prehistoric Celts who emerged from the primeval gloom of Eastern Europe had an opportunity to come to life again.

Patterns of Celtic survival (which led to the eventual emergence of the Celtic fringe) appear clearer by the beginning of the eighth century. The Irish influence remained pervasive, with a history of regular invasion and occupation of Scotland and Wales. Brittany promised to be more Celtic than the Celts themselves. Overall, the Christian Church had taken firm root in the wake of the Romans and preached to a diluting Celtic community which, though still largely agricultural, had now begun to acquire learning based on literature and Latin. The old family system of the kindred had changed and enlarged, bringing greater legal and social sophistication.

The monastery played a powerful part in the scheme of things and the practice of religion, popular and colloquial, gathered together the essentials of life, birth, marriage and death, and used them as lynchpins. Away from the monasteries, in converted parts of Britain and all across Ireland, a physical pattern of rural Christian Celtic life emerged which remains substantially unchanged to this day – the village or community church with the local cemetery, crosses, commemorative stones.

The great abbeys, such as Clonmacnoise on the River Shannon, rose as centres of wealth and learning – the abbot held power comparable with the local chieftain or petty king. In his care he had many young men whose families deemed it an honour to have a son in the service of God. Within the monastery walls, expressing worship through art, lay many objects of great beauty, chalices, croziers, reliquaries, golden, silver, jewelled. The flourishing of learning rose wonderfully, especially in Ireland, with the Church acting as principal patron. In several hundred years of peace Ireland had become a settled and relatively placid island, enjoying all the affluence and self-confidence that comes to a land free of invasions and conquests. In this 'Isle of Saints and Scholars', images, legends and memorable piety became notes in the cadences of the word 'Celtic'. On quiet sea inlets, or in their own water-meadows by broad rivers, the monastery communities scribed the tales of the heroes (doodled poems or cartoons into the margins), copied the Latin texts which formed the basic literature of the Christian religion, sang the praises of God and gave thanks for their sweet and untroubled life.

Sudden ferocity: the Vikings struck. Their longships raided along the coastlines and up the river estuaries, penetrating far inland with speed and rapaciousness. The sanctity of the abbeys meant nothing to them: they disrespected all beliefs, defiled all altars. In 842, the wife of one Viking raider committed – in the monk's eyes – a sacrilege of pagan magical ritual by posturing herself on the altar of Clonmacnoise where she 'gave oracles'. No place seemed safe from these accomplished sea-warriors. From the monastic settlement on Skellig Michael, a wild and inaccessible crag out in the Atlantic, Etgall, a monk, was captured and died of neglect at their hands. The Norsemen looted and pillaged and burnt and murdered: so comprehensively dreadful was their reputation that one monkish poet could even find comfort in a stormy night, secure from the Viking's axe.

> Harsh and cruel the wind this night;
> Turning and tossing the sea's locks white.
> On a night like this I gain some peace
> Proud Vikings will only sail calm seas.

All monasteries, large or small, offered plunder; huge quantities of silver and gold objects, precious and invaluable manuscripts disappeared, as whole communities were put to the sword and the torch. Many of the metalworked treasures were borne back to Scandinavia where they still turn up in excavations: some, especially the books, in which the Norsemen had no interest, were lost for ever, thrown into lakes or burned.

As extensive as they were ferocious, the raids terrified the island. One recorder of 'the invasion of Ireland by the Danes and other Norsemen' described the scene in his own native province of Munster, in the south:

... immense floods and countless sea-vomitings of ships and boats and fleets so that there was not a harbour nor a land-port nor a dun nor a fortress nor a fastness in all Munster without floods of Danes and pirates ... they made spoil-land and sword-land and conquered-land of her throughout her breadth and generally. And they ravaged her chieftainries and her privileged churches and her sanctuaries; and they rent her shrines and her reliquaries and her books ...

Ireland's celebrated chronological record, The Annals of the Four Masters, laconically records some of the most devastating early attacks, which took place in 'the Age of Christ, 802' (a date which varies, according to other accounts, by several years).

The church of Colum-Cille at Ceannannus was destroyed. Inis-Muiredaigh was burned by foreigners, and they attacked Ros-Commain.

Such brevity fails to convey the extent of the Viking incursions: Ceannannus (Kells) is located in County Meath in the east of Ireland, Inishmurray in County Sligo in the far west, Roscommon, inland in the north-west midlands of the country.

An appealing by-product of the invasion (although earlier attributions have been made) hallmarks later Celtic Ireland – the Round Tower, belfry, sanctuary, symbol. It stood between twenty and forty metres tall, made of cut stone and tapering upwards to a conical cap. From its uppermost floors the monks rang their handbells and guided pilgrims to the dignified refuge. The door opened several feet up in the wall. If the raiders appeared on the river or came in from the sea, the monks fled, taking the monastery's precious vessels with them. They drew the ladder up behind them, and perhaps fought back by pouring scalding substances down upon the looters. (The most exciting moments in my early education derived from the incongruity of saintly men pouring boiling oil down from the high windows.)

The Viking invasions of Britain and Ireland led to a new style of settlement. Where they gained hold they built towns, especially at sea ports as, in Ireland, Waterford, Wexford – and Dublin which became their headquarters for raids on all territories in the Irish Sea. In Scotland their extensive influence led to chieftainries such as the Lordship of the Isles, offering allegiance to a Norse rather than a Scottish king. In England they established substantial communities and even effected peaceful colonisation in other regions. In Wales they sacked Anglesey and overran the Isle of Man. But their greatest and most visible effect changed Ireland – logically enough, as the country had had no recent history of such devastating invasion. In the coastal towns which they built, they introduced – as the Romans did in Britain – a form of urbanisation. They capitalised upon Dublin's position, as a port on the Irish Sea, sixty miles from the Welsh coast. They established the commerce of shipping trade, they gave the country her first coinage – and made deep inroads into the rich, existing, and largely Celtic culture.

The Celts fought back. A number of Irish chieftains conducted campaigns against the Vikings, sometimes ranging far out of their own territories to do so. Finally, Brian Boru, a Munster king, defeated the Danes at the Battle of Clontarf in Dublin in 1014. The Norse threat to Ireland was broken, but Irish Celtic culture, flourishing under the leadership and patronage of the Christian religion, had been disturbed. A European people, even more mobile and adventurous, had now discovered this relatively wealthy and placid island, whose legendary and heroic and saintly reputation had travelled abroad, whose missionaries had already travelled France and Italy. The rural areas still retained the tribal way of life, with petty kingships, surviving or regenerated monasteries – but for how long could this descended Celtic system last?

By the time the Irish had broken the Norse hold, Celtic Gaul was an echo, several centuries distant. New methods of government, new tribal groupings, with kings and courts and chivalries evolving from the Celtic, Romano-Gallo and invading Germanic influences had comprehensively eclipsed the Gaulish tribal identity. England, too, comprised an amalgam of Celtic, Roman, Romano-Celtic, Germanic, Norse. Scotland had acquired several layers of cultures – some Roman and Anglian influence in the Lowlands, the Irish settlers and kingships in the west and the Highlands, a large Pictish presence sharing the east, partly with Anglo-Saxons: other tribes with British antecedents scattered through some border areas and into northern England. Wales had been caught between Anglo-Saxons from inland and invaders from the sea, first the Irish and then the Danes - and often split further internally by the continuous disagreements between North and South Wales. Eventually, in a series of agreements rather than battles, based on English sympathies rather than old Celtic traditions, the alliances between Wales and the Saxon overlords, such as Alfred the Great, grew stronger.

Much of history is geography. The Celts, tribal and travelling, could never have established a political entity. They fought too frequently among themselves; in a kindred system too intensive and introverted, the collective personality remained too individual, too undisciplined, too lacking in organisation, to permit the global ambition necessary to found an empire. They never created a lasting political nation: Ireland, the most cohesive single Celtic national presence, owed any autonomy as much to the country's geography — a lone circumscribed island territory — as to any national political impulse among the Irish people or their leaders.

The Norman system of feudalism, with a central power deriving from the kingship and government, dealt the final blow to a society which had been founded on the triumph of the individual. Where the Roman empire had been a machine which cut deep into the civilisation, changing the face of great tracts of it, and where the Norse invaders had been a series of detonations which fundamentally altered the sites where they exploded, the Normans moved straight and smooth through all existing structures, leaving nothing unaltered in a thorough and deep colonisation. The power was visible; the manner undeniable; the culture irresistible; the effect irredeemable — and all from the moment that William of Normandy killed Harold of England at Hastings in 1066, and from the moment that Dermot McMurrough invited Henry II to consider Ireland.

Ireland resisted strongly and for several centuries. The Irish of the Scots kingdoms fought back with their foot soldiers and other well-drilled infantry. A rebarbative resistance — two hundred years after their arrival the Normans depended for their defences upon a strip of colonised fencing radiating from Dublin, thirty miles long and twenty miles deep, called 'the Pale'. Inside this region the Normans lived comparatively safely, still unaffected by contact with the native Irish - outside the Pale nothing was secure. Then a new assimilation began as the Normans intermarried with the local Irish, and became *Hibernicis ipsis hiberniores* — 'more Irish than the Irish themselves'. The cultures had begun to merge. Some Norman gentlemen in their limestone keeps appreciated the remnants of the Golden Celtic Age — another dimension had been added to the inexorable erosion.

In Wales, the alliances formed with Alfred the Great weakened the chances of any future resistance of England, or movement towards monarchical or political independence. The last natural Prince of Wales, Llywelyn II, died in 1282. Previous or subsequent resistance to Angle or Saxon or English rule petered out. Some independent-minded chieftains, like Owain Glyndyr, held out for a time, endeavouring to keep Wales Welsh. However, the exchange in Shakespeare's *Henry*

BATTLE OF CULLODEN.

The Battle of Culloden resembled in many ways a traditional engagement between Celts and Romans. The forces of the English, under the Duke of Cumberland, were arrayed neatly and in disciplined ranks. The Scots set themselves out along tribal lines, and so individual were the personalities of the clans that no clear leader could emerge to give orders. The battle went as decisively against the last Celts of Scotland as it had against Vercingetorix and Boudicca sixteen centuries before.

IV between Glendower (sic) and the cool Englishman, Hotspur, epitomises, if satirically, the reasons behind the eventual defeat of the Welshman.

Glendower: I can call spirits from the vasty deep.
Hotspur: Why, so can I, or so can any man;
             But will they come when you do call for them?

In Scotland, from the eleventh century onwards, a centralised kingship pushed such Celts as then remained further and further from the centre of power. After centuries of strife, at chieftain and clan level – 'they spend all their time in wars and when there is no war they fight one another' – and at regal level, in the sagas of the Stuart kings and pretenders to the throne of England and Scotland, any lingering Celtic aspiration or influence ended with 'the 45'. The rebellion of Bonnie Prince Charlie, the Stuart pretender, terminated glumly when his ragged forces lost one bloody day on the battlefield at Culloden in 1746 – in a rout whose shape so characterises the whole nature and failure of Celtic combat. Terrain had assisted both Scotland and Wales – as insularity had assisted Ireland – to remain Celtic for longer than the South of England or the fat midlands of Gaul. But by the time improved transport had made these regions more accessible the power bases ceased to be Celtic and the remaining Celts diminished ever further. Scottish or Welsh political reality based on the ancient cultural identity became unthinkable.

Brittany actually achieved a parliament in Rennes, and for several hundred years after the defeat of the Viking raiders enjoyed a prosperous and independent existence. Breton aristocrats married into Norman ruling families and assumed Norman manners and speech. The Bretons trod a delicate line between the English and the French, but succeeded in maintaining their independence from both – even during the Hundred Years' War – until the end of the fifteenth century. A defeat for Breton rulers in 1488 brought Breton independence to an end. Some internal administration survived by agreement but the impact three centuries later of the French Revolution – liberty, equality and fraternity – destroyed Brittany's pretence to independence by centralising all French government. The irony redoubled: Brittany had supported the Revolution enthusiastically, but yet had to hear – in 1792 – that French was to become the language of the new Republic and no other language possessed official status.

Ireland, especially the Republic of the twenty-six counties of Southern Ireland, claims to be the only sovereign state descended from the Celts. An historic, linguistic, archaeological truth – but at the point of independence the country did not revert to the kindred system of government employed by the ancient Celts. In 1922, at the foundation of the Republic, following the signing of the Anglo-Irish Treaty, a democratic system of elected government came into power, with the President as a titular Head of State. The Celtic traditions receive lip service: the Prime Minister's official title, *Taoiseach*, means 'chieftain', his deputy, *Tanaiste*; the House of Parliament, the forum, is *Dail*, as in the ancient tribal discussion chamber. Other similarities to the old Celtic ways of government do not exist except in vestigial or honorary form.

Using geographical, archaeological and perhaps even anthropological evidence, an argument may be sustained that the Celts are to be found all over Europe: some may even be traced in vivid migrations, such as the Irish in North America, or the curious, intensively Welsh colony in Patagonia. A particularly strong case may be made for England, which even though diluted by successive waves of conquerors, has the right to be called Anglo-Celtic as much as Anglo-Saxon. But the most prevalent definition of a Celt, the linguistic one to which we must keep returning, means that 'true' Celts – in reality the descendants of those earliest Europeans – may only be found now on the Atlantic fringes of Europe.

In Brittany they struggled for survival: occasional bombs, jail sentences and protests witness the impulse for independence which has persisted since Celtic times. In Wales the language revival has been remarkable – even if some of the 'cultural' activities given the name 'Celtic' have, to say the least, doubtful origins. In Scotland, despite a serious erosion, and a bare clinging to the islands of the west, signs of a renewal, or, at the least, a search for Celtic roots has appeared, especially among students who wish to learn the language of their ancestors. In Ireland the spirit receives vivid, if patchy support. The language revival offers a good example, cynically handled by generations of politicians despite a written political intent to have Gaelic as the first official language.

All the countries bear some witnesses to a Celtic heritage – in music, literature, form of expression, thought, even in physical characteristics as reported by scribes from the Greeks and Romans onwards. But in truth there can be no accuracy in discussing Celtic political or national identity as a living form. All that ended when the Roman trumpets blew, when the Viking longboats sailed up the river estuaries, when the Norman knights drew their longbows. Certainly the original Celts earned the appellation 'Fathers of Europe', in that they pushed across the Continent in the wake of the Ice Age, then went – literally – as far as they could.

The Celtic presence, without any effective traces of the old magical qualities, only persists identifiably – but vaguely – now on the Atlantic shores of Western Europe, in Brittany, Wales, the west of Scotland and on the island of Ireland. To argue otherwise is to bow to the mythology. The division between the genuine, ancient Celtic peoples and their modern, diluted namesakes remains clear and can no longer be relevantly bridged.

3

THE FIRST SORROW OF STORYTELLING – THE CHILDREN OF TURENN

Three sorrows of storytelling enlarge me with pity:
The telling of them harsh upon my ear.
First the fate of the Children of Turenn –
So woeful for me to hear.

When beauty and magic governed the land of Ireland a young man–god appeared in whose face the light shone, in whose stride power reigned. Lugh of the Long Arm, he called himself, raised by magic hosts and lately come to live among the Tuatha De Danaan, the people of the Goddess Dana. The most glorious of all the Celts, in Lugh the sun radiated. Even the king of the evil Formorians, whose cruel reign Lugh set himself to destroy, wondered why the sun rose one morning in the west, instead of the customary east, and the king's Druids told him that the sun did not enter the question: this golden light came from the face of Lugh.

And Lugh's possessions belonged to the heavens and the earth and all that gleamed in between. He wore the Milky Way as his silver chain: he carried the rainbow as his seven-coloured sling: his sword, the Answerer, could sever any armour or weapon: his boat, the Wave-Sweeper, could read a mariner's thoughts and navigate without instructions: his horse, borrowed from Mannanaan MacLir, the god of the ocean, bore the rider equally over land or foam.

Lugh's father, Cian, and Cian's two brothers, Cu and Ceithinn, were ranged in permanent and deadly rivalry against three other brothers, Brian, Iuchar and Iucharba, the Sons of Turenn. The coldness of their feud could only be answered in blood. One day, when Lugh learned of a fresh threat from the ravages of the Formorians, he asked his father, Cian, and his two uncles, Cu and Ceithinn, to muster forces. All split up to cover the country, and when Cian was crossing the plain of Muirhevna whom should he see coming towards him but the three deadly rivals, the Sons of Turenn, Brian, Iuchar and Iucharba.

Outnumbered three to one, Cian resorted to magic, changed his shape into a pig and concealed himself in a herd of swine, who were at that moment grazing and snuffling the clay and tree-roots of the plain of Muirhevna. Too late, though: the Sons of Turenn had seen the riding warrior and wondered where he had disappeared. Soon they deduced that he had numbered himself among the pigs, and fearful of the times that reigned, decided to seek out the warrior and kill him. But which pig? Even to slay them all might still result in escape for the warrior in the magic mêlée? Brian drew his magic wand across the air and turned his two brothers, Iuchar and Iucharba, into hounds, who smelt the pig and chased it. Brian got there first: with one cast of his spear he wounded the pig in the chest. The pig called out in Cian's voice and asked for quarter, but the brothers knew they had uncovered the warrior and gave no mercy. Then Cian asked that he might be changed back into his own human form and the brothers consented, with Brian saying he found it less difficult to kill a man than a pig.

Cian stood before them and assumed that the moment of his death had come: when the Sons of Turenn recognised their deadly enemy, they could only be satisfied with his blood. But in one last gesture Cian told them that he had outwitted them – because the debt of honour and blood to be paid for the murder of a man would amount to many times the sum required to avenge the death of a pig. And not only that, for the killing of a pig ordinary punishment would seem appropriate: for Cian's murder such a revenge would be exacted as never before thought or imagined – his son Lugh would come and hunt down his father's killers, and would recognise them from the weapon-marks on Cian's body. To this stratagem the Sons of Turenn responded by using not their weapons but the stones which lay scattered across the plain of Muirhevna. Rock after rock they rained down on the doomed Cian. They gathered round him in a circle, one to the east of him and one to the west of him and one to the south of him, and they further shut out his light with the rocks they raised above their heads and hurled down upon his breaking and bleeding body. And the Sons of Turenn did not desist from their wild, relentless murder until Cian, the father of Lugh, lay bleeding into the dust and clay of the plain of Muirhevna. Even the snuffling pigs stood silent afar, watching the last faint writhings of the pulped bones and flesh. Then the Sons of Turenn dug a grave into the earth of the plain, a pit deep enough to accommodate a standing man, and in it they buried their victim: on top they piled a cairn of the killing stones and then rode for the rest of the day to engage in battle alongside the others who were fighting the Formorians.

Lugh of the Shining Face, Lugh of the Long Arm, won a great victory in that battle: the Formorians retreated in wild confusion, and hid in the fogs of their northern fastnesses. But all through the fighting a doubt nagged Lugh. In the moments after victory he gathered his family and asked whether anybody had seen his father, Cian. Nobody had, so Lugh feared the worst and set forth, without food, without drink, without sleep, and refusing all until he found his father. On the plain of Muirhevna Lugh's natural magic made the stones cry out: the blooded rocks called Lugh over and told him of the death of Cian – and by whose hands he had perished. Lugh's men lifted Cian's body out of the grave and laid it before the grieving son, who kissed the broken, stiffened corpse and wept over it. Then he turned his face back to whence he had come and vowed revenge upon the Sons of Turenn and all their generations.

They buried Cian's body sadly but with honour. Lugh sang a long keening lament over the grave, raised a prouder cairn than the grievous stones that had already marked the spot and rode back to Tara. Here the Sons of Turenn sat with the King of the Tuatha De Danaan, for they too had played a part in the great victory, and they too were welcome guests at the celebrations and the games. Lugh, however, received the place of the guest of honour and ate the Champion's

Portion. Before the eulogies and satires were due to begin, Lugh, to the astonishment of everybody, begged – and was granted – the King's permission to speak.

The light from him shone brighter than ever: his broad chest seemed like a gleaming shield, fire and sadness played in his eyes and his voice trembled.

'My king; fine champions; Bards and Druids. Let me ask you each in honour: if your noble father dies at the hand of a vile murderer, do you seek vengeance?' All murmured yeas, including the Sons of Turenn.

But the assembly registered surprise – both at the question and the disposition of Lugh. Cian's absence had been observed and the King asked Lugh whether Cian had been murdered. When Lugh said he had, the King said that by no single blow, on no single day should such a revenge be exacted, but rather, blow by blow, limb by limb, organ by organ – and day by day, a long, slow and violent revenge. All murmured their yeas again, including the Sons of Turenn.

Then Lugh told the King that Cian's murderers sat among them and therefore he could not slay them, but he would impose a great *eric,* a fine, upon them. At this, the Sons of Turenn stood up, fast and firm, and asked their fine. Lugh demanded that they should pay him three apples, a pigskin, a spear, a pair of horses yoked to a chariot, swine to the magical number of seven, a young dog, a spit to cook upon and to give three shouts atop a hill. The Sons of Turenn, Brian, Iuchar and Iucharba, had no choice but to accept, for the fine seemed so small they would otherwise lose face greatly, but Brian feared some trickery. Indeed his instinct paid him well, for then Lugh filled in some details.

The apples, he said, hung in the Garden of the Light in the East, each the size of a small child's head, each gleaming in gold, each a cure for all wound and ill. The pigskin sat in the house of the King of a far southern land and when laid upon the hurt cured all wound and ill. The spear stood in another land of the South and East: it fought the greatest battles with such eagerness and force that it must remain always preserved in blocks of ice lest all around be melted in the heat from its point. The horses and their chariot, all of unequalled power and exquisiteness, race in a faraway King's court, and all travel easily over land or water. The seven swine of the King of the Golden Pillars possess the magical property of regeneration: though killed and eaten one day they reappear the following morning. The young dog from the King of the East frightens all beasts in the universe: the cooking-spit belongs to the underwater women of an island deep in the green ocean between England and Ireland and the three shouts must echo on a hill in the North. This hill was owned by a King, Michan, and his three sons in whose dear companionship Lugh's father, Cian, had trained as a warrior, and that court has pledged never to permit a shout from their hill: double, therefore, the danger to the Sons of Turenn, protection of the hill and revenge for their dead friend, Cian.

The Sons of Turenn, despite their deadly deed and their hatred of Cian, Cu and Ceithinn, possessed great power and magic and cleverness. To gain the golden apples they changed themselves into hawks and flew like arrows out of the sun, grabbing an apple each in their deep talons. Though the daughters of the King changed themselves into bigger hawks and followed the brothers out to sea and ventured fiercely to regain the apples, they failed and so the Sons of Turenn accomplished their first task.

To gain the pigskin they presented themselves at that court as poets, because the King there was known to have music and words respected in his land. After reciting for him a wondrous praise-poem, they asked as their prize the magic pigskin. The King refused but offered them the fill of it with gold. As they presided over this operation, the Sons of Turenn drew their swords and began to fight a way back through the guards with the gold-filled pigskin. The battle swung ferociously and ended when Brian killed the King himself with one mighty blow, and when the Sons of Turenn escaped they cured their wounds by laying the magic pigskin upon their bodies.

To gain the world-hot spear, in their third year of these seven-year-long tasks, the brothers again appeared as poets, again praise-singing the King who possessed the spear, again asking for the sought object as their prize. This time, though, no graciousness attended upon their host's refusal: his rage rose, and fighting broke out. Brian hurled one of the golden apples at the King and shattered his head. The Sons of Turenn then fought their way out across the courtyard to the ice-house where the spear stood, tore it from the blocks which cooled it and used it to fight their way to safety.

To gain the horses and chariot the brothers disguised themselves as mercenary soldiers and offered themselves to the court of the King who possessed them. For seven weeks they stood at arms, but never glimpsed the object of their quest. But they had begun to prove immensely valuable as warriors, and so they went to the King and told him they would leave unless he displayed to them the famous horses and chariot of which they had heard. The flattered King had his charioteer drive furiously around the circus, and the horses went over water and earth, and the chariot moved as quickly as the March wind. Then Brian leapt into the chariot, slaughtered the charioteer, picked up his two brothers, Iuchar and Iucharba, and drove away in laughing triumph.

By now the Sons of Turenn had earned a reputation across the world for their famed deeds. Success attended them everywhere they went, so that when they arrived in the Kingdom of the Golden Pillars to capture the seven magic swine, the King at the advice of his court gave up the pigs, and celebrated the three champions. Indeed, he assisted them – he could accompany them, he said, to the land where they sought the magically fearful golden dog, as his daughter had married the King there, and he felt he could persuade them to surrender their dog without bitter fighting. This did not occur: the distant King guarded his dog too jealously – and paid the price. In fierce combat the Sons of Turenn carried the day again, but eventually managed to make peace with the King and were given his dog.

Now they had accomplished six tasks, five had been attended by fighting, one by talking, many by the use of some sorcery. Lugh knew of all this, and needed some of the treasures so far captured to fight on against the Formorians. He threw a spell over the Sons of Turenn, they forgot the nature of the remaining tasks and returned to Ireland in confusion. There Lugh possessed from them the magic

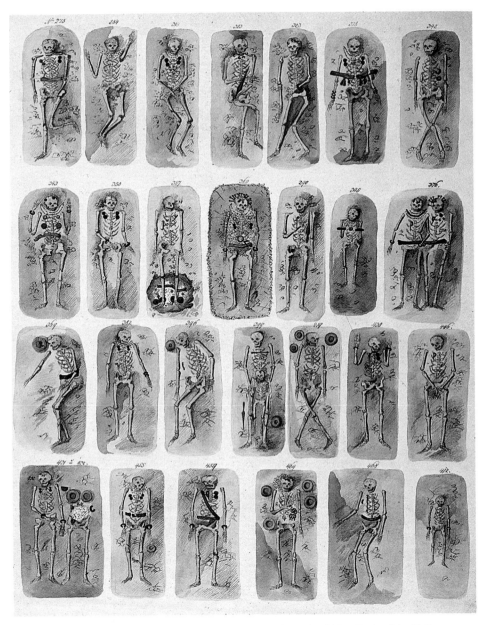

Above and on page 68: Detailed impressions by the Austrian artist, Isidor Engl, of the Hallstatt graves excavated by Georg Ramsauer.

Overleaf: A salt-miner's hod used for transporting salt to the collection point, and preserved in the salt since prehistory.

Page 67: A painting (again by Engl) of Hallstatt, seen from across the lake.

Early archaeological identification of any people who might have been called (or have called themselves) 'Keltoi' drew upon the excavation of burials all across Europe, from eastern regions such as Bohemia and Silesia, to as far west as the Marne in France. The form of burial, the manner in which the bodies or their cremated remains lay within the graves, and the disposition and nature of the grave goods all combined to form a picture of their culture. Within the actual mines, other valuable details – food traces, mining artefacts and implements – had already suggested useful archaeological sources of information regarding the workers of the society. The combination of the gravefield discoveries and the articles preserved in the deeps of the mines led to the nomination of a European material culture, perceived from the reports of ancient writers, to be Celtic – the Hallstatt Culture. The mountains behind the village contain the salt mines (still in production today) which form a great part of the local economy, and which contributed to the region's name, Salzkammergut, 'the place of good salt'. The definition of a society divided into the workers whose traces turned up in the salt, and the wealthy who lived off the profits of the salt trading, and whose wealth could be seen in the excavated graves on the hillside, cast a clear light upon a hierarchical social structure eight centuries BC.

Tab. XVIII.

ALTERTHUMS AUSGRABUNGEN am SALZBERG zu HALLSTATT am 19ᵗᵉⁿ OCTOBER 1856.

In Beisein Seiner k.k. Apostolischen Majestaet des Kaisers FRANZ JOSEF, Ihrer Majestaet der Kaiserin ELISABETH S.ᵗ kaiserl. Hoheit FERDINAND MAX von Österreich, Ihre königl. Hoheiten des Prinzen THEODOR, Prinzen KARL, Prinzeße JCELENE, MARIA und MATHILDE von Baiern nebst hoher Suitte.

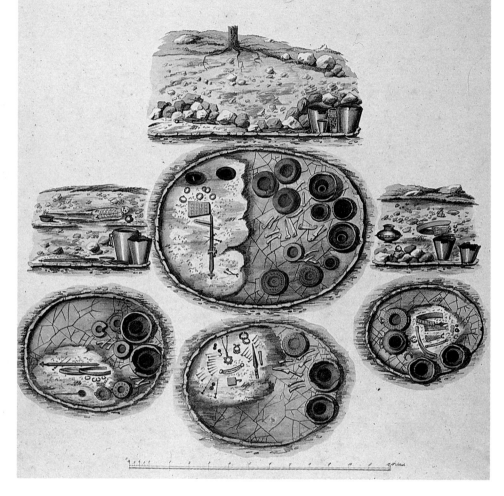

Despite the collapse of the wooden beams which had held
up the heavy boulder roof, the tomb at Hochdorf was still capable
of full excavation. The major item, a bronze bier, on which the body of the
gold-bedecked chieftain had lain in state before final inhumation, has been almost
fully restored. The long panels which form the high back are illustrated with designs and
patterns in a punched style depicting horses, and human figures engaged in battle or dance ritual.

One of the eight unicyclists (see previous page) upon whose hands and wheels the chieftain's bier rested. The grave also contained (*right*) a massive cauldron with a capacity of four hundred and fifty litres, in which were found the sediments of mead made from the pollen of a hundred and twenty-five local plants. When one of the handles, a mass-produced lion broke off, a local Celtic craftsman of the period made a wittier, more individual replacement.

71

La Tene, in translation, 'the shallows', on the shores of Lake Neuchatel in Switzerland, the archaeological site which gave its name to the second great period of Celtic civilisation. The site, believed to be a populous Celtic habitation for at least two or three hundred years around the fifth century BC, has disappeared under the waters and the name La Tene now represents a period of development rather than the specific place. 'La Tene Culture' identifies the Celts at a time of great flowering, of beautiful expression, when they had developed a sophistication, when their metalworkers began to produce exquisite designs like the bronze harness disc (*opposite*) with punched and curvilinear decorations, found in a chariot grave at St Jean-sur-Tourbe, France, and now in the museum at St Germain-en-Laye in Paris.

Butser Farm in the South of England (*left*), where in a detailed reconstruction, Dr Peter Reynolds conducts extensive agriculture, both realistic and experimental, along Iron-Age lines. The grain crops, the herbs, the cattle and sheep have all been developed to represent identically the farming conducted by the Celtic tribes who populated Britain extensively – especially in the south – before the Romans. In country communities such as Butser and the hillfort of Maiden Castle in Dorset (*above*) the tribes of Britons lived off the land in a system of food production that was as sophisticated as any in Europe, and which would still be effective, in part at least, today.

Few citadels with such direct Celtic connections have remained so impressive and exciting as the Rock of Cashel, County Tipperary, a limestone pile rising out of Munster's Golden Vale. Now a mixture of architectural styles, and indelibly Christian in its perceived intent, Cashel of the Kings commanded a powerful place in the government of Celtic Ireland. Here the kings of the south sat, with a wide view over some of the richest land in Ireland. Ancient pagan associations, with astronomical emphasis, were taken into account in the various phases of building, and the legends associated with Cashel still have a unique and odd combination of the pagan and post–pagan Celtic traditions.

Proud above the plains of Royal Meath, Tara drew together all the legends and politics of Celtic Ireland, all the romance and power. Once the seat of the High Kings of Ireland and the fifth province of the country, all that remains of Tara are a few earthworks, mounds and an unattractive, intrusive statue of Saint Patrick. The most legendary of all the sites in Celtic mythology, the major figures in the cycles of gods, heroes and beautiful women frequently transacted their colourful, involved and paradoxical business on Tara's dominating hillside.

The Paps of Anu (*top*): two small mountains in the West of Ireland epitomise the Celtic principle of worshipping in the natural world. Mountains, crags, trees, rivers, such presences either became deified in themselves or contained deities.

Hadrian's Wall (*above*) marks the last line of Rome's Western Empire. In weather hostile to soldiers and generals who had been bred in the hotter Mediterranean, and under pressure from fierce tribes coming over the hills, the dynamic by which Rome had expanded came to a halt and petered out.

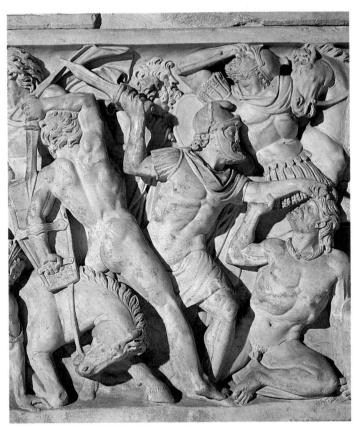

History written by the winners: a sarcophagus carrying scenes of Romans defeating Celts. The Celts ran into battle singly and naked, and eventually, despite extraordinary courage, fell before the calm and organised legions. The short slashing Roman sword proved more effective than the long weapon usually carried (though not in this carving) by the Celtic warrior, and even though the Celts were frequently far more numerous on the battlefield they rarely responded to leadership and could not be effective in formal war.

History written by the losers. The nineteenth-century statue of Vercingetorix erected at Alesia, site of the Celts' last stand against the Romans in 52 BC. The French Emperor, Napoleon III, used Celtic themes to portray to his people the proud history of France, and even managed to turn the greatest defeat ever experienced by the Celts into an inspiration.

The Dying Gaul: one of the many later heroic representations of Celtic warriorhood. The warrior cult informed all Celtic mythology, and each champion who represented his tribe understood the principle that it was better to have a short and heroic life than a long and uneventful one. In legend, the aspiring champion had to undergo several tests of valour, physical skill, stamina and ingenuity and the manner of completing the tasks became as important as the proficiency which the warrior was required to display.

apples, spear, pigskin: they, unknowing that they had forgotten, boasted of how they had fulfilled their quests, paid their *eric* for the blood of Cian. Lugh, though, asked them where had they placed the cooking-spit from the ocean's depths, and he had not yet heard their three shouts. They saw through his trick, and sank disconsolate to their knees.

When they had gathered their hopes about them again, the Sons of Turenn set off to complete their last tasks. They found the cooking-spit down among the lamps and flowers of the green ocean, and the thrice fifty water-maidens who guarded it gave it to Brian with a smile. But the hill of the King Michan, where Cian, the slain father of Lugh, had learned his young combat, proved their undoing.

On this, their last task, the Sons of Turenn walked up the hill. King Michan greeted them, demanded to know their business and under his own pledge forbade them to shout. Battle commenced, fierce and bloody: the heavens rang to the sound of swords, the hill flowed red with warriors' blood. King Michan perished on the blade of Brian's sword and when that hand-to-hand combat had ended, the King's three sons engaged Brian, Iuchar and Iucharba with swords and javelins. Across the mountains to the north, to the ocean in the far west, among the clouds of the south could the fighting be heard, until the Sons of Turenn overcame the Sons of Michan and killed them. But the Sons of Turenn, though they had paid their blood-fine for the death of Cian, had suffered terrible wounds. Still they managed to raise their feeble shout on the Hill of Michan: the last deed had been accomplished, their fine paid, their bond freed.

Their father Turenn brought this news to Lugh of the Long Arm, and asked for the loan of the magic pigskin to heal his three sons – they were dying of their wounds. Lugh considered the request and then denied it. He made the excuse that so great had been their valour, better now that they die and have the poets remember them in great glory, than that they live and be diminished in their vitality: better a short glorious life than venerable old age, all deeds wilt in the face of daily existence. But in this answer Lugh merely concealed his own refusal to forgive, and the Sons of Turenn, killers and heroes, murderers and valiant fulfillers of a quest, died side by side, with their father's sorrowful blessing.

4

BELIEFS

When Christian met Celt – who assimilated whom? By the time of Christ, Celtic 'pagan' belief had been long and sophisticatedly personified, and satisfied the early Celt's principal spiritual requirements. The ancient Celt's mythology responded to his need for morality. He had to impose order – upon life, within himself, on his relationship with his tribe. His mythology also directed his growth, enabled him to decide his position, reduce his bewilderment. And when it all ended – as he saw it did, brutally and often – what happened? How could the terror of death be allayed? The mythology provided a structure in which answers were made available – not just to such fundamental questions, but to the moral enquiries of every day.

In my Irish Catholic boyhood we drank a curious soup of religion and mythology, rich and viscous but with a bitter-sweet taste, comforting yet warning. The ingredients – though never officially twinned – were the sober Christianity of Patrick and the wild paganism of the Celts. So close the relationship, so alive the pagan history of this Isle of Saints and Scholars, that if a bunch of time-travelling, horse-borne Celtic warriors had turned up at Mass on a Sunday morning my eyes would have been surprised – but not my imagination, nor my faith. They would have been welcomed, baptised, Christened, and sent away as newly meek as that king at Cashel who suffered a crozier through his foot. Then, the ruined abbeys in the fields monumentalised the merger of ancient Celt and modern Christian. In the centuries after Patrick's fieldwork, this taming and melding of the pagans and their beliefs had been stamped, given the seal of approval, by the monks: as they illuminated the word of God they also transcribed the epic cycles.

The duality – although I did not then see it as such – was tangible. On the one hand, the gospel of Christ was sung and rampantly preached, while on the other hand it seemed as if those 'barbaric' beliefs, which Patrick's Christianity supposedly had superseded, still lurked. The parish tingled frequently with dark murmurings of *pishogues* or *pishrogues*, a kind of malevolent local magic muttered not just upon humans, but to destroy crops: eggshells found in a potato garden were intended to call down blight. Disease could be daubed upon livestock, too, riddling the herds with warble fly, or causing a cow to miscarry. Christianity countered with Easter Water, not abundantly more efficacious than normal Holy Water, merely differently directed. Other ailments and requests were serviced by novenas of prayers, relics, blessings galore.

My Irish ancestors took to Christianity with ease, adroitness and piety. Given that the Celts were otherwise rebarbative in their own defence, spiritually and practically, it seemed to me at first glance surprising that they embraced the story of Christ with such facility – alacrity even. Not at all: religious belief supplied the oxygen in the Celtic aspiration to immortality, in their ambition to defeat death and the terror it brought. Christianity produced the hardest and most pragmatic development in the chain of reconciliation, interpretation, morality and growth. Furthermore, it offered everything the Celts already had – and more.

In the beginning, the ancient Celt, a fearful man, like any of his prehistoric fellows, lit a fire in his clearing to ward off dangerous animals. But to protect against the inexplicable terrors, thunderstorms, the sudden wind in the winter branches, the feeling of being watched, he required some kind of inner fire, personal magic. A small, particularly caressable stone, a stick of egregious shape, a totem – these could be invested with equally inexplicable powers. And the protection increased if expressed in a place of special feeling, a hushed and powerful atmosphere, such as a grove, or river-pool, or sea-creek. The journey there added to, and made more deliberate, the statement of belief. The twentieth-century successor, a pilgrim before the grotto in Lourdes, or attending Mass, rosary beads in hand, on a Sunday morning in a packed church in the west of Ireland also seeks to have his fears allayed, his ailments cured, the chaos of his world made sensible, his death fended off, his after-life in the sweet fields of Elysium assured.

The voyage from oaken grove to communion with Christ took several thousand years. Like a cabalistic scroll it charts the Celtic spiritual ascent through personal magic, tribal ritual, mythology, scripture. The earth itself was worshipped in dumb fright, and the spirit connected in awe with the inanimate – tree, river, rock. Ritualised recognition of the animate – beast and bird – was followed by a slow mythological shifting of shapes between animal and human. Finally, just as Celtic civilisation reached its apogee, the Celts encountered this Son of God. And – glory be! – he, it was found, was human like themselves and he surrounded himself with real people, the saints. Here stood the ultimate compliment to Man for having made it safely out of the ooze. Now any mere human, frail and flawed, could become immortal – and important for Heaven's sake! The terror of death was seen off by the promise of better things in a beautiful place, an alcove on the golden stairway. And was all this new – this religion, this belief, this mythology, this faith? No: many of the impulses and the symbols of Celtic paganism received answer in Christianity.

In the beginning was the clay – Celtic worship was inspired by natural sources. It began with the mysterious earth itself, the source of fertility, of life, of support. In the mythology, heroes and kings are mated with the earth-goddess, the earth-mother, from whom we spring and to whom we return. Gods watched over the fertility of the ground and were rightly owed reverence. Gods inhabited rocks, heights, natural ramparts, individual mountains: sometimes the peaks of mountains represented the breasts of a great mother-goddess. Gods illuminated rivers and their sources and their confluences, and the darkness of lakes. Gods belonged to trees; across the years and the Celtic lands, the tree attracted cults of worship and the tribal tree stood on the most sacred site, where the tribal leader was inaugurated. The ash, the yew and particularly the oak frequently appear in the poems and the annals – especially those of Irish origin, seat of the greatest concentration of Celtic mythology. Sometimes the tree represented a rallying-point for the tribe, to be attacked, therefore, and cut down by a marauding tribe – the capture, so to speak, of the enemy standard. Elsewhere it appears as a garlanded signpost: at the mouth of a cave which marked the entrance to the Otherworld stood a tree laden with silver flowers, and in whose branches birds sang sweetly and for ever.

Prayer typically took place in a copse of oak trees on a grassy knoll, with the waters of a pool or small stream glistening nearby. Such a grove seemed already sacred, the residence of a god, or made holy by association: at the water or under the trees they invoked the deity and made offerings. As the family expanded the site became the place of tribal ritual; a sanctuary was built, in some cases the dead of the tribe were buried nearby. Certain days attracted singular worship, connected with the change in the seasons, or the storing of food for the winter, or the birth of animals. Such special days promoted the thoughtful feelings, a sense of difference, festive days on which the gods were given their full importance. On such occasions, all except the most essential activities were suspended. The ritual included votive offerings, human and animal sacrifices.

Celtic worship venerated the animate world – the raven, the swan, the bull, the stag, the boar, the horse. The bull, for instance, courses through Celtic mythology as a powerful symbol of strength, virility, sexuality, an object of wealth and desire and stature. The bull defended the herds from rustlers and thereby became a god of battle, since most warfare originated in search and defence of property, including sources of food.

Horns frequently betokened deity. Cernunnos, the horned god whose many echoes include Herne the Hunter, appears as chief of the animals, surrounded by a stag, a ram, a wolf, a bear, a snake. Scholars make two claims for his sitting posture – that it stems from the Celts' own custom of squatting on the ground within their dwellings, and, more powerfully, that Cernunnos reverberates from within the ancient East. But in later Christian belief, his high antlers were made to correspond with the horns of Lucifer.

Many deities assumed the form of a raven – a goddess of war, or a harbinger of doom or a messenger of the gods. When Cuchulainn was dying from his wounds, rather than concede to his enemies he strapped himself to a pillar in order to remain upright and fight on. Only when the raven perched on his shoulder did his enemies finally dare to draw near. And elsewhere across the mythology, boars, fish, horses appear, whether individually used as objects of veneration, or associated with particular gods.

An analysis of the range of Celtic deities, supported as they were by animals, suggests a religion which had a sound practical base – earth, water, fruit, meat, wool, fur. The presence of the horse, beast of burden, warrior's ally, adds a further utilitarian dimension. And all were invested with a magical otherworldliness — as if within each object of worship there lay depths of secrets, mysteries.

The mythology developed by way of anthropomorphic shape-shifting, the creature who inhabited several human or animal forms. The greatest of the Irish Celtic legends, *Tain Bo Cuailgne,* tells the story of the Cattle Raid of Cooley, in which Cuchulainn defends the province — and honour — of Ulster against the men of Connaught, who seek to bear away the great brown bull of Cooley, the Donn Cuailgne. When Cuchulainn continues to rout every form of combat flung against him, Queen Maeve of Connaught (not unconnected with England's Queen Mab of the Fairies) resorts to magic and calls up various malign spirits.

Cuchulainn beheld at this time a young woman of noble figure coming towards him, wrapped in garments of many colours.

'Who are you?' he said.

'I am King Buan's daughter,' she said, 'and I have brought you my treasure and cattle. I love you because of the great tales I have heard.'

'You come at a bad time. We no longer flourish here, but famish. I can't attend to a woman during a struggle like this.'

'But I might be a help.'

'It wasn't for a woman's backside I took on this ordeal!'

'Then I'll hinder,' she said. 'When you are busiest in the fight I'll come against you. I'll get under your feet in the shape of an eel and trip you in the ford.'

'That is easier to believe. You are no king's daughter. But I'll catch and crack your eel's ribs with my toes and you'll carry that mark for ever unless I lift it from you with a blessing.'

'I'll come before you in the shape of a grey she-wolf, to stampede the beasts into the ford against you.'

'Then I'll hurl a sling-stone at you and burst the eye in your head, and you'll carry that mark for ever unless I lift it from you with a blessing.'

'I'll come before you in the shape of a hornless red heifer and lead the cattle-herd to trample you in the waters, by ford and pool, and you won't know me.'

'Then I'll hurl a stone at you,' he said, 'and shatter your leg, and you'll carry that mark for ever unless I lift it from you with a blessing.'

Then she left him.

From *Tain Bo Cuailgne* (The Cattle Raid of Cooley), trans. Thomas Kinsella

Cuchulainn's tormentor, the Morrigan, appears as the goddess of war, and when the Christians arrived such vivid legendary fare clearly offered a challenge to any new belief.

The Celts based their worship on their social structure: divine organisation mirrored that of their society. Just as they never organised into one political unit, they never created a single religion or pantheon. Gods had many features in common, but, whether in Gaul or in Ireland, each belonged to the particular tribe. At the top of the hierarchy sat a father-figure; he may have been their ancestor, certainly their protector, who made the harvests fruitful, inhibited enemies, averted plague and famine. In Irish mythology he was called the Daghda, and he wielded a huge club; his opposite number in Gaul has several representatives who qualify for the description, including Sucellos, 'the good striker', portrayed carrying a hammer. This omnipotent father-figure headed the family of gods. His mate, an earth-goddess, further ensured the fertility of the earth, and employed magic. In the early Irish myths, the Morrigan mated with the Daghda; in Gaul, Sucellos coupled with Nantsovelta, 'She of the Winding Stream': both goddesses have as their representation the raven. Female deities usually indicated sexuality, fertility and maternity – with powerful magical or warlike connotations. Flidais, the huntress, was possessed of a great sexual appetite; Epona, the horse-goddess, rode sidesaddle, associated by Welsh Celts with their goddess, Rhiannon: Sulis presided over the healing springs at Bath. Celtic statuary and tradition record dozens of such goddesses across the civilisation who resemble each other strongly, both in name and efficacy. Localisation of the gods satisfied the human ambition for divine association. 'Our Lady of Limerick', a radiant-blue representation of the Mother of Christ, found only in the mid-south-west of Ireland, and hanging on the walls of my parents' bedroom, had no need of official Vatican sanction – or denial.

Lugh of the Long Arm commanded particularly numerous cults, Lugh the Shining One, who gave his name to such European places as Lyon, Loudun, Leiden, and whom the Romans equated with Mercury. Lugh, a handsome hero, fathered (in some versions) Cuchulainn, and did other great, versatile deeds. When he presented himself at Tara's halls to join the people of the goddess Dana, he was refused entry until he stated his calling. He said that he was a carpenter. They already had one. He said he was a smith. They already had one. He said he was a warrior. They had several. He then said he was, in turn, a musician, a scholar, a poet, a magician, a hero – the job descriptions came thick and fast but the gatekeeper remained unimpressed. As a last resort Lugh asked whether the Tuatha De Danaan had in their company any one person who could do all of these things with wondrous skill, and so Lugh was permitted entry. His exploits are famous: he killed Balor of the Baleful Eye, with – according to which version you believe – a slingshot, or (as with Ulysses and the Cyclops) by driving a stake through Balor's single eye.

Above all, Lugh gives his name to one of the four principal pagan Celtic feasts, the festival of Lughnasa, celebrated on August 1st (which corresponds with the Anglo-Saxon Lammas). Nature's logic suggests this as a harvest festival, although specific mention of any such association does not arise until the Christian era. The feast of Lugh, in several guises, survives. On the Sunday next to August 1st, thousands of pilgrims climb a mountain in the far west of Ireland, Croagh Patrick: they may be commemorating Saint Patrick, but Lugh, too, was worshipped on high ground – while in other parts of the country on the same day, pilgrimages take place to holy wells and other local shrines. In Lyon (Lugdunum, the fort of Lugh) when Gaul was occupied by the Romans, an annual commemoration of the Emperor Augustus was held on the same date.

Samhain, the greatest Celtic festival, marked the beginning of the year, celebrated on the night of October 31st, now Hallowe'en. The earth opened, the spirits stalked the land. Darkness reigned, godly matings shook the ground, a spirit of eeriness prevailed, the night of All Souls. Samhain echoes the chaos from which man emerged and to which he must never return, the night of magic most effective. When the air fills with cries and incantations, the moment turns between the light time of the year and the dark time, the fertility of the earth must be renewed, the future of the tribe guaranteed.

> The night is cold on the Great Bog.
> The storm is lashing – no small matter.
> The sharp wind is laughing at the groans
> Echoing through the cowering wood.

The eeriness, sense of woe, persisted; they hang about me still. Round and round the concrete yards of the local church, praying outside and praying inside, we called down the love of God for the souls in that resolving place, Purgatory, and we prayed for the dead, 'that they may be loosed from their sins'. A unique rhythm, a bizarre sight, the worship continues to this day, fog of prayer on the November air.

The six-month period between Samhain and the lighted half of the year which began on Bealtaine, May 1st, was bisected by the pastoral feast of Imbolg, February 1st. Bealtaine contained more magic than Imbolg, but less than Samhain. The god Belenos encouraged the growth of crops, the health of cattle. The universal magic of the beginning of May shimmered in Celtic settlements of Northern Italy, in France and Britain and in Ireland, where ceremonies of cattle purification are still practised: between twin fires beasts are driven to propitiate the gods.

When Christianity arrived, it offered to the Celts a faith constructed upon systems which they recognised – beginning with an all-seeing, all-powerful, all-knowing paternal deity, a Zeus–God-the-Father. His son, the hero-god, the Apollo-Christ, had descended by remarkable or morally meaningful conception, a human figure of divine birth, who actually lived and who was capable of all skills, even performed miracles, and who died in his young and glorious prime. The Christian calendar reinforced the regularity of worship, with recognition of the social and practical relevance of the Celtic festivals. This was development, not conversion, acknowledgment not revolution, an embrace of the motion of time, not a disturbance of an existing order. A natural order, too: in an increasingly overwhelming world how could a man retain his own importance? Christianity, however global, also offered a private relationship with God for each individual. Tribal worship may have been public and ritualised – but archaeological evidence indicates a more personal, and often touching connection.

The River Seine, whose name derives from the local Celtic goddess Sequanna, rises in wooded farmland, thirty-eight kilometres from Dijon in the midlands of France: in the nineteenth century Napoleon III enshrined the pool at the source. In 1963 nearly two hundred waterlogged wooden objects, small carvings, entire statues or limbs, trunks and organs, grotesque and crude but not crass, turned up in an excavation. Made of oak heart-wood, they had been created both to appease the gods and to ask for favours. One figurine displays a club foot: another a

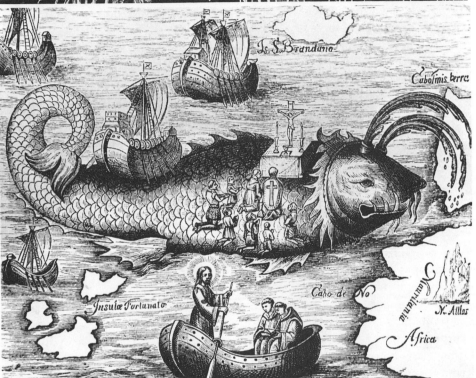

Above: An artist's (rather loose) impression of the voyage of the Irish saint, Brendan, or Brandon, to the New World. Although strenuous efforts have been made to establish that he discovered America in the sixth century AD, the voyage must also be considered in the context of an earlier mythological voyage, of an Irish Celt called Bran (see page 100).

Top: Stonehenge, where, in the words of a nineteenth century writer, 'the mazes of wild opinion are more complex and intricate than the ruin.' The Wiltshire site remains one of the most-documented, speculated-upon – and inevitably ill-judged – places in all Celtic lore. (See page 93).

Left: A Gallo-Roman bronze figure found in Premeaux, France. The deity represented here possessed several identities. In Ireland he goes by the name of the Daghda, who carried a massive club, had inexhaustible appetites for porridge and sexual intercourse and remained permanently rejuvenated.

crudely accurate representation of the lungs and respiratory system. Carvings of breasts, eyes and – most numerously – genitals indicate ailments or fertility requirements: all suggest personal worship on a massive scale over a long period of time.

What did they wish to achieve with this offering of their ailments to the goddess of the waters? At Doon Well, a holy spring in County Donegal, a bush bears – all the year round – anxious garlands of asthma ventilators, spectacles, kerchiefs, menstrual tampons. At Faughart in County Louth, every August, thousands of Irish people celebrate open-air Mass to honour Saint Brigid at her shrine. Those afflicted with eye ailments tie rags on a thorn fence or bathe their eyes in small, naturally-formed pools upon rocks which they have hallowed with Brigidine legends. Some random observations thrust forward their puzzles: in Greek churches altars are hung with tiny metal icons of eyes and limbs and organs: and was there not a pagan Brigid, daughter of the Irish god, the Daghda? He, indeed, had three daughters, all named Brigid, a trinity of goddesses. And – further resonances – the feast of Saint Brigid occurs on February 1st, the pagan Celtic Imbolg: the Brigantes, a Celtic tribe in Britain, worshipped Briganti, who gave her name to the River Brent, once significant, now merely a North London trickle.

Other votive places, richer than the source of the Seine – La Tene, for instance – influenced the definition of the Celtic civilisation. The term 'La Tene Culture' might never have become scholarly parlance had a site in North Wales been excavated first. On the island of Anglesey, the Royal Air Force operate an extensive training base at RAF Valley, whose real name, Llyn Cerrig Bach, has as much right to Celtic headlines as Hallstatt or La Tene. In 1943 the construction of the airfield had proceeded at the pace of wartime urgency.

On the building site a digging tractor was arrested by an old chain. Archaeologists made a necessarily hurried investigation. They discovered that, from a rock projecting over the pool, a huge assortment of objects had been consigned to the waters centuries before. Sufficient portions of a chariot were recovered to permit a reconstruction: harness pieces, weaponry, utensils, tools and trumpets bore testimony to vast prayer. The bones of cattle, sheep, pigs, horses and dogs suggested animal sacrifice and clinched the interpretation of the find as votive; the pool disappeared, covered in to make one of the principal runways. And the circle thereby closed – scholars speculate that the Llyn Cerrig Bach deposit gave sacrificial thanks for successful combat.

The irony of the Celts' votive offerings is superb. Sacrificial prayer immortalised them. No gift ever seemed too precious, no price too high: La Tene, Llyn Cerrig Bach, the Seine – such exaggerations of coins in a fountain. Near Toulouse in France the Romans plundered one shrine which, according to Posidonius, contained one hundred thousand pounds of gold bullion and one hundred and ten thousand pounds of silver. Near Lake Velence, in trans-Danubian Hungary, south of Budapest, relics included a child, a man in his early twenties, a middle-aged woman, an elderly male, all excavated in a sacrificial pit at a stream. Animal traces found in the waters there included a dog skeleton, and the antlers of a stag.

The element of earth received offerings too – cauldrons and jewels and chariots, the slain bodies of slaves and beasts. The most peculiar propitiation took the form of a shaft, driven deep into the ground – dramatic, powerful, suggestive. The logic seems clear: as children fear the mischievous spirit who dwells in a dank well, gods might be contacted in their lairs beneath the clay. The ancient Greeks believed the deities could be thus reached, likewise the Romans. And the Celts, in Germany, France and Britain, plunged their ritual devotion many metres deep into the earth, burying in the shafts fragments and votive offerings, specifically manufactured, or chosen at random from the life of the tribe.

At Ewell in Surrey, in the mid-nineteenth century, eight shafts were discovered, detailed, neat, orderly. They varied in depth between four and twelve metres and contained a wide variety of objects – the skeleton of a large dog with the head severed from the body; a quantity of iron nails distributed equally between the pits; apple pips, cherry stones; some burnt human bones, numerous unburnt animal bones, of stag, boar, hare, cow, sheep; brooches, a bronze ring, glassware; an iron hammer, two stakes made of oak, oyster shells, vessels and shards of pottery. At Carrawburgh in Northumbria, a well two metres deep and measuring two and a half metres by two metres, dedicated to the goddess Coventina, contained over thirteen thousand coins, a human skull, rings, vessels, bells and two dozen miniature altars.

Later in the nineteenth century, two shafts were found at Ashill in Norfolk: one twelve metres deep and one metre square, the second – uncompleted – had been sunk to six metres. The greater shaft had been finished and lined with oak planks, and in descending order various deposits transpired: at a metre a wicker basket, the bones of oxen and deer, some pottery; at three metres a knife and whetstone; at four and a half metres mussel and oyster shells. From six metres down the temperament changed, with, in deepening layers, symmetrically-arranged urns laid on beds of hazel leaves and nuts; between eight and nine metres down, more vessels, again laid carefully on beds of hazel and oak leaves; at ten metres, other, similarly-arranged vessels, with pieces of antler and a boar's tusk; half a metre further, more urns and leaves, laid beneath a layer of large stones; then, downwards, a bucket with an iron handle: a quern stone for grinding corn: stones bearing marks of burning: vessels banded in sedge or encased in basketwork near the bottom – which had been carefully lined with flints on which lay the haunch-bone of a deer.

Other wells and shafts contained – in Scotland – the skeleton of a man standing upright three metres down, his spear placed conveniently by; elsewhere, the skeleton of a dwarf, the bones of those birds which the Celts used as portents, ravens, buzzards, starlings; the combination of cock and hare – Boudicca released a hare to propitiate her goddess before a battle – knives, statues, tiles, bracelets, tools, hooks, chains, harness-pieces. Many date from the time of the Roman legions – who included many Celts in their ranks.

On mainland Europe, spectacular shafts were dug in Bavaria; one plunged forty metres deep, another nearby contained a wooden pole surrounded by the traces of blood and decomposed human flesh. A deep shaft in the Vendée, in central

France, (which today, though covered in like a disused mine, carries a warning notice) contained bones, stones, charcoal and pottery.

The votive deposits maintained vital contact with the elements, bodies in Earth, other offerings dispatched to Water. To the element of Fire they made an extraordinary and spectacular donation. Julius Caesar observed it among the Gauls:

They judge that the only way of saving a man's life is to placate the anger of the gods by rendering another life in its place, and they have regular instituted sacrifices of the same kind. Some tribes have colossal images made of wickerwork, the extremities of which they fill with live men; they are then set on fire, and the men burnt to death.

And according to Strabo:

There are also other accounts of their human sacrifices; for they used to shoot men down with arrows, and impale them in the temples, or making a large statue of straw and wood, throw into it cattle and all sorts of wild animals, and human beings, and thus make a burnt-offering ... They used to stab a human being, whom they had devoted to death, in the back with a dagger, and foretell the future from his convulsions. They offered their sacrifices not without a Druid ...

The Greek word *drus*, according to one school of thought among linguists and philologists, contributed to the words the Celts used for an oak tree, or oak-wood. The other half of the word 'Druid' derived, supposedly, from an Indo-European word, *wid*, meaning 'to know'. Different arguments reach for ancient words meaning 'true', encouraged by the Druidic requirement to soothsay accurately. The definition of 'Druid' thereby acquired, in any combination of meanings, a pleasing fullness: 'the man by the sacred oak tree who knew the truth'. The sanctity of the oak dictated the material for such statuary as the Celts practised – they never carved icons in stone until the Roman example became widespread. Stone occupied a different place in Celtic spiritual emphasis, and ironically many of the more doubtful beliefs and latter-day 'Celtic' practices spring from their use of stone – as well as from the oak and from the connotations of the word 'Druid'.

On a hill on Salisbury Plain in the rich South of England stands Stonehenge. Few prehistoric locations have attracted such mixed attentions, few have had such variety of (alleged) pedigree – such as that Stonehenge had been transported by magic, intact and as it stands, from Ireland: Inigo Jones, the seventeenth-century London architect, believed Stonehenge to be a Roman temple and attempted to 'restore' what he described as 'THE moft notable ANTIQUITY OF GREAT BRITAIN vulgarly called STONE-HENG ON SALISBURY PLAIN'. Another writer claimed it as the tomb of Boudicca. The Vikings have been credited with it, and more modern speculation argues that 'ley lines', those imaginative magical networks running across the earth and atmosphere of Britain, connect Stonehenge with other groups of standing stones, including Avebury in Wiltshire to the east, Stanton Drew in Somerset to the west, Rollright in Oxfordshire to the north, even Carnac in Brittany.

Whether Stonehenge – like the earlier cemetery at Newgrange in Ireland – demonstrably pre-dates the Celts, academic opinion agrees that stones of all dimensions, standing in groups, or egregious among mountains, or lone in the middle of the fields, have survived as Celtic totems. In Connemara, in the west of Ireland, old people still murmur, according to a priest who ministers among

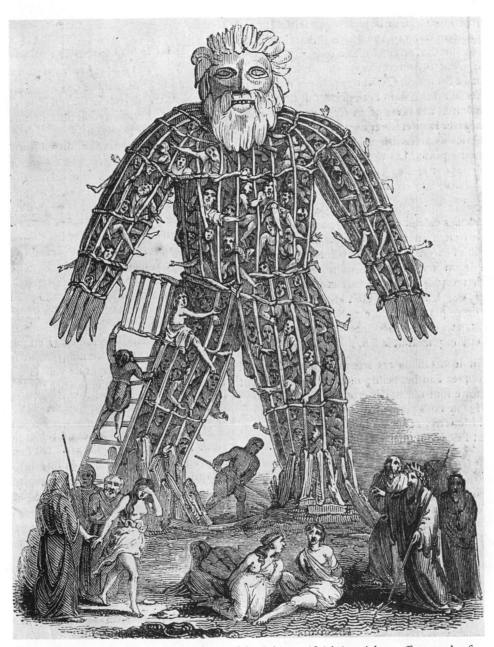

The wicker man, one of the most terrifying of the Celtic sacrificial rites. A huge effigy, made of cane and reed, constructed with a hollow torso, hollow arms and legs stood large enough to take the bodies of humans, men, women and children, and of animals. When suitably packed, the effigy was set on fire by the Druid, and all the creatures within burnt to death.

them, 'in ainm Chrom' – 'in the name of Crom', in place of the more usual invocation, 'in ainm De' – 'in the name of God'. Crom, or Cromm, or Crom Cruaich or Crom Dubh – Crom the Black – identified a stone deity worshipped widely. Early Christian synods denounced stone worship, yet the practice persists. Near Lochronan in Brittany, annual gatherings – some of which included a reluctant local Christian clergy – have been photographed as they processed, with incantations, round a large boulder. England crowns the monarchy astride the Coronation Stone, the Stone of Scone, in Westminster Abbey. The screaming Stone of Destiny at Tara chose kings of Ireland. Arthur drew Excalibur from a stone – he, and only he, had the power to do so. In Ireland, the myth descended and perpetuated – perhaps unconsciously, but who knows what the recesses of folk memory dredged up – when the Catholic priests on the run from the post-Reformation British rule celebrated Mass in the wilds upon large rocks which later took on local monumental significance.

The involvement of Stonehenge, and of other mysterious standing stones, in latter-day 'Celtic' cults reincarnates the Druid – a figure who still informs and excites the imagination. Julius Caesar, fascinated, observed at length in his *De Bello Gallico,* the power of the Druidic system.

The Druids officiate at the worship of the gods, regulate public and private sacrifices, and give rulings on all religious questions. Large numbers of young men flock to them for instruction, and they are held in great honour by the people. They act as judges in practically all disputes, whether between tribes or between individuals; when any crime is committed or a murder takes place, or a dispute arises about an inheritance or a boundary, it is they who adjudicate the matter and appoint the compensation to be paid and received by the parties concerned. Any individual or tribe failing to accept their award is banned from taking part in sacrifice – the heaviest punishment that can be inflicted upon a Gaul. Those who are laid under such a ban are regarded as impious criminals. Everyone shuns them and avoids going near or speaking to them, for fear of taking some harm by contact with what is unclean; if they appear as plaintiffs, justice is denied them, and they are excluded from a share in any honour. All the Druids are under one head, whom they hold in the highest respect. On his death, if any one of the rest is of outstanding merit, he succeeds to the vacant place; if several have equal claims, the Druids usually decide the election by voting, though sometimes they actually fight it out. On a fixed date in each year they hold a session in a consecrated spot in the country of the Carnutes, which is supposed to be the centre of Gaul. Those who are involved in disputes assemble here from all parts, and accept the Druids' judgments and awards. The Druidic doctrine is believed to have been found existing in Britain and thence imported into Gaul; even today those who want to make a profound study of it generally go to Britain for the purpose.

The Druids are exempt from military service and do not pay taxes like other citizens. These important privileges are naturally attractive: many present themselves of their own accord to become students of Druidism, and others are sent by their parents or relatives. It is said that these pupils have to memorise a great number of verses – so many that some spend twenty years at their studies. The Druids believe that their religion forbids them to commit their teachings to writing, although for most other purposes, such as public and private accounts, the Gauls use the Greek alphabet. But I imagine that this rule was originally established for other reasons – because they did not want their doctrine to become public property, and in order to prevent their pupils from relying on the written word and neglecting to train their memories; for it is usually found that when people have the help of texts, they are less diligent in learning by heart, and let their memories rust. A lesson which they take particular pains to inculcate is that the soul does not perish, but after death passes from one body to another; they think that this is the best incentive to bravery, because it teaches men to disregard the terrors of death. They also hold long discussions about the heavenly bodies and their movements, the size of the universe and of the earth, the physical constitution of the world, and the powers and properties of the gods; and they instruct the young men in all these subjects.

De Bello Gallico, Book VI: 13 and 14

The comprehensiveness of Caesar's description liberates several truths. The Druids relied absolutely on oral record. Caesar displayed generosity in suggesting that they wished their students to use brainpower rather than texts. Druidic influence lay in secrecy. Mystery, their energy, gave them the means of gaining and retaining power. Their moral disapproval, their ability and permission to excommunicate, gave them control of the minds and souls of their people. In some Celtic tribes no member of the lauded warrior-knight class, or below, could speak until the Druid had uttered first. In a rural society, the man who interpreted the elements, who had access to the gods, held power.

The parish priest in the largely agricultural community in which I was raised, commanded respect amounting to fear – a tall, thin man, austere, harsh and hooked of face and voice, a crude man, who sweated with impressive intensity while praying. He filled his sermons with hectoring emotional brutality, commenting upon every aspect of life, sexuality, politics, weather, death. He withheld communion from women who wore lipstick, he distributed the black *largesse* of disapprobation, he eliminated from the possibility of salvation all those who shared not his views. His sense of his own force was exemplified in the management of his gaunt presence: children and adults alike were frightened by his severity of walk, posture, clothing, mien. He (albeit untypically) provided an individual additional dimension which more than ever suggested his Druidic forebears: he practised herbalism, and was to be observed trawling the hedgerows for appropriate leaves and roots, which he then boiled in a stew to offer ailing parishioners who lined the roads by his house on Sunday afternoons. The Sacrament reposed in an oratory in his house, obliging us by custom to make the Sign of the Cross as we cycled past – awe by remote control.

Twin poles of power magnetised him – learning, and an access to the Supernatural. They coalesced in his worship – conducted in Latin, a sound of shamans. In the light of flickering candles, dressed in robes of white and purple and red and black, the mystic cadences rose and fell. Then, the congregation, shuffling, and with muted, infrequent coughing, moved towards the altar rail to receive from his intense presence the Bread of Life. The mysteries which reposed in him took on yet another dimension in his confessional. In a small community he had more knowledge than anybody else: in him were confided the darkest, most lubricious secrets of the fields and bedrooms, and even though the teaching insisted that a priest neither registered nor recalled the confidences offered in Confession, the process nevertheless added cubits to his stature as a figure possessing knowledge.

Other rituals he was called upon to practise in the course of his ministry enhanced his vividness. He blessed animals and crops, offered Extreme Unction to the dying – oil of chrism anointing the contact points of the five senses. He prayed for dry, harvesting weather, assisted at the side of a visiting prelate, caused bells to be rung and lamps to be lit and votes to be cast and banns to be called and people to be named in disapproval, excoriation, excommunication. Several times a year he read aloud the many collections – lists of names preceded by the amounts which they had contributed to the support of their pastors. And at the end came an ominous list heard in total silence, names with no amount registered, parishioners who had not, did not or could not give money, when formally requested, at the church door.

One more facet of his behaviour encourages an impression of the parish priest's presence as continued Druidism. My mind still rings with tales of our priest's eerie experiences. Once, as a young curate in South Africa where he had spent his first ordained years – and he told us this story from the altar – he was called out to administer last rites to a Catholic long lapsed. His horse baulked abruptly, refused to go further, the priest had to turn back. Upon later enquiry he learned that the soul to be saved had expired, unabsolved, at the precise moment of the horse's shying – the work of the forces of darkness. Such stories heightened the association with the supernatural, commanded deeper power over the listeners. Likewise the Druids reported ominous events known only to them, and thereby reinforced the effects of their arcane rituals. One account of a ceremony relates it to the progress of the moon, and describes the ingredients as a pair of white bulls, a golden sickle used by the white-robed Druid to cut mistletoe (parasite of the revered oak) which conveniently fell on a ready white cloak. More sinisterly, they conducted human sacrifice – although opinion differs as to the extent. To repeat Strabo, 'They used to stab a human being whom they had devoted to death, in the back with a dagger, and foretell the future from his convulsions.'

The most exaggeratedly distinctive of all Celtic ritual concerned the severing of the head from the body. At Entremont in Provence, a Celtic tribe, the Salii, constructed a sanctuary based on the cult of the severed head. When the Romans routed the tribe, some time after 125 BC, they found assorted statues and actual remains of human heads. Several adult male heads had been cut from dried bodies, some with curly hair, some still bearing the nails with which they had been first fixed to wooden posts elsewhere. A child's gentle head, a woman's head veiled and ear-ringed, several primitively carved representations of heads – twelve on a single perpendicular column – added up to a weird and distressing (even to the Romans) atmosphere of extreme religious practice. At Roquepertuse, in Bouches-du-Rhone, stone pillars beneath a lintel contained skulls and severed heads, enshrined to echo the Celtic reverence for the part of the body which they believed contained the soul.

Such veneration was never confined to the Celts: head-hunting tribes in Malaysia, scalping as trophy-taking by the North American Indians, cults from the Mesolithic period in Eastern Europe, bear archaeological and colloquial testimony. The Celts, perhaps more explicit and lively in the practice, gathered the heads of enemies and displayed them in the tribal settlement, and the more eminent the slain enemy the greater value did the head possess. In one encounter, the Celts killed a Roman official: they

stripped his corpse, severed the head, and bore their prize in triumph to their most sacred temple. There, acording to their habit, they cleaned it, decorated the skull with gold, and employed it as a sacred vessel for the pouring of libations, for the priests and acolytes of the temple to drink from.

Other descriptions portray the Celtic warriors returning from battle, waving their weapons in the air, shouting chants of victory, with severed heads of the enemy host dripping at their bridles. The legends contain many descriptions: in the *Tain Bo Cuailgne*, one of Cuchulainn's early victories occurred 'when the warriors Err and Innel, and their two charioteers, Foich and Fochlam, came upon him. He cut off their four heads and tossed them onto the four points of the tree-fork.' On another day, twelve opposing warriors 'fought foul and fell on him all twelve together. But Cuchulainn turned on them and instantly struck off their twelve heads. He planted twelve stones for them in the ground and set a head on each stone.'

At Mass on a Sunday morning in an Irish hillside church, the community took over. Though each individual worshipper was encouraged to contact God directly, all of us nonetheless belonged in communion – literally and figuratively. The mythology, whether Christian or pagan, or that vague and delicious brew of both, led us towards the stability created by belief. The system brought into play all the five senses – seeing the icons, the altar, the priest; hearing the prayers and hymns; smelling the incense, and even the damp of the church's fabric; tasting the Communion wafer, a flat dry taste, and of a substance which more often than not clung to the roof of the mouth; touching the rosary beads, the pew, the kneeler, the altar rails. Inculcation led towards communal harmony and moral coexistence. But at the basis, as the principal way and means, stood verbal communication. Narrative predominated: all the lessons taken from the higher authority, God or Jesus Christ, were transmitted as legend. Each and every Mass contained a Gospel, frequently a specific re-telling of some remarkable event in the life of Christ: between the human and the divine, identification was glimpsed, imitation and aspiration advised.

The Celtic tales re-echoed. Christ, the moral warrior, was exemplified in teaching, preaching, parable-telling, sacrifice and, finally, immense suffering in the Crucifixion. The lines between his divinity and humanity never became clear: the deliberate blurring contributed mythic power. But from the earliest age his childhood in the house at Nazareth received full display – as, in the Irish cycles, the childhood of Cuchulainn brought wondrous tales of silver hurley and golden ball and as, elsewhere, young Arthur and his wizard mentor Merlin appeared enchantingly. Extraordinariness offered a common bond between pagan Celtic and Christian god/hero. Lugh of the Long Arm could leap on a bubble without bursting it: Christ walked on water. All had remarkable births – immaculately conceived or the progeny of earth-goddess and beast. All had cycles of tales told of their exploits: the Christian Gospels were preceded in the Irish consciousness by legends such as the Fenian cycles – the stories of Finn McCool. These accounts depended upon miraculous accomplishments, or triumphing over the forces of darkness, or profound insight and knowledge.

One of the legends, Finn McCool and the Salmon of Knowledge, struck to the very root of the system common to both Christian and pagan. The ancient Irish worshipped the River Boyne, a goddess with Brigidine and other associations: in some philological discussions the word 'Boyne' comes from Boann or Bo Fionn, 'the white cow', an Indo–European connotation. The Boyne flowed from a sacred pool which sprang out of the earth in a grove of nine wise hazel-trees: their fallen nuts made the water rich with knowledge. Thus, the salmon in the Boyne gained renown for wisdom.

But one fish prized above all was 'the Salmon of Knowledge'. Now, Finn McCool was apprenticed to a learned teacher (a king in some versions) near the Boyne pool, a priest who had for seven years sought to capture the magical fish and gain from it all the truth of the world. One day, success came: the fish was landed and roasting commenced. The seer withdrew to meditate and prepare himself for the imbibing of the miraculous powers, leaving young Finn to supervise the cooking, but warning him not to taste. A blister arose on the fish's scales and the boy, conscientious, depressed it with his thumb – which he burnt and thrust suddenly into his mouth for coolness. In a flash, he, by virtue of being the first to taste the Salmon of Knowledge, gained total knowing. Thereafter, when he wished to perceive the truth of life he merely pressed his thumb to his mouth – touched his wisdom tooth – and the deepest mysteries were unfurled towards him. The story resonated vividly in Christian tales with the symbolism of the fish, the anointing by taste, the mystical properties of a river-pool, the early omnipotence of an emergent hero-god. Across Celtic mythology other legends reverberated: in the Mabinogion, Teirnyon Twryv Vliant, Lord of Gwent Is Coed, who was 'the best man in the world', found on his doorstep a boy-child wrapped in satin swaddling-clothes. The boy, by virtue of his fine appearance, seemed to come of gallant lineage and was raised accordingly until he became ruler of seven kingdoms and seven kingdoms more. And Arthur gazed upon his sword as if it were a cross and when he drew it from the stone he did so under the guidance of Merlin.

In the Irish branch of the mythology, the portrait of Cuchulainn as SuperCelt exemplified requirements that a hero should possess a spiritual or sacral dimension. When Christianity assimilated the oral tradition, Cuchulainn's legends were taught in such a way that his morality never came into question. In the *Tain*, his involvement as defender of Ulster against the forces of Maeve of Connaught, portrayed him only in a good light. The legends (transcribed, after all, largely by monks) emphasised the immorality of womankind: the entire epic of the Cattle Raid of Cooley came about through a woman's greed for her husband's possessions. Within their royal fort, Ailill the king and his wife Maeve lay, comparing in their pillow-talk their individual wealth.

Then the lowliest of their possessions were brought out, to see who had more property and jewels and precious things; their buckets and tubs and iron pots, jugs and wash-pails and vessels with handles. Then their finger-rings, bracelets, thumb-rings and gold treasures were brought out, and their cloth of purple, blue, black, green and yellow, plain grey and many-coloured, yellow-brown, checked and striped. Their herds of sheep were taken in off the fields and meadows and plains. They were measured and matched and found to be the same in numbers and size. Even the great ram leading Maeve's sheep, the worth of one bondmaid by himself, had a ram to match him leading Ailill's sheep. From pasture and paddock their teams and herds of horses were brought in. For the finest stallion in Maeve's stud, worth one bondmaid by himself, Ailill had a stallion to match. Their vast herds of pigs were taken in from the woods and gullies and waste places. They were measured and matched and noted, and Maeve had one fine boar, but Ailill had another. Then their droves and free-wandering herds of cattle were brought in from the woods and wastes of the province. These were matched and measured and noted also, and found to be the same in number and size. But there was one great bull in Ailill's herd, that had been a calf of one of Maeve's cows – Finnbennach was his name, the White Horned – and Finnbennach, refusing to be led by a woman, had gone over to the king's herd. Maeve couldn't find in her herd the equal of this bull, and her spirits dropped as though she hadn't a single penny. Maeve had the messenger MacRoth called, and she told him to see where the match of the bull might be found, in any province in Ireland. 'I know where to find such a bull and better,' MacRoth said. 'In the province of Ulster, in the territory of Cuailgne, in Daire Mac Fiachna's house. Donn Cuailgne is the bull's name, the Brown Bull of Cuailgne.'

But the owner of the bull would not yield his beast, and war commenced. The role of Cuchulainn – who alone defends his tribesmen against the evils and wiles of Maeve and her army, while all the time exhibiting the highest of moral virtues – is soothsaid by a poet with yellow hair and speckled cloak who held a light gold weaving-rod in her hand, and whose eyes had triple irises:

> I see a battle: a blond man
> with much blood about his belt
> and a hero-halo round his head.
> His brow is full of victories.

No wonder the Celts of Ireland were ready for Jesus Christ. The pacifism of Christianity blended cunningly with the sense of moral courage which only heroes may possess and to which, with humility and denial, mortals may aspire. Cuchulainn, the halo-ed warrior who did not fear death, who as a young man laid down his life for his people, provided a legitimate figurehead. In the fledgling State established in 1922 after the Anglo-Irish Treaty the dimension of national pride, when added to a legendary mysticism, made Cuchulainn a hero for all seasons. The General Post Office in Dublin, from which the Insurrection of 1916 was launched, contains within it a resplendent statue of Cuchulainn: the raven, messenger of doom, perches on his dying shoulder. His posture recalls the (albeit recumbent) Dying Gaul, who likewise evokes the aspiration to early glorious death rather than long unexceptional life. In the statue, three vital ingredients, mysticism, epic and patriotism, meld and display the sacral nature of Celtic mythology.

Likewise, Arthur's place in the consciousness of the later 'Celtic' mythology combined all the virtues to which a man should aspire – patriotism, morality, spirituality, chivalry. The identity of King Arthur, whether Welsh or French, never created the same force as his mythology – the Knights of the Round Table, the sword in the stone, the arm emerging from the lake, 'clothed in white samite, mystic wonderful'. The real Arthur may, mundanely, have been Artorius, a Romano-Celt, born about AD 470, a skilled cavalry warrior, who exploited the traditional metalworking abilities of the native Celts towards making armour, who then gathered around him other horsemen, dressed them in this armour and set off to repel marauding bands. And were his real-life exploits against the invading Saxons later invested with many of the attributes and legends already current in the Celtic oral tradition? Arthur has all the properties of the quintessentially Celtic hero; the associations with supernatural birth, essential for someone greater than normal mortals: the link with Tintagel, surely the ultimate hillfort, a rocky Cornish outcrop overlooking the Atlantic where still stand the remains of a medieval castle above the cave of Merlin, who ordained Arthur 'King of the Britons'.

Within all such cross-fertilisation did the Christian and pagan streams merge? The long, stylised stories which the monks wrote down were still orally current when Patrick, Columba, Bede, and other Christians began to evangelise. Occasionally, Christian zeal crept into the transcription of a bardic tale, but the colour of tribal life before Christianity – especially at the chieftain's table – remained perceptible. The monks' activities effected more devastating change. The Druids depended upon word of mouth – and, conversely, to their silence they owed their mystery. The arrival of literacy terminated this power. Ironically, priest defeated priest. Ultimately, the assimilation of Christianity resided in the transfer of lore. In a community which lived strapped to the elemental wheel, nothing that wrought fast and radical change could hope to adhere; success came about in embrace rather than confrontation.

The motivation – salvation – remained the same; only the destination altered. The ancient Celts had always hoped for a sweet life somewhere beyond the waves or the mountains, Tir-na-nOg, the Land of Eternal Youth. Sometimes the journey there took the form of a practical voyage – as when Brendan the Irish monk set sail from Kerry to find the New World. Here again the myths cross-fertilised between pagan and Christian: on the night Brendan was born a bright light shone over his village in south-western Ireland. On that same night, thirty cows dropped thirty calves and the farmer who owned them found the new-born babe. (In the farmyard cemetery associated with Brendan's mentor and ordainer, a bishop called Erc, a blue light still shines when a member of the farmhouse family dies anywhere in the world.) And as if such associations with the birth of Christ did not offer enough mythology, Brendan grew up in the shadow of a mountain range which was the playground of mighty Finn McCool. Brendan's voyage to America echoed the voyage of Bran whom Mananaan, the god of the sea (for whom the Isle of Man is named) instructed to seek a fair land. The voyage of Bran, and the later voyage of Brendan – both concerned with that most basic of spiritual impulses, the Quest – informed much of European literature. They and many others like them 'sailed over the wave-cries of the strong-haired sea, and over the tempest of the green waves, and over the jaws of the wondrous and bitter ocean'. Up as far as the nineteenth century, poets, in allegory or sentimental ballad form or epic poem, continued this sense of miraculous journey which, legendarily, so many Celts on the western seaboard of the Atlantic felt compelled to take:

> On the ocean that hollows the rocks where ye dwell
> A shadowy land has appeared as they tell;
> Men thought it a region of sunshine and rest
> And they called it Hy-Brasil, the Isle of the Blest.

For Hy-Brasil read Heaven – a golden palace somewhere in the sky, a combination of Atlantis and Elysium, sweet birdsong, flowers, permanent youth and peace.

The personification had changed little either. Saints replaced deities and heroes, and this facet more than any other completed the assimilation. The Celtic saint represented the point at which paganism lost the balance of power. Where the Celtic god or goddess had been a hero or a figure of efficacy, the saint replaced him or her – and with equal properties. The most basic similarities remained: above all, the localisation which had characterised the deities now spread to the saints. They proliferated, almost at field level – as even the shortest visit to Cornwall, Ireland or Brittany will testify. These saints offered a new heroism – the anchorite tradition of isolation from the community, moral courage. In remote corners of the countryside they built huts in woods and lived in stillness and contemplation:

> My heart stirs quietly now to think
> of a small hut that no one visits
> in which I will travel to death in silence
>
> Nothing will draw my eyes away
> there, from repentance for evil done
> or hinder my view of Heaven and Earth

On islands, in rivers, or offshore, on barely accessible rocks out in the ocean like Skellig Michael off the south-west coast of Ireland, they prayed and fasted in rigour, diligence and faith.

> On some island I long to be,
> a rocky promontory, looking on
> the coiling surface of the sea.
>
> To see the waves, crest on crest
> of the great shining ocean, composing
> a hymn to the creator, without rest.

Affection, rather than heroic admiration or overweening awe, characterised the opinion in which these saints were held. Their exploits registered more personally – endurance and self-denial, rather than epic valour in great battles. The scale of regard ascended in a mirror image of the society. Local figures, accessible as the Druid or chieftain, were celebrated in a personal and neighbourly way – pilgrims still walk around their holy wells, or sacred stones associated with them. Their legends wrought local heroes: it is said, for instance, that in the parish of Lemanaghan, on the banks of the Shannon in the midlands of Ireland, you cannot purchase milk, because a local saint, Managhan, owned a magical cow which was stolen, killed, quartered and reduced to bones. But Managhan prayed over it, brought it back to life and in thanksgiving decreed that evermore milk in his parish should be given free – an edict to which the community claims it adheres.

Further up the scale, if the saints were attached to large monasteries, such as Kieran at Clonmacnoise, or Kevin at Glendalough, the legends reflected their status as powerful figures – an abbot had the same influence as a local king. Kieran at Clonmacnoise entered into a dispute with the same Managhan of the regenerated cow as to the extent of the land boundaries of their respective abbeys. They decided to solve the problem by setting out to meet each other at a certain time on a certain day and where they met was thereafter to be reckoned as the agreed dividing point of their territories. But Managhan made it all the way to Clonmacnoise wherein Kieran had fallen asleep and therefore Managhan insisted upon his right to take his abbey's boundaries right up to the monastery walls. Kieran agreed but begged for a little leniency by asking for a reclaim of his land in so far as he could throw his cap. Then a magic wind sprang up and carried and carried and carried Saint Kieran's cap far, far away.

At the top of the hierarchy, as with a High King, wonder crept into the regard of the saints, and their stories took on decidedly epic tones, many of which reflected the preoccupations of the people. Brigid, for instance, became the heroine of a story dear to any farmer's heart. When she sought to establish a monastery in Kildare she was promised land by a local rich man, who mocked her by offering as much land as her cloak would encompass. But when Brigid cast her cloak upon the ground it spread and spread and spread until a large tract of countryside, sufficient to maintain and feed a sizeable community, had been marked out. Welsh and Breton legends reflect the same combination of practical and mystical, which originally lay at the root of the earliest Celtic belief.

In mystery we begin, in mystery we end: we supply our own solutions. Beneath a tumulus in the Boyne valley at Dowth a stone dish sits in the middle of the floor, as it has done for thousands of years. What destiny did those bones achieve? A gleaming land of golden peace, or a wild and noisome place of neither rest nor deliverance? Later, how did this belief greet and inform the incoming Celts? Where did the Christian and Celt become one – in the legends?

At the tower of Babel an Irish monk listened carefully, chose the best bits of all the languages, bore them home and manufactured Gaelic. Saint Brigid was cast adrift in a basket, a helpless infant. Where she fetched up Druids dwelt, and they raised her until the day came when she was summoned by a white dove who guided her through a grove of hawthorns to a desert. There she assisted at the birth of a Divine Child, and on his forehead she placed three drops of water. One Friday nearly twenty centuries ago, the High King of Ireland, sitting with his Druid, saw the sun darken, felt the earth tremble, heard a great rending noise, and his enquiries revealed the death in the East of the Son of God. When Columba prayed on Iona, fire surrounded him and angels were seen to whisper in his ear.

Hindsight occupies much of the Celtic religious experience – after the event the holy scribes imposed timeless connections upon Christianity. Arrogance – and innocence – persuaded them of their right to be included in the general Christian testament, and their capacity for invention filled the Christian legends with evidence of a Celtic presence. This recognition by the monks of their own Celtic forebears gave their Christian worship a distinctive feeling, and led them to a uniquely-flavoured, symbolistic vision. When Christianity received their acceptance, they married to it many of the ancient legends, put themselves, so to speak, in the picture. In the Mabinogion, Taliesin tells the King, Maelgwn:

> I was with my Lord in the highest sphere.
> On the fall of Lucifer into the depth of Hell;

I know the names of the stars from north to south;
I have been on the galaxy at the throne of the Distributor;
I was in Canaan when Absalom was slain;
I conveyed the Divine Spirit to the level of the vale of Hebron

and conveys further that he was 'at the place of the Crucifixion of the merciful Son of God', that he had been with 'my Lord in the manger of the ass: I strengthened Moses through the water of Jordan'. On a practical level, sacrifice, once offered in human blood, gave way to the blood of Christ. Natural forces drew forth their echoes: does the circle on the Celtic High Cross, for instance, resonate a sun-god, the face of Lugh whose festival pilgrims now re-create – in time, if not in name – on Croagh Patrick? Or merely a practical echo of early carpentry? At the holy place of Faughart, to honour Saint Brigid, water offers votive force in a stream that flows through the grove. Tennyson's *Morte d'Arthur* took the fabled king 'from the deep to the great deep'. Belief, whether mythological or Christian, built a bridge across which the fearful Celt might walk in safety. The worshipper, king or bondsman, praying to hero-god or saint, sought, like the artist, the safety of immortality, the defeat of death and power over the one uncontrollable dimension – time.

5

THE SECOND SORROW
OF STORYTELLING – THE
CHILDREN OF LIR

Second the bird-cursed Children of Lir;
I curse the mouth that made young lives in vain.
Conn, Fionnuala, Fiachra and Aedh –
Theirs is the second pain.

Tall and gracefully strong, the sons of Mil, also known as the Milesians, sailed up
the seas of Europe from Iberia to Ireland and engaged in battle with the Tuatha
De Danaan, the people of the goddess Dana. These magical tribes had inhabited
all the countryside for many enchanted generations: deities, wizards and makers
of spells. The greatest of their powers finally evaporated during the two great
battles of Moytura, in which they succumbed to the Milesians – who became the
new rulers. They all agreed to a division of the country, with the Milesians, the
new Gaels, taking everything above the ground and Dana's people commanding
everything beneath. Now, to the hollowed-out palaces beneath the hills and
mounds the Tuatha De Danaan repaired, where they constructed elaborate palaces
of pearl and silver, and surrounded themselves with elegance and beauty. In this
new land, time had no meaning, space had no dominion, all that counted was the
eternal youth of the people, and the timeless summer where the birds sang until
twilight.

The Tuatha De Danaan, in time, came to elect a new king. They chose Bov
Dearg, Bov the Red-Haired, a good and decent man whose candidacy for the
throne was challenged at the election by Lir, a chieftain from the north. Lir lived
at Finaghy, a powerful and excitable leader, whose son, Manannan MacLir, ruled
the sea. When Lir lost the election, he declared that he would pay neither tribute
nor fealty to Bov the new king, and no envoy from Finaghy ever journeyed to
Bov's court. After some years had passed, Lir's beloved wife died, leaving him
inconsolable. Bov Dearg sent a messenger to Lir, bearing sympathy and gentle
offers of reconciliation: Lir embraced the messenger and sent him back to Bov's
court on the shores of Lough Derg, the greatest lake on the River Shannon, with
word that he, Lir, was about to make a journey of fealty to Bov. Lir set out
shortly after the messenger and by the time he arrived at Bov's court, a great and
splendid welcome had been made ready, of feasting, dancing, tribute and song.
The two leaders greeted each other with love and tenderness and talked long and
simply in friendship.

The grief of Lir at the loss of his beloved wife still hung about him and with
great tact Bov suggested that Lir take another wife, to be chosen from Bov's own

three foster-daughters, Eve, Aoife and Alva. Lir granted that all three were of identical and unsurpassable beauty and after much deliberation chose Eve – on the grounds that as the eldest she must possess the greatest wisdom among the three. He took Eve back to Finaghy for a fine wedding, at which all Lir's subjects danced with joy both to see their king happy again and in appreciation of their new, beautiful and wise queen.

Within a year Eve bore Lir twin children, a girl, Fionnuala, and a boy, Aedh. Within another year Eve bore twins again, two boys Fiachra and Conn – but in their difficult birth Eve died and the children of Lir, Fionnuala, Aedh, Fiachra and Conn, walked through their childhood world motherless and lonely. Lir had loved Eve even more than his first wife and now his grief knew no bounds. He moaned wildly and walked the night wailing to the stars and the gaunt trees and his grief brought him near to passionate death for love of Eve. His impulse to live, however, received life from the observations and attentions of his sweet small children who adored their father, and he them. Such beautiful children had never before been seen among the Tuatha De Danaan, and when they laughed and played among the fountains of the great, gleaming underground palaces, the people who saw them marvelled at their perfection, at the simplicity of their utter beauty, the perfect formation of their foreheads and lips and limbs. Lir the king embraced their beauty and their gentle, loving nature and slowly the wound of bereavement began to heal within him, though his heart remained sore after the loss of lovely Eve.

In due course, when decency and respect for the dead queen permitted, Bov Dearg again sent a messenger to Lir, suggesting another marriage, to provide Lir with a loving companion and to offer a mother towards the children. Who could be more suitable than Aoife, his second foster-daughter, sister to the lamented Eve and equally beautiful? Such a suitable marriage: Aoife must surely feel love for her dead sister's children – and upon acquaintance, she and Lir loved each other more and more. The match seemed enchanted when Aoife travelled north with Lir to his palace at Finaghy: his people and his courtiers welcomed her with happy enthusiasm.

To begin with, Aoife loved the children, shared their time with Lir, listened enthralled with them as Lir told them the tales of the old days and far-off battles and golden champions. Aoife's father, Bov Dearg, also loved his four beautiful grandchildren, and spent almost as much time at Lir's court in Finaghy as in his own court beneath Lough Derg. Surrounded by her father, Bov, her husband, Lir and her four step-children – who were, after all, her niece and nephews – Aoife's life fulfilled her, made her content, she had the love of her loved ones.

But a canker grew in her soul, the ridged and knotted worm of envy. Aoife felt that Lir and his people, and even her own dear foster-father, Bov Dearg, regarded the four children more highly than her. When the notion took root she became ill and went to her bed, where she languished for many months. During that time a plan was born in her newly-twisted mind, and in detail she worked it through, until every turn of it was given shape, every move of it made feasible. Finally she rose from her bed, and told the four children that she was taking them in her chariot to the court of Bov Dearg, their grandfather, for a long and pleasurable visit. Alone among the children, Fionnuala had observed Aoife's change of heart, the new hidden barb towards her step-children, had even dreamt warning dreams with danger in them. Now she hung back, reluctant to take her place in the chariot of Aoife, but eventually she felt obliged to join her excited three young brothers.

Lir bade them goodbye, loving father and husband, but when they had gone but a short distance on the journey south, Aoife ordered the charioteer to stop. She then instructed her appalled servants to put the four children to the sword, since they had robbed her of the love of her husband: Lir, she insisted, loved his children more than her. The servants refused to comply, three times she gave the order, three times they drew back. Aoife's cunning took over, she appeared to subside and the journey continued.

But soon, when they had reached the shores of Lough Derravaragh, the lake of the oaks, sedge-bound and lonesome in the very middle of Ireland, she again bade the charioteer stop. The children were told they must refresh and clean themselves in the waters of the lake while the horses drank. They undressed, waded gingerly in, and suddenly – Aoife, remember, as one of the Tuatha De Danaan, still possessed sorcerer's powers – they became transformed at her wand's waving into four white swans.

Tall-necked, and whitest of the colour white, and of the serenest appearance, the Children of Lir in their new form sat on the waters of Derravaragh, sad, and moaning low. Fionnuala spoke for all, her voice echoing with the pain in her heart, and begged to understand why Aoife had done this to them, who had all and each loved her, their stepmother, their aunt, so much? And when would this new and awful burden of a swan's shape fall from them, and when would they be restored to their dear father? Of a sudden, the awfulness of what she had done struck Aoife, the worm of envy exploded within her heart and fizzled away, leaving her consumed with an agonised remorse. But there was little she could do: in casting the spell she had been definite, all she could attempt now was an amelioration of the sentence. And she told Fionnuala that the spell need not be borne for ever but would nonetheless carry them for three hundred years on Lough Derravaragh, three hundred years on the cruel Sea of Moyle, between the wild north coasts of Ireland and Scotland, and three hundred years on the rocks and waters of Inish Gluaire, again in the far and hostile northern seas.

No matter how terrible the sentence, at least the Children of Lir now knew the length of it, a small but genuine relief. And as further concession, Aoife, desperate to make any amends, gave them the gift of song such as never had been heard before, as well as all their human gifts, including speech. As a parting word Aoife told them that they would be released from their swan's bondage when a chieftain from the north took the hand in marriage of a princess from the south, and when a bell of new sound could be heard ringing over the land of Ireland.

Aoife continued her journey to the house of Bov Dearg where she told her foster-father that Lir no longer trusted her with the care of the children. Bov, angry but at the same time suspicious, sent a messenger to Lir's court to enquire the truth of this: in the exchange of information the wickedness of Aoife became apparent. Bov raised his wand, and with the most awful magic available to the King of the Tuatha De Danaan, turned Aoife into the cold and whistling demon who still inhabits that air which comes from the east. Then Bov set out with all haste to Lough Derravaragh where Lir had also hurried.

When the two men arrived they saw the four great white swans, the four beloved children, out on the water. Fionnuala observed the commotion on the shore, and among the crowd of courtiers then recognised the figures of her father and grandfather. She turned and led her brothers, Aedh, Fiachra and Conn, slowly and beautifully across the lake, singing as they went, in music which reached to the stars, reverberated with aching sweetness among the planets. Then the swans spoke from the sedges at the edge of the lake and told the assembled company, including their beloved forebears, of their sentence. Despite the sadness and pain in the hearts of Lir and Bov, their anguish eased when they heard the voices of the swans, and this effect came over everybody who heard them. For three hundred years they sailed in their majestic sadness across the waters of the lake and each night the people of Ireland, from far and near, journeyed to Derravaragh to have their hearts eased by the singing of the swans.

The day came when Fionnuala told her brothers that their time on Derravaragh had ended, and they must leave. They rose slowly into the air, watched by the sad crowds beneath and, wheeling low over the sedges, climbed into the sky towards the north.

> Silent, O Moyle, be the roar of thy water;
> Break not, ye breezes, your chain of repose,
> While, murmuring mournfully, Lir's lonely daughter
> Tells to the night-star her tale of woes.
> When shall the swan, her death-note singing,
> Sleep, with wings in darkness furl'd?
> When will my heaven, its sweet bells ringing,
> Call my spirit from this stormy world?

Not a human, not a soul, not a friendly face or sound did they find on the wild Sea of Moyle. In the waves and the black rocks the Children of Lir found only cruel misery. Occasionally a party from their own dear people would call by, but could only shout wishes and affection from afar, and the cries often died away on the wind. The storms of Moyle raged fierce and famously: in one, Fionnuala and her three brothers were forced apart, and for several days lost all sight of each other. Fionnuala found safety on the hollow of a great rock where she huddled against the wind, just out of reach of the lashing spray. One by one, but slowly, her brothers came to her, and crept under her wingspan for her warmth and comfort. Indeed, many anxious moments walked by until she saw the last one, Aedh, appear falteringly over the edge of the cleft, his wing damaged, and limping, his face twisted from the way the wind forced it while he had been listening out for their calls. Hardly a crueller place than Moyle existed on the face of the earth, and the anguish of their existence there intensified when they recalled the sweet and perfumed times they spent in the land of their father Lir, or playing in the bright courtyards of their grandfather, Bov Dearg.

The day when they left for Inish Gluaire seemed a bright and hopeful one: Moyle, savage Moyle, fell away behind them, and though Inish Gluaire seemed even more remote, the Children of Lir appreciated that the last term of Aoife's malicious spell had been entered. By now, no news ever reached them from Finaghy or from Lough Derg, and they resigned themselves to the fact that their people had completely forgotten them, or had passed into another existence. They looked longingly at the mounds of earth over which they flew on the way to Inish Gluaire, thinking of the friends and days they had known beneath these hills, and would now, perhaps, never find again. On Inish Gluaire, the wind blew harsh and cold, the nights and the waters darker even than on Moyle, yet still the swans sang sweetly and spoke fondly to each other. Then the day dawned and with Fionnuala leading, they wheeled into the skies and made for the land of Ireland.

As they landed, two events occurred: in the south a wedding took place – of a prince of northern Connaught, and a maiden of high birth from the province of Munster. And a saint came forth from his tiny cell and rang a bell to tell all who might chance by, animal or human, that prayer could be shared. The spell of Aoife shattered in the two occurrences: the swans landed in the clearing by the saint's cell. Immediately, as they had hoped and prayed for nine hundred years, they began to change shape. But, alas, they did not appear as they had been: on the grass stood four ancient and wizened people. In the casting of the spell of jealousy, all beauty and timelessness had been taken from them, and their magic lived no more. Barely had the saintly monk time to bless them than they had linked arms, lay on the ground and died.

Ever since in Ireland, when the singing of a swan is heard, the people know that this is not just the death of the swan's lifelong partner, but the last day of another of Lir's children.

6

EXPRESSIONS

Goethe wrote: 'The artist determines beauty. He does not take it over.' Did this axiom govern the Celtic artist? Suspicion arises – especially if you gaze across the breadth of La Tene metalworking, or at one of the great artefacts in a European museum, or examine an Irish illuminated manuscript. The exuberant profuseness of the decoration, the tendency to ornament every square millimetre of surface, the excursion into the abstract, suggest a rampant, unimpeded, overwhelming artistic imagination.

Never. Celtic art combined the dark and uncanny with the abundant and simplistic: above all else it responded to the natural world. Like Nature itself, Celtic art abhorred a straight line, pushed organic influences – observed in trees, plants, water, the earth – to deliciously abstracted infinity. It expressed them in happy, or humorous, or practical or beautiful terms, and never concerned itself too seriously with accurate pictorial representation. A coin, for instance offered an opportunity to the Celtic artist to break down the component parts of the head illustration into an abstract group of images until only the impression of the head's shape remained – and the eye might then interpret the image as it wished. And – perhaps most important of all – each expression within an artistic statement depended utterly upon the tension created by its neighbour.

Most frequently, the term 'La Tene' is used to define quintessential Celtic art. And understandably, when, for those four centuries or so before Christ, the Celts made such great beauty dance across surfaces of gold and clay, with fabulous and freeflowing skill. If taken as a sole description the term misleads. La Tene Culture certainly drew the Celts' artistic expression to a pinnacle. But Hallstatt Culture, though less cosmetically glorious, must take precedence both in chronology and as an originating contributor. Both periods and subsequent developments reflect the progress of their civilisation as clearly as any written record might have done, had the Celts been literate. And even more accurately, perhaps; the very word 'illumination', while describing one aspect of Celtic art, also defines a major service which Celtic art now performs for us.

The French artist, Marcel Duchamp, provoked Paris in the years after the First World War with his 'readymades' – the presentation of everyday objects, a wine-bottle rack, a urinal, a bicycle-wheel – as artistic expression. Further, he permitted ordinary occurrences – the dust in his studio, or natural damage, such as cracks – to become part of the work of art which he had set out to create. In this wild and seemingly random fashion he pursued his belief that life had no meaning other than absurdity.

Half a century later, an American, Robert Rauschenberg, insisted that art can exist anywhere, in any form, for any purpose. In the Moderna Museum in Stockholm stands his work, Monogram – a stuffed goat, midriff encircled by a car tyre. For his materials Rauschenberg drew upon his own natural world – of Manhattan. 'If I walked completely around the block and didn't find enough to work with, I could take one other block and walk around it in any direction – but that was it. The work had to look at least as interesting as anything that was going on outside the window.' He found the stuffed goat in a shop that sold used typewriters. He was, he said, 'mainly interested in other people's facts'.

In principle – but most certainly not in execution – the Celts seem close to the artistic values of both Duchamp and Rauschenberg, believing, as they did, in the natural breathing of art and in the utter availability of it, all around them, domestically and environmentally. However, they differ in that the objects which the two modern artists used, despite their domesticity and commonplace presence, never became art in themselves, until they were deliberately placed in an artistic context. Whereas what the Celts left behind seems now to have an immortal glory, derived from more than the mere patina of time, or from their precious metals and jewelling techniques. The commonplace element, utensils, weapons, household objects, which we now regard as constituent parts of Celtic art, belonged to exactly the same principle of everyday life as Duchamp's urinal or Rauschenberg's stuffed goat. To what extent would the domestic utensils born of our mass-production techniques ever acquire the same legendary aura? It seems impossible to think that two thousand years hence the world will marvel in the same way at the rusting washing-machine or refrigerator a farmer's plough has just turned up. We accept mass-production, permit it in our lives. Admittedly, we have no evidence that the Celts would not have done likewise: whether they would remains as conjecture – all we have is the fact, plain in their artefacts, that they did not. We therefore have to proceed upon their evidence of what they created, rather than with our hindsight suggesting what – given the facilities of our mass-production – they might have created.

The air base at Valley on the North Wales island of Anglesey hums and roars, a major RAF training station. Unknowing, the young pilots fly their small red-and-white planes above the site of famous encounters where Celtic women with white faces, in long black robes, once screamed terrifying defiance at the invading Romans. The pilots wear flying-suits designed to cope with the lethal wildness of uncontrolled atmospheric forces; the helmet, if incompetently donned, can snap the neck. Careering, careening through the skies, each aircraft, if seen in conjunction with the place directly below, assumes the aura of a godly chariot – because that remarkable find in 1943, beneath what is now runway One-Nine of RAF Valley, responds directly, almost ghostily, to these powerful and elegant instruments of war.

In the pool of Llyn Cerrig Bach the huge cache of weapons which the wartime

The Basse-Yutz Flagons (4th century BC)
found at Nieder-Jutz, France, dug up by
workmen who at first stole them: now in
the British Museum. In form, content,
expression and humour these wine vessels
stand as important contributions to Celtic
Art. The metalworking artist who
executed them used coral, worked in tiny
pattern, expanded into comic themes,
reflected animals and birds, while
creating elegant and original objects for
some chieftain's table.

The Durrnberg Flagon which echoes the same style as the Basse-Yutz Flagons. Ornamented details, long shaping and fluting display the influences which came, via the wine trade, to Celtic craftsmen who lived and worked in the rich river valleys of France and Southern Germany.

The Aylesford Bucket, found
in 1886 in the cemetery of a
Belgic tribe in Kent, and
dated to approximately
50 BC. The bulging eyes, the
little slitted mouth and long
wedge-shaped nose typify
human representation in
La Tene expression.

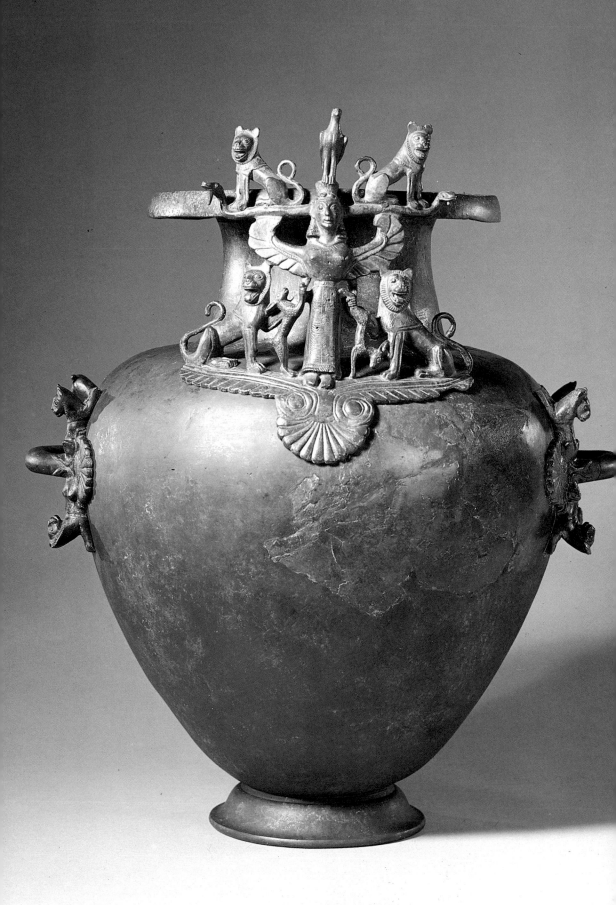

The Desborough Mirror. Dated to the first century AD, found in Northamptonshire, 1908, 26 cm wide, 35 cm high, now in the British Museum. Exemplifying one of the specialities of the Celtic craftsmen, it is described as part of the 'Western mirror school'. The crescent rings and other symmetrical designs were probably traced out with a compass.

Opposite: A bronze hydria, approximately 60 cm tall, dated to the sixth century BC, found in Switzerland, and now in the museum in Bern. Trade between the Celts and the rest of Europe grew extensively, and the influence of such contacts became evident in the possessions of the Celtic chieftains, and therefore in the work of their craftsmen.

Personal decorations, glass and amber beads from Slovenia (*left*), gold rings and fasteners from Hallstatt (*right*), jewellery from a princess's grave in the Saar region (*below*), testify to the Celtic belief that death represented not an end but a beginning. The journey to the 'Otherworld' required style and the impression of stature and therefore had to be dressed and catered for, as if going on an important journey or meeting influential people in this life.

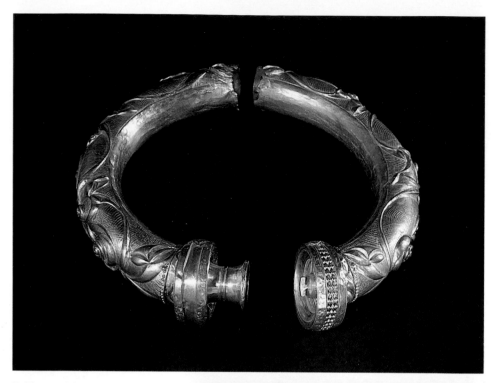

Gold torcs (*above and right*) worn usually as ornamental jewellery, but with, originally, a more sinister purpose. Wrapped around the neck, the torc broke the unsuspected attacking blow of an enemy sword on the back of the neck.

Assorted coins (*opposite*) of the Celtic era, depicting kings and horsemen, derived from Roman and Macedonian models.

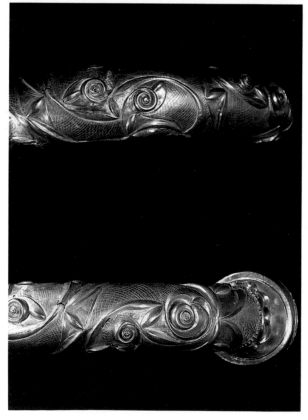

Harness-mounts and other horse furniture bore lavish decoration and colour, and reflected not only the style and stature of the horseman, but the esteem in which the horse, beast of burden and heroic companion was held. Many graves, all across the different periods of Celtic civilisation, contained the trappings of the chieftain's horse – such as the coloured harness-piece (*top*) dated approximately first century BC and (*below*) an earlier, late 5th century BC openwork harness disc. In some cases the bones or skeletons of entire horses were found in the graves, still harnessed and decorated, and in certain gypsy and itinerant customs, the tradition of burying a horse with its dead owner survived until well into the 20th century.

The Witham Shield – found in the River Witham near Lincoln, now in the British Museum. The figure of a boar, in outline, had once been pinned to the shield: note the holes which held the boar in place.

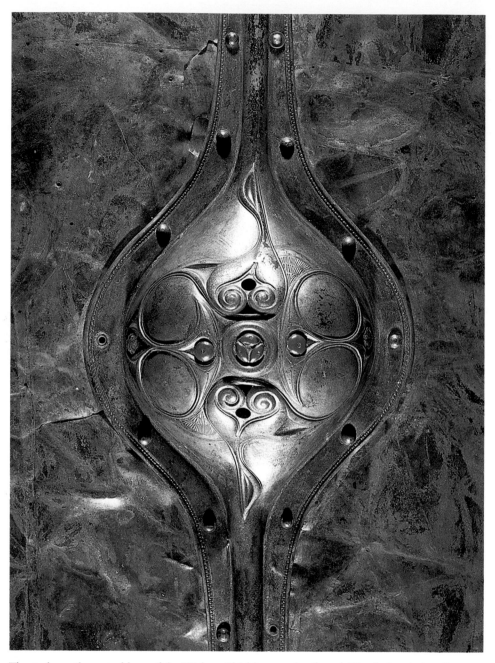

The studs on the central boss of the Witham Shield are made of coral. The dating derives from similar styles current in Europe at approximately the end of the third century BC, and continuing in Britain into the first century AD.

The Battersea Shield – described by an Edwardian antiquarian as 'the noblest creation of Late Celtic art', found in the River Thames circa 1855 by a labourer who made his living by searching out and selling such discoveries, dated – amid much discussion – to the first century BC and now in the British Museum. Made of bronze, with panels and enamelled roundels, the shield may have been too lightly fitted and ornamental for other than ornamental or ceremonial purposes.

Top: Helmets from the Marne district of north-eastern France. *Above:* The Amfreville Helmet, taken from the River Seine. *Right:* Bronze pony helmet from Kircudbright in Scotland. All come from La Tene Culture, 400–200 BC approx. and bear witness to the Celtic impulse for ornamented headgear. More than one enemy commented upon the Celts' liking for helmets which impressed either by their grandeur or their fearsomeness.

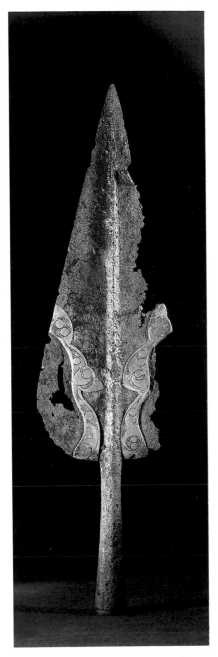

The earliest development which gave the Celts an advantage over any other prehistoric peoples came in their use of iron – especially in weaponry, where harder, more varied cutting edges could be introduced. Again, the marriage of the practical to the beautiful took place, whether in a Hallstatt dagger, or short sword with holes punched across the hilt or in a later spear found in the River Thames in London, and bearing bronze *applique* embellishments.

overleaf: A bronze harness plaque, found in a chariot burial in the Marne district of France, dated to the fifth century BC. The flower-shapes intertwine in the characteristic Celtic curvilinear impulse, each depends upon the shape next to it and the whole piece represents a fine example of La Tene art in typical mood.

archaeologists managed to excavate seems to have had votive intent. The power of that slave chain, which drew attention to the deposit, may suit as a metaphor: it arrested the progress of the tractor clearing the ground for the building of the runway. And thus, by a bondsman's relic, our understanding of the Celts strengthened. Swords, spears, shields, harness-pieces, trumpets, cauldrons and other vessels came to our attention – the readymades of Celtic Anglesey, circa AD 100.

Now, in light of the aircraft making circles in the skies overhead, reflect upon the famous Llyn Cerrig Bach chariot relics, abundant enough to permit an elaborate reconstruction. Consider how shape has been related to the aircraft's task, sleek and beautiful aerodynamic design in pursuit of a deadly purpose, absolute correspondence between form and function. Only to be expected, you argue, in the latter half of the twentieth century. But two thousand years ago, the form and function of the items lodged in the pool at Llyn Cerrig Bach – loot, some scholars have suggested, taken in a victorious battle and then offered in thanksgiving to the gods of war – possessed just as much synthesis.

Such power and style married together offers another classification of the Celts, another illumination, another means of capturing their spirit and of regarding them as being entirely in observance of Goethe's point – the artist determining, but never dominating beauty and putting the work of art to useful purpose. Celtic artists produced work which even today, despite our post-Renaissance advances in artistic expression and design, retains a unique quality derived from a marriage of the beautiful to the practical.

Any survey of Celtic art leaves the eye dazzled. In the National Museum of Ireland in Kildare Street, Dublin, the exhibition, 'Treasures of Ireland,' on permanent display after an extensive international tour, displays sumptuous beauty. The official description summarises the collection of objects and their pathway to preservation:

The illuminated manuscripts owe their survival to having been jealously treasured in churches and monasteries; nearly all the other objects are of the noble metals – gold, silver and bronze – and so resisted destruction from both exposure to the air and burying in the ground. The many objects of wood, iron, leather and fabric that must have been their companions have disappeared. Those objects that did survive the attacks of nature had to face other constant perils in the course of Ireland's long and turbulent history: to be buried hastily without much chance of discovery; to be stolen and used to decorate the hall of a different lord or the altar of a rival monastery; to be plundered, broken up, and divided among a marauding gang who might mount the fragments as trophies; to be melted down and vanish forever in a pool of bullion metal.

The same story reverberates across Celtic Europe, no different from the tale of many ancient valuables: invasion reaches all corners of a culture. Luckily, Celtic relics continue to turn up, largely by domestic or agricultural accident.

In any consideration of Celtic treasures, remember the place of the metalworker. The Celts granted him stature of almost sacred proportions. In a world which was still blurring the lines between the natural and the supernatural the craftsman, like the Druid, performed a role which suggested mystical properties. His power came through his visible gifts and their abstract, often arcane results. And his force persisted; even in the Christian era, when Irish Celtic art flourished to unprecedented heights, hints of the dark and haunted precincts of pagan expression remained. Despite great and obvious regional differences, in motif, in structure and shape, a bowl from La Tene and a brooch from Saint Patrick's Ireland appear cousins – not just in the obvious designs, but in the atmosphere which each conveys, in a flexibility of line, a comfortableness of feeling and a sense of excitement. The continuity of instinct – perceptible across the entire range of their art – which unites the European Celts of six centuries before Christ with Irish monks of thirteen centuries later, provides the basic body of work in which we can see the full adventure of Celtic expression.

Using the shortest of shorthand, the tangible examples of Celtic art fall into a series of styles. They date from the end of the Bronze Age, through the Hallstatt style of eight centuries BC, followed by the polish of La Tene Culture, ending with the post-La Tene British and (more lavish) Irish work which continued for several centuries after Christ.

Early Celtic art drew the following from one renowned scholar Paul Jacobsthal:

The repertory is narrow; the image of man is limited to huge menhir-like statues in stone, in bronze to a few busts or miniature doll-like men and a multitude of heads. There are very few natural animals; most of them are fantastic and highly stylised … to the Greeks a spiral is a spiral and a face is a face and it is always clear where the one ends and the other begins, whereas the Celts 'see' the faces 'into' the spirals or tendrils; ambiguity is a characteristic of Celtic art.

Where did it come from? What caused the ideas, what visions guided the expression that led to the beautiful decoration of an early pot or bucket from Hallstatt, or the freeflowing line of a honeysuckle tendril captured unself-consciously in a cloak-fastener or armlet?

The deepest basis of Celtic art grew from a primordial dependence upon the natural life experienced in the emergent Europe north of the Alps, east of, and along the Danube valley – or, come to that, in the sloping fields of what is now Hertfordshire, or Northumbria, or Wicklow. The early motifs showed great consistency of pattern, geometric, angular shapes, concentric circles, whorls, lozenges, revolving spirals, chevrons, cross-hatched repeating patterns – mechanical, auto-suggested means of filling a blank space on a pot. Later, the images of small creatures begin to materialise, swans, ducks, horses: on the lid of a Hallstatt bucket, a goat, a sphinx, a lion, a deer. A full, annotated catalogue of Celtic art would fill several huge volumes. Add in the innumerable dissertations, learned proceedings, 'dig' reports, theses, essays, breakthroughs, claims to original interpretation – the catalogue becomes a library. And so it should. But by selecting a handful of the more famous Celtic artefacts 'signposts' will appear, tracing that vital, chronological, regional record of development which led to an identifiable school called 'Celtic Art'.

Take, therefore, four moments which will also represent the range of Celtic work and purpose: a Hallstatt scabbard belonging to the fourth century BC, but echoing from a much more ancient date; a pair of French wine receptacles from fifth/fourth century BC; a shield from Britain, the dating of which, agreed by investigators to be a subjective matter, ranges through parameters of fifty years

The Hallstatt scabbard: the style of drawing and illustration echoes across the earliest artefacts which characterise the word 'Celtic,' and the faces and shapes of the figures and horses persisted in some branches of European illustration for many centuries, up to and including the Bayeux Tapestry.

either side of the birth of Christ; and an illuminated manuscript dated to northern Britain and Ireland between the seventh and tenth centuries AD.

From the Salzkammergut graves of Hallstatt a scabbard appeared, decorated concisely with figures of men with recognisable personalities, small, almost comic, engaged in wrestling (if such it is), discussing a spoked wheel, marching on foot, carrying decorated shields, spears, bound for battle, charging on horseback, helmeted, with their ritualised horses trampling enemies *en route*. The comparative evidence suggests an accidental provenance in Hallstatt – that the scabbard had been manufactured well outside the territory, perhaps in the Adriatic region. Therefore, the very presence of the piece surely offers proof that the Celts of many centuries before Christ knew the Greeks, the Romans, the Etruscans. But already a difference from the artists of the Mediterranean, a loosening-up, becomes apparent. Unlike the Greeks, in whose art of the period every picture had to tell a story, the narrative in the Hallstatt scabbard seems less important than the manner of telling. For instance, in the horses' exaggerated tails, more personality, more dramatisation, more observation of individuality, more wit, comes through.

In a case in the British Museum in London stand two of the most exquisite objects ever produced by a Celtic artist – the Basse-Yutz flagons, thirty-eight centimetres high, bronze, with much inlay. Delicate, graceful, dignified – and even the rough trade of time has cost them little. Their greatest scholarly value lies in the fact that they stand at a junction. They epitomise and draw together the main sources of La Tene inspiration, art created at native, local level, beaten and finger-worked, but with pattern and shape influenced from trade with the Greeks and Etruscans, and a debt acknowledged to 'the Most Ancient East' of the Celts' ancestry – *ex oriente lux*, 'out of the east came light'.

The Basse-Yutz flagons, dated to the beginning of the fourth century BC, display the Celts as a maturing, sophisticating, civilising people, prepared to respond to influences from outside their own regional sphere, aware of other cultures, observing those with whom they traded. The detail on the flagons adds, in immediate fashion, to the understanding of how Celtic art evolved. The spout thrusts forward the representation of a bird – in this case a merrily-swimming duck, bulging eyes made of bright coral – pursued, unknown to itself, by exotically ferocious beasts, one of whom, an enormous dog-like figure, hair or fur clearly configured, forms the handle, and grips in its teeth the chain which lifts the lid. The spirals at the animal's joints echo the whorls of the horses' haunches on the Hallstatt scabbard. The flagons probably graced the table of a European Celtic chieftain. The handles have lost much of their original enamelling, although, according to analysis, might regain a deep red colour if saturated in water. The overall effect conveys lightness, and a delicacy much advanced – suddenly, almost – upon the heaviness, deliberateness, bulkiness of the artefacts found in Hallstatt, or any other material classified mainly as belonging to the Hallstatt Culture.

The Basse-Yutz flagons communicate several facts central to Celtic art – curvilinear ornamentation, Mediterranean influence, a spirit of decoration which did not fear to reach for playful shapes – in turn derived from natural, animal or vegetal forms, heading in the direction of the unreal or the surreal, inventive, abstract. Full of colour and prepared to experiment with different material, their creator experienced no great intellectual consideration, religious thought, or symbolic depth. But one major development presents itself too – the permission taken by the Celtic artist, rare up to that moment, to leave surfaces free of ornamentation, to have the courage to leave open space to speak for itself.

Final touch of pleasure – the flagon-maker was influenced by the Celts' dealings with the wine traders of the South, so that the eventual contents of the flagons had a say in their delicacy of appearance – form and function felicitously interdependent.

The Basse-Yutz flagons graced the tables of some warlord, some swaggering Celtic chieftain who took enormous pride in displaying such sophistication, such obvious style and wealth to neighbouring statesmen, to Roman, Greek or Etruscan visitors, or to connections encountered in the wine trade. The aristocracy commissioned such work – even when travelling, a Celtic leader frequently included his metal-working craftsman in his entourage.

Another imperative, more practical but no less luxurious, governed the crafts-man's stature. Legends describe the light glinting off a weapon on a hill in the distance before battle, the flashing herald of an enemy's presence, or the encouragement of the gods. Seated upon his horse, his champion near him, a Celtic king drew pride, morale and adrenaline from the beauty of his weapons – they displayed his stature, echoed his courage, marked him out as a leader of exception.

On March 10th 1858, H. Syer Cuming offered a paper to the British Archae-ological Association, to which he had the honour of being secretary. He included in the document a note from one, Thomas Bateman, describing some finds 'dredged up from the bed of the river' – the Thames at Battersea – in particular what Cuming called 'a veritable Celtic shield ... now deposited in the British Museum'. Where it still reposes, a distinctive piece of armoury, seventy-seven centimetres long, of bronze and enamel panels attached to the shield by twenty-four rivets with washers. Each of the three panels had been decorated with nine roundels, inlaid with red enamel: each roundel had been built on a circular framework of bronze, on which a decoration suggesting a swastika had been executed. The central boss of the shield rises above the surrounding surface, roundel-decorated too, a gleaming centrepiece, and so lavish and delicate seems the whole work, with inlaid glass and vivid colour, and abstract suggestions of fearsome facial expressions, that much speculation has focused on whether it was designed for battle at all. The craftsman who made it departed from any previous or current vogue in Celtic shield manufacture and thereby became his own mystery.

All the interpretations of the Battersea Shield discuss the exact dating. The influences evident in the work confuse any chronology: some of the designs could have come straight from the fourth century BC, the enamelled roundels have associations with both the fifth and first centuries BC. The lightness of the handle pinnings further raised the question as to whether the shield had ever been intended for combat, whether it possessed ceremonial or decoration status only. The most frequently-expressed opinions infer that the Battersea Shield came from between the first centuries BC and AD. This suggests that British art, having 'caught up' with mainstream European La Tene genres, took on a life entirely unto itself, with great individuality. But it never forgot the old alliance with ancient Celtic curvilinear form whose basis lay in suggestion, in abstract intention, rather than in any portrayal of reality. The Battersea Shield while belonging clearly to the freeflowing world of all Celtic art, expressed a regional departure among the Celts of the West, and made a triumphant appearance on the arm of some south-eastern English chieftain at a time when Celtic culture on mainland Europe had already begun to decline.

Of all the Celtic artefacts the most famous (certainly from Western Europe) and the most-examined piece comes from the last great period of Celtic civilisation, from Christian Ireland in approximately the eighth century AD. The Book of Kells lies in Trinity College, Dublin, an official tourist attraction, six hundred and seventy-eight pages of illuminated brilliance: the two remaining pages bear no illustrations. (A further sixty pages from the original book have disappeared.) The basic text comprises the Gospels of Matthew, Mark, Luke and John – but did the book ever have a function in daily prayer? Rather it belonged in the same category as sacred vessels and shrines, designed to grace the altar on great Christian feast-days and celebrations. (When Queen Victoria saw it, during a famous visit to Ireland, she missed the point: she asked for a pen, under the impression that she would be expected to sign it.)

It emanated from a *scriptorium*: the monastery at Kells in County Meath which belonged to the settlement of abbeys established in the tradition of Columba of Iona. The Book of Kells may even have been begun in Iona and brought to Ireland for safety from the Vikings. Several different scribal influences appear, embracing illustrative styles from the monasteries of northern England and continental Europe, to a summary of almost all that had gone before in Irish Celtic art. The book raises the same difficulty as, say, the paintings of Fra Angelico or the more powerfully reverential works of Piero della Francesca. How can you worship through the art?

Originally the makers contained it within a golden cover, long lost. But such a vast and wondrous range of expression – forests of scrolls, spirals, trumpet-shapes, interlacings of ribbons, dropped capitals, elaborately-wrought letters, each one a charming and peaceful excursion for the eye, in colours of yellow, green, blue, red, and, most of all, purple. Within these idyllic mazes tiny faces and shapes dance about and peer out with an unconcerned inquisitiveness, sometimes mischievous, sometimes querulous, sometimes terrifying, sometimes happy, always alive – old men, cantankerous-looking groups (caricatures, perhaps, sneaked into the body of the work by younger scribes), mice, butterflies, kittens, fish, peacocks, horses, supple, lissome, elastic creatures, an entire population derived from the work of the Creator and given back to him in honour.

By tradition, Trinity College Library turned a page per day: dwell upon any one of them, contemplate, consider, let your imagination go on a long and exquisite voyage. Furthermore – and vitally – within the Book of Kells, so comprehensive, so lavish, so deeply, utterly and comprehensively generic, traces of all Celtic art appear. The faces seem blood-related to those on the scabbard at Hallstatt. The creatures whistle up the blissful duck and wild pursuers on the Basse-Yutz flagons. The whorled designs confirm the red and glass roundels on the Battersea Shield. Virtually every piece of Celtic decoration, since Hallstatt, all through La Tene Culture, or taken from the warlike votive pool at Llyn Cerrig Bach, achieves representation of some sort in the Book of Kells. It refers to, reaches into every corner of the Celtic artistic experience, with hints of legend, appreciation of the human and commonplace, but ultimately exotically abstract in the concentration of massive, fantastic imagery.

Tremendous though it appears to the eye, the great value of the Book of Kells lies not in the illuminations, nor even in the reverential value, nor even in the technical accomplishment of the scribes. Even though it arrived long after the decline of Celtic mainland Europe – or perhaps because of that fact – see it as the ultimate image of everything that Celtic artistic expression intended, stood for, attempted: the epitome of attempting to define the undefinable. The scribes' objective – great and grand celebration and worship – draws from the deep well of human experience, not just Christianity. The bewildering, ordered chaos of pattern, design and illumination conveys something of the mind's perplexity and the imagination's colourful response when faced with magic, hallucination or inexplicable mysteries of religion – 'those revealed truths which we cannot understand.' Wordless communication, too, that same principle which led the Celts to ornament their bodies and their belongings. Every brooch, every armlet, every bracelet, every ornamentation of a sword, every movement upon the clay of a pot, every curl, curve and curlicue ever contemplated, attempted, completed by a Celtic artist – once the Celtic civilisation had come into its own – may be perceived within the Book of Kells. See it, too, as the paradigm of all other kinds of Celtic artistic expression, including those still extant, flourishing, in the nations of the European West – music, dance, song, story and the later literary expressions such as the impossibly intricate patterns of James Joyce's 'novel' *Finnegans Wake* and, to a lesser extent, his *Ulysses*, or the simple and profound synthesis of so many Celtic poets. The pages of the Book of Kells simply call to mind a love of pattern, intricacy, colourful expression drawn from everyday life and embellished to – literally – fantastic extremes. And each moment within each page depends and relies upon the moment next to it: in the tension dwells the soul.

An Irish or Scottish or Breton traditional dancer performs intricate patterns of steps, weaving inwards and outwards, tracing circles and spirals on the floor in time to a music which comes down in a straight line of folk descent. Freedom seems all, yet the requirements of the dance technique remain rigid. (So, alas, in a different meaning, do the arms and bodies of the dancers – usually as a result of censorious teaching: the music and the movement of the feet and legs confirm the original erotic intent; many of these were dances of courtship performed in kitchens.) The feet batter the floor, the legs sway and flash and they say you can tell where a dancer comes from, on which side of the hill or valley he or she was born, from the steps of their dance. Once upon a time, journeymen dancing-masters wandered the countryside bringing their own steps, contentiously at times, into areas already proud with dancing, so that, as with art, regional influences abound. As to whether the modern form resembles the steps danced in legendary courts of the great Celtic warlords we have no proof. Commercialism, drawing-room fashion and that restraint among teachers have each brought corruption.

Instead, listen to the music, and the primary, primitive instrument, the voice. The ancient writers refer frequently to the way the Celts used their voices as instruments of war: the champion dashing into battle yelled terrifyingly. One military historian believes that in the American Civil War, the famed 'rebel yell' heard among the armies of the South derived directly from that ancient battle-cry of the Celtic warrior – the Confederates' Army had many Scots and Welshmen. Describing the Celts' custom of severing enemy heads, Diodorus Siculus added, 'The blood-stained spoils they hand over to their attendants and carry off as booty, while striking up a paean and singing a song of victory.' In *Tain Bo Cuailgne*, Cuchulainn indulges in numerous power-driven chants, some heroic, some filled with angst, as when he feared even his own great strength might not prevail against the enemy hordes:

I am alone against hordes.
I can neither halt nor let pass.
I watch through the long hours
alone against all men.

Tell Conchobor★ to come now.
It wouldn't be too soon.
Magach's sons have stolen our cattle
to divide between them.

I have held them single-handed,
but one stick won't make fire.
Give me two or three
And torches will blaze!

I am almost worn out
by single contests.
I can't kill all their best
alone as I am.

From *Tain Bo Cuailgne* – (The Cattle Raid of Cooley),
transl. Thomas Kinsella

By his chanting the warrior inspired himself in combat, or love, or thoughtful contemplation of his own prowess. Music became an heroic consideration, a matter

★Conchobor, the King of Ulster, stood in such high repute, 'that every man in Ulster that took a girl in marriage let her sleep the first night with Conchobor, so as to have him first in the family … Any Ulsterman who gave him a bed for the night gave him his wife as well to sleep with. His household was very handsome. He had three houses: Craebruad, the Red Branch; Tete Brec, the Twinkling Hoard; and Craebderg, the Ruddy Branch.'

for thought among gods and champions. When Finn McCool and his band of Fianna lay resting upon the grass of the mountainside one day after a hunt, debate began as to the sweetness of sounds. Finn's son, Ossian, declared that the blithest sound in all the world was made by the cuckoo calling from the highest tree in the hedge. Oscar, Ossian's son, Finn's grandson, favoured the sound made by the ringing of a spear upon a shield. The other warriors delighted in such melodies as the belling of a stag across water, the baying of a tuneful pack heard in the distance, the song of a lark, and the laughter of a gleeful girl or the whisper of a moved one. Then they turned and waited for their leader's opinion, and Finn said: 'The music of what happens – that is the finest music in the world.'

Like all primitive music everywhere, the Celtic 'music of what happens' – associated now with the countries of the Western European seaboard – never sprang from a notated or formal system. The voice, the primary musical form, responded spontaneously – lullaby, jubilation. And lament, called 'keening', a remarkable expression, which has all but died out. The word derives from '*caoine*', in roughest phonetics 'queen-yeh', meaning 'sorrow' or 'lamentation' or 'mournful sound'. Those who ever heard it chilled to the eeriness of the sound, the wailing and the repetition, the wildness contained in the controlled howling. The chant often seemed to meld with the elements in the graveyard. One nineteenth-century collector of Irish music described the principle of *Caoine*.

There are usually in a neighbourhood two or three women, who are skilled beyond others in keening, and who make a practice of attending at wakes and funerals. These often pour forth over the dead person a lament in Irish – partly extempore, partly prepared – delivered in a kind of plaintive recitative; and at the conclusion of each verse, they lead a choral cry, in which others who are present join, repeating throughout, 'Och-Ochone!' or some such words.

Another contemporary description described a larger group keening

… in the open air, winding round some mountain pass, when a priest, or person greatly beloved and respected, is carried to the grave, and the keen, swelled by a thousand voices, is borne upon the mountain echoes – it is then absolutely magnificent.

Later scholars defined the Irish *Caoine* as having three parts, a salutation in which the mourner or professional keener wails over and over again the name of the deceased, or some appropriate loving term; next, a verse or dirge praising the dead person, sentiments of admiration and respect; lastly the cry at the end of each verse in which the keener(s) lead the assembled company in a repetitive chant, with the meaning contained in the sound. This structure permitted internal change, especially in the music of the verse, where improvisation frequently came into use: otherwise the central chant of the keening, especially the repetition, had common usage in many regions. Another observer of life in nineteenth-century Ireland described such a keening comprehensively.

I once heard in West Muskerry, in the county of Cork, a dirge of this kind, excellent in point of both music and words, improvised over the body of a man (who had been killed by a fall from a horse) by a young man, the brother of the deceased. He first recounted his genealogy, eulogised the spotless honour of his family, described in the tones of a sweet lullaby his childhood and boyhood, then changing the air suddenly, he spoke of his wrestling and hurling, his skill at ploughing, his horsemanship, his prowess at a fight in a fair, his wooing and marriage, and ended by suddenly bursting into a loud piercing, but exquisitely beautiful wail, which was again and again taken up by the bystanders. Sometimes the panegyric on the deceased was begun by one and continued by another and so on, as many as three or four taking part in the improvisation.

The practice of keening, widely reported in Ireland and Scotland during the eighteenth and nineteenth centuries, later fell into disfavour: it smacked, the priests said, of official, paid mourners. The most recent reports came from the Aran Islands and other remote west coast regions during the 1950s. In effect, keening differed little, and may have derived from the deep and ancient tradition of heroic poetry. Here the Celtic connection introduces itself with some force.

Heroic poetry seems always to be chanted, [wrote the scholar Maurice Bowra] usually to some simple stringed instrument, like the Greek lyre, the Serbian *gusle*, the Russian *balalaika*, the Tartar *koboz*, or the Albanian *lahuta*. The music to which poems are sung is usually not a real or a regular tune, but a monotonous chant in which the bard often keeps whole lines on a single note. Such indeed is said to be the regular practice in Albania – and heroic Yugoslav chants ... are monotonous and lacking in melody. There certainly seems to be no evidence that a special poem has its own tune ... Heroic poetry puts the words first and subordinates the music to them. What it uses is really no more than recitative. To use a regular tune like that of a song would have made the task of heroic poets much more difficult and have interfered with the clear presentation of the tales which they have to tell.

Some traditional singing (even when sung in non-Celtic languages, such as English) resonates with these ancient influences: musicologists have discussed at length the way in which the same notes, tonal and vocal embellishments appear in Celtic and Asian music. Both traditions have one vital property in common: no matter how often a singer will perform a song, he or she will never sing it in the same way twice. Like a jazz player's tune, the song becomes the singer's own property. The expression, the ornamentations, the permutations, belong to infinity, and the marriage of the singer and the song becomes primal art.

The earliest varieties of this music and its performance occupied a special place in the life of the Celtic family. Each king or chieftain of substance had at court his own poet, praise singer, wordsmith. According to Posidonius:

The Celts have in their company even in war (as well as in peace) companions whom they call parasites. These men pronounce their praises before the whole assembly and before each of the chieftains in turn as they listen. Their entertainers are called Bards. These are poets who deliver eulogies in song.

And Diodorus Siculus described '... lyric poets whom they call Bards. They sing to the accompaniment of instruments resembling lyres, sometimes a eulogy, sometimes a satire.'

The Bard, like the Druid – far from being a 'parasite' – commanded an important and clearly identifiable place in Celtic society. The role carried with it considerable distinction, depending, first of all, upon the degree of inspiration, skill and creativity which the Bard possessed. Training, education – for seven to twelve years – further enhanced the status, which in early Ireland had an extra cachet, and went under the name of *filid*, pronounced 'filleh'. The superior, third-level version, as it were, of the Bard and *filid*, the *ollam* (pronounced 'ull-uv', now the name given in Ireland to a University Professor) bore high rank, which entitled the bearer to a retinue of up to two dozen men. And by law he received a reward – usually in kind – for his verses: a good horse, a jewelled sword.

Whether Bard, *filid* or *ollam*, the role had a fundamental importance, sufficient to have the position classified as that of Court Official. His principal duty entailed the specific and unlimited praise of the king; during this lengthy and involved process, he contributed, as a deliberately calculated by-product, to the morale of the tribe. History and genealogy came next – and out of such tribal and kingly chronicles grew the oral tradition. In the fireside performances the legends became incandescent, as gods, heroes, princes, beasts and mysteries staggered and rose and rampaged into life in the space between the firelight and the wall.

Do not imagine, though, that the poet's verses arrived spontaneously, *ex tempore*. Composition, in specific and precise metres, formed part of the training in the great bardic schools. The students – in this non-literate system – attempted their compositions while lying on their beds in the dark, and then handed up their homework orally for correction and further instruction. This system persisted in Ireland and Gaelic Scotland up to the seventeenth century: one description of life in the Western Isles recounts how

... they shut their Doors and Windows for a Day's time, and lie on their backs with a Stone upon their Belly, and Plaids about their heads, and their Eyes being covered, they pump their Brains for Rhetorical Encomium or Panegyrick; and indeed they furnish such a Style from this Dark Cell as is understood by very few; and if they purchase a couple of Horses as the reward of their Meditation they think they have done a great Matter.

The poems discussed in detail the chieftain's (alleged) greatness, in war and peace, tremendous battles he had fought and won. The poet advised the king, set before him principles, moral and kingly, to which he should aspire. Conversely, and equally flatteringly, he mocked the vileness, stupidity and incompetence of the enemy. Such satire achieved a reputation – perhaps exaggerated – for power and fury, credited with strength enough to maim and kill. Poems uncoiled, too, from the humour implicit in the discommodation of any other hostile or unpopular person; or from the dearth of hospitality in a house encountered by the poet on his travels (especially by comparison with the generous household which he now addressed); or from the wonder of great mysteries, such as storms, floods, beauty of landscape, other natural phenomena. In other words, the poets of the Celts – like their artists – found their art in material drawn from everyday life. In copious verses, witty or wise, saccharine or vitriolic, the poet fulfilled a role as the entertainer and commemorator of his people, their catharsis, their subjective reporter – a resident combination of after-dinner speaker, local newspaper editor, preacher and laureate.

We owe wonders to the bardic tradition. Many of the clues into the living of the Celts came from the great tales of the Ulster Cycle, or the several legends of Lugh and Cuchulainn, or the resonances thrust forth by the Welsh tales collected in the Mabinogion. Whether they all belong in the same era, or many centuries apart, their pre-Christian existence gives them a pagan purity. Further, they amplify many of the connections with ancient Europe: scholars have proven impressive links between their events and those in Homer and Beowulf. Academics also debate whether the Celtic cycles ever had a realistic background, a basis in history. But their depictions of an aristocratic and heroic society echo the glorious commissioned objects such as the Basse-Yutz flagons or the Battersea Shield.

When the Romans overran Celtic Gaul and Britain, they disrupted the ancient culture. Ireland never experienced such devastation and consequently Celtic scholarship relies heavily upon Irish 'literature'. The term has a wider-than-literal application because the earliest writings included much material transcribed from the oral tradition. The greatest comes from the Ulster Cycle – *Tain Bo Cuailgne*, the Cattle Raid of Cooley, described by Thomas Kinsella as 'the oldest vernacular epic in Western literature'. The main body of the epic was discovered in the Book of the Dun Cow, a twelfth-century manuscript made in the monastery of Saint Kieran in Clonmacnoise, and a further, partial version in the fourteenth-century Yellow Book of Lecan. But in the Introduction to his translation Kinsella remarks:

The origins of the *Tain* are far more ancient than these manuscripts. The language of the earliest form of the story is dated to the eighth century, but some of the verse passages may be two centuries older and it is held by most Celtic scholars that the Ulster Cycle, with the rest of early Irish literature, must have had a long oral existence before it received a literary shape, and a few traces of Christian colour, at the hands of the monastic scribes. As to the background of the *Tain* the Ulster Cycle was traditionally believed to refer to the time of Christ. This might seem to be supported by the similarity between the barbaric world of the stories, uninfluenced by Greece or Rome, and the La Tene Iron Age civilisation of Gaul and Britain. The *Tain* and certain descriptions of Gaulish society by Classical authors have many details in common: in warfare alone, the individual weapons, the boastfulness and courage of the warriors, the practices of cattle-raiding, chariot-fighting and beheading. Ireland, however, by its isolated position, could retain traits and customs that had disappeared elsewhere centuries before, and it is possible that the kind of culture the *Tain* describes may have lasted in Ireland up to the introduction of Christianity in the fifth century.

All through its considerable length, the *Tain* distils an essence clear in taste and colour. Despite the monkish sanitising, the raciness and vivid heat come through – 'the easy references', in Kinsella's words, 'to seduction, copulation, urination, the picking of vermin, the suggestion of incest'. And contemporary relevance – how the province of Ulster waged war against the rest of Ireland. But descriptive excitement takes precedence over everything else. (Even Lady Gregory, in her attempts to clean the body of the tale, to make it fit for admission into her romantic Celtic Twilight, could not keep the energy out of it. Kinsella recalls how she wrote to her tenants and villagers in Kiltartan in County Galway, 'I left out a good deal I thought you would not care about for one reason or another'.) Conveyed still more powerfully by Kinsella's poetic gifts, the *Tain* remains clearly an epic narrative – the perfect vehicle for the ancient storyteller on the evenings between Samhain and Bealtaine, between the beginning of winter and the end of spring, the storytelling season. Thus did the bardic tradition persist, and when such entertainment sprang from a background of acknowledged learning, the poet and storyteller achieved a status which has never fully died in Wales, Ireland or the West of Scotland.

That oral tradition lingers – albeit greatly diminished, almost eradicated, by mass communications. 'In my father's time', began many of the tales told in country kitchens, and truly in my father's time storytelling survived, especially on the western seaboard: formal, structured storytelling, that is – not the mere everyday gift of communicating mundane information in narrative form. The storyteller, perhaps a local figure, perhaps a journeyman, occupied – literally – a cherished place by the fireside, slowly turning the wheel of the bellows which made the flames on the hearth leap. With hindsight – and astute but authentic remembrance by members of the theatrical profession – the storyteller has been turned into a romantic figure, though in truth many a housewife, still choring at the day's end, and with children yet to put to bed, felt less than pleased to hear the familiar step, the lifting of the latch and the 'God Save All Here' which announced him.

The style of the storytelling contained many Homerisms – especially in devices, such as rhythm or repetition, called 'runs', those repeated phrases designed to give the narrator a resting, collecting pause; to offer signposts to the listeners; to repeat the adventures of well-known characters; to prepare the ground for the entry of new ones. As Homer repeated 'dawn came with rosy fingers' or 'the wine-darkening seas' – the Irish storyteller tapped his blackthorn stick upon the floor for percussive emphasis and repeated phrases such as 'things rested so', and 'so he chewed his finger, chewed the nail to the quick, the quick to the flesh, the flesh to the blood and the blood to the bone and the bone to the marrow'. The material of the stories also deviated little from Homeric intention, or from the most ancient Celtic flavour: champions and their chieftains and their chariots rode through the tales, Cuchulainn and Ferdia fought again, or a lissom woman came to the poet in his dreams of whitened beauty, and invited him to lands over the waves in the way that Oisin, the son of Finn McCool, fled with Niamh Cinn Oir, Niamh of the Head of Gold.

The storyteller represented the last living vestiges of a Celtic past in Western Europe. He harked back to the non-literate Celts in his oral preservation of life's records. Prodigious feats of memory assisted: Professor J. H. Delargy, then Director of the Irish Folklore Commission, described a fisherman he met in Kerry in 1923:

He had never been to school, was illiterate so far as unimaginative census-officials were concerned, and he could neither speak nor understand English. But he was one of the best-read men in the unwritten literature of the people whom I have ever known, his mind a storehouse of tradition of all kinds, pithy anecdotes, and intricate hero-tales, proverbs and rhymes and riddles, and other features of the rich orally preserved lore common to all Ireland three hundred years ago. He was a conscious literary artist. He took deep pleasure in telling his tales; his language was clear and vigorous, and had in it the stuff of literature.

At the point when the oral tradition became formalised into literature, matters of loss and gain become impossible to quantify. We do not know how much of the colour and force of the past would have survived in the telling alone. On the other hand, did the holy scribes dilute so much of the material they transcribed? Unlikely – given the evidence of, for instance, the strong meat in the *Tain*. Admittedly, downright collusion with the past could hardly be expected, especially since the Bards and *filidhe* belonged so closely to the Druids – but some complementary feeling applied. And for obvious reasons: the monks already knew the stories, and naturally wished to preserve them: with luck all pleasing traditions die slowly. From their own culture they now had the opportunity of contributing something important, something with literary or artistic value – not necessarily in any self-conscious way. And the sheer enjoyment of the tales made them suitable cases for *scriptorium* treatment: the heroism, the graphic trumpetings; the vaguely Byzantine convolutions of the illuminatory form corresponded with the legendary content.

An irony bubbles. Christianity, their ultimate coloniser and eroder, contributed, in the illuminated manuscripts, one of the finest art forms of the Celts: then, by capturing in writing some great essentials from the oral tradition, they preserved the very root of communication, source material. This new artistic expression, Celtic literature, observed many of the same basic principles as the art of Hallstatt and La Tene – the marriage of form and function, stimulation plucked from the immediate and natural world, the obvious influences from wider, more sophisticated constituencies. Therefore – the irony congeals – long after the Celts had ceased to be a European cultural force, Celtic art took a major step forward. And Christianity, whose intention, *per se*, was precisely the opposite, became the only conqueror to contribute to their culture in an intrinsically, spiritually, Celtic way.

First of summer, lovely sight,
season of perfection!
At the slightest ray the sun sends
blackbirds sing their full song.

The hardy vigorous cuckoo calls
all hail to high summer.
The bitter weather is abated
when the branched woods were torn.

Summer dries the stream down small,
the swift herd searches for a pool.
Heather spreads its hair afar.
The pale bog-cotton, faint, flourishes.

Buds break out on the hawthorn bush.
The sea runs its calm course
– the salt sea the season soothes.
Blossom blankets the world.

Bees' feet, with tiny strength,
carry their bundles, sucked from blossom.
The hill-fields call to the cattle.
Ants are active in swarming plenty.

The woods' harp works its music;
the harmony brings total peace.
Dust blows out of all our houses,
haze blows from the brimming lake.

The sturdy corncrake-poet speaks.
The cold cataract calls its greeting
down to the warm pool from on high.
Rushes begin to rustle.

In a ninth-century poem the echoes ring and clang – evocations of all the animals and animations, all the whorls, coils and tendrils, all the colours and tracings of growth in the handiwork of the oldest Celtic artists. Lyric poetry and nature poetry, complete in their concrete descriptions, descended in a straight line from those earliest decorating workers who made the reputations of Hallstatt and La Tene.

The fourteenth-century Welsh poet, Dafydd ap Gwilym received from a neighbouring poet the accolade, 'the nightingale of Dyfed', a considerable compliment for any citizen of that part of Wales, where poetry flowed plentifully as water. Dafydd, born a few miles to the north-east of Aberystwyth, travelled extensively, wrote beautifully. His poems celebrated love via nature – and nature via love.

> I woo a softly-spoken girl,
> pale as fine snow on the field's edge;
> God sees that she is radiant
> and brighter than the crest of foam.

In his general complexion, Dafydd might well have been auditioning for the role of the archetypal Celt. Every popularly-acknowledged facet of the Celtic personality and behaviour – the humour, the wryness, the boasting, the praising, the drinking, the hospitality, the fear of the supernatural – raise themselves eagerly in his verses. Any one poem may contain all or several of such characteristics – none will be without any of them. Six centuries later he still bestows rich colour, amusement, self-awareness. The texture of his work descends from the earliest Celtic mythologies, and clearly informs much of the jollier or romantic medieval literature.

> I came to a choice city
> With my fine young servant after me,
> a place of lavish entertainment, liberal meals;
> I was proud from childhood, so I took
> a public lodging, dignified enough,
> and I took some wine.
>
> I perceived a slim and lovely girl
> in that house, my pretty darling:
> I had set my heart entirely on my blessed slender dear
> who had an aspect like the rising sun.
> It was not just to show off that I had bought a roast
> and costly wine for me and for that girl.
>
> Young men love sport, and so I called the girl,
> a modest creature, to join me at the bench.
> Truth to say, I whispered to her
> two words of magic – I was bold and pressing
> nor was love with her idle – and I made
> agreements to come to the sprightly lass
> when all the company should have gone off
> to sleep: she was a black-browed girl.

The adventure continues at length and in robust fashion, redolent of Dafydd's contemporary in England, Geoffrey Chaucer. And it ends in useful flight, as three

English tinkers and an ostler seek out this Welshman who 'prowls around here bent on treachery'. More seriously however, Dafydd draws into his own bardic medium mighty strands of the romantic expression favoured by his European contemporaries, and weaves praise-poems of elegiac beauty:

> He is descended from a race of heroes,
> a noble band, gold-helmed and generous.
> Honoured, wealthy, hawk of men,
> sturdy his limbs upon his horse;
> swift to accomplish overthrow in battle,
> a falcon excellently wise in argument,
> a stag who does not die ...

Dafydd ap Gwilym's poems exhilarate and invigorate: the lack of self-consciousness, the awareness of fun and heroism, the sheer beauty of his observations on the landscape make him a most charming companion. But he also provides a powerful link back through Europe, through the deadening hand of the Anglo-Saxons, through the arrogant meretriciousness and commerce of the Romans, into the heart of colourful La Tene: one may easily imagine him or his direct ancestor resident at, or visiting the court of, the prince of Hochdorf – perhaps making a poem in praise of the prince's golden shoes. The faces of his drinking or walking companions could have come from the Hallstatt scabbard: likewise, the birds and animals he encounters in the greenwood – 'you, Roebuck, antlered fugitive, with the cloud's swiftness, in trousers of pale grey' – might have travelled live from the pages of the Book of Kells, wherein also dwells the deity to whom Dafydd prays; 'Arise, God's brilliant glory – keep me from the sin of drunkenness'.

With wit, happy self-abnegation and an understanding of the general predicament of life, he anticipates Goethe's remark by determining beauty and reporting it – without ever trying to dominate it. And as a completion of the Celtic capacity to synthesise form with function, to wed the practical and the beautiful, he innovated, experimented with metre and set standards by which the poets in Wales measure themselves to this day. Even more pleasingly, Dafydd the son of Gwilym perpetuated the golden tradition of the ancient Celts. They set standards for those parts of Europe where their presence became part of the fabric: his poetry reached into France and Germany, from which – whether he ever travelled there – he also derived evident stimulation. His view of himself as lovelorn poet, rather than heroic courtier, owes much to French rose-tinted love: the impression gained from his work calls up pictures of those brilliantly-illuminated Books of Hours commissioned by court figures such as Joan the Mad – brilliant blues and purples, distant hills and the gleam of armour, drawbridges and hounds, but somehow, always, an awareness that life offers less pompous, more important matters, such as the next girl or the next bottle of wine, or preferably both – and together. His art came from the life around him: his ready-made attempts at lovemaking, sometimes with sublime results, sometimes comic, place him at the centre of the tradition of that arena of Celtic expression which enjoyed the sense of the absurd available all around, every day.

But sadly Dafydd also stands at the very end of that world which produced the Basse-Yutz flagons and the Battersea Shield. The decline of the grand elements in the Celtic social order, which lingered in Ireland and Scotland until the seventeenth century, killed off those Bards in whose tradition he belonged: the courts in which they entertained disappeared. The lavish palaces of the mythologies, the settings of honour bonds and great challenges, had no place in lands where the government now came from outside, and where the native traditions of leadership and language barely survived. As the Celts necessarily mutated, forced from grandeur into vassaldom, reduced from membership of the king's extended family into abject and insecure tenantship often of an absentee landlord – how could their poets reflect gold when the people needed bread?

To look, therefore, for the same wondrous style of the flagons or weaponry or illuminations among the later Celtic peoples is to look in vain. But another part of the spirit survived – that ability to wring art from the life on the ground. The poets had always spoken their verses or sung them. The Bards – in the true sense of the word 'bard', not the hopelessly romantic, pseudo-antiquarian nineteenth-century notion – may have made poems for kings but they also made them for people, and now necessarily so.

The birth of Bryan Merriman, tentatively put at 1749, took place in a village in the west of Ireland, Ennistymon in County Clare. Still poor, Clare takes the full force of the Atlantic Ocean: much of the county offers a long shank westward. Merriman's (alleged) father, a journeyman stonemason, moved twenty miles, to the village of Feakle where Bryan Merriman grew up. Here he received an education among the hedge-schools, those furtive leafy academies which were obliged to flourish in a country where education of the peasantry was forbidden by law. In turn he taught among them himself, otherwise grew prize-winning flax crops, and married a woman from his own parish. None of these good and decent things necessarily distinguishes a man beyond the bounds of his own kitchen table, but Merriman became immortal on account of a long poem he wrote, which first circulated locally, in handwriting and by word of mouth, and then received publication in 1850, forty-five years after his death.

> I liked to walk in the river meadows
> In the thick of the dew and the morning shadows,
> At the edge of the woods in a deep defile
> At peace with myself in the first sunshine.
> When I looked at Lough Graney my heart grew bright,
> Ploughed lands, and green, in the morning light,
> Mountains in rows with crimson borders
> Peering above their neighbours' shoulders.

The poem, *Cuirt an Mhean-Oiche*, The Midnight Court, describes how the poet, out on an easy walk through the lush countryside, seeks the cool of the hedgerow and falls into a deep sleep. In his reverie, he receives a fright – in the shape of a welterweight hag who shocks him from his comforts and summons him to justice.

She cried in a voice with a brassy ring:
'Get up out of that, you lazy thing!
That a man like you could think 'tis fitting
To lie in a ditch while the court is sitting!'

The poet appears before the court, charged as a single man with not servicing the women of the nation sufficiently, despite their undoubted desire for his prowess.

Shame on you without chick or child
With women in thousands running wild!
The blossoming tree and the green young shoot,
The strap that would sleep with any old root,
The little white saint at the altar rail,
And the proud, cold girl like a ship in sail –
And what matter to you if their beauty founder,
If belly and breast will never be rounder,
If ready and glad to be mother and wife,
They drop unplucked from the boughs of life?

In long, bawdy arguments the poet comes under fire from various witnesses, who accuse the poet, and each other, and their fellows of sexual misdemeanours, social and physical defects, general global dishevelment – and all at a wild and tearing pace. At one point, an old man whose young wife had cuckolded him before they were wed, a marriage he had entered upon despite the jingle of gossip, comes forward as a bitter witness for the defence:

And I smiled and I nodded and off I tripped
Till my wedding night when I saw her stripped,
And knew too late that this was no libel
Spread in the pub by a jealous rival –
By God, 'twas a fact and well-supported:
I was a father before I started!

Notwithstanding this tirade, the verdict comes from the princess who presides over the court:

I do enact according then
That all the present unmarried men
Shall be arrested by the guard,
Detained inside the chapel yard
And stripped and tied beside the gate
Until you decide upon their fate.
Those that you find whom the years have thwarted
With masculine parts that were never exerted
To the palpable loss of some woman's employment,
The thrill of the milk and their own enjoyment;
Who, having the chance of wife and home
Went wild and took to the hills to roam,
Are only a burden on the earth
So give it to them for all you're worth.
Roast or pickle them, some reflection
Will frame a suitable correction,
But this you can choose at your own tribunal,
And whatever you do will have my approval.

Not long afterwards the poet – happily – wakes up with a shiver and all that remains is the memory and the dream. The Midnight Court, in conception, form and enjoyment presents a dilemma which crops up over and over again in any consideration of the Celts: surely, in voice, rhythm, intent and performance it must echo similar poems in other civilisations, India, Russia, Persia, Turkey. Merriman may have been a humble but brilliant man, living in a remote locality of Stone Age and Celtic descent, but in his metre and pace and power he reflects the force of the Celtic drift, as it was in the earliest oral tradition, as it continued right into his own era and beyond, art as poetry, as song, as satire, as ballad, as social comment – and in undisputedly individual, rural tone. The dilemma intensifies: how much fancy may one permit when considering whether Bryan Merriman's voice has come straight through the Celtic ages – as much a part of Celtic expression as the pastoral poets or the poems of courtly love which form the early cornerstones of the genre? And if a Celtic artist could be employed to visualise in abstract form the events and sentiments in Merriman's poem, would he not find them compatible with the kind of expression already evident in the metalwork or the illuminations? Merriman in his racy, bawdy balladry, with its rich and colourful imagery, was drawing straight from the well of his own life. The old man's outburst has been interpreted as an indication that Merriman's own birth may have been illegitimate: a physical description of the poet-narrator has been taken as a self-portrait; the atmosphere conjured can be made to fit the noisome and grotesque society of his time and environment. To emphasise further his qualifications to be included among the Celtic artists who reach from La Tene to Dafydd ap Gwilym, the metre he chose fitted perfectly the story he was telling, function again matching form. Therefore he advances the dilemma facing anyone who wishes to unravel Celtic expression. To put it succinctly – may you trust to instinct that what you perceive here is a Celtic voice, as authentic as those once audible in Austria or Switzerland or Bohemia or France or England? The evidence overwhelmingly says 'Yes': and at the simplest technical level stands the final, irrefutable proof that Merriman wrote *Cuirt an Mhean Oiche* in a Celtic language. Any doubts about the authenticity, in Celtic terms, of a voice sounding out as late as the eighteenth century wanes somewhat in face of the repeated definition: 'A Celt is someone who speaks a Celtic language.' The glory may be gone, the gleam of the ancient gold may have been crushed to powder politically – but still a voice can be heard, converted and quieter now, and only available to the people to whom it means something, no longer an influence in Europe the way Irish monks or Dafydd ap Gwilym's verses once made an impression, but nonetheless belonging to the same tradition.

The language, in terms of what can be called Celtic 'literature' – embracing what eventually came to be written down among the people of the Celtic fringe – must finally be the arbiter of the authenticity. Celtic poets ply their trade in Celtic languages. This definition may seem ruthless – therefore shadings and variations have to be allowed. Permission must be given for those sincerely motivated followers who wrote in a non-Celtic language, and their case can be largely pleaded by the huge presence of a poet such as William Butler Yeats, who

Lady Augusta Gregory, 1859–1932. Her influence upon drama and literature in Ireland, emphasised by her contribution to the founding of the Abbey Theatre, ensured at least an awareness of the roots of Celtic mythology and oral tradition as a source of cultural ideas.
Right: William Butler Yeats 1865–1939. In his County Sligo family connections, and on childhood holidays, Yeats heard the stories which had descended partly through local superstition and folklore, and undoubtedly had been recited aeons earlier in the ancient Celtic bardic tales. The heroic and romantic themes and imagery of Celtic mythology contributed to some of his greatest poems.

consciously drew upon the influences of the Celtic mythologies. From childhood he had been made aware of their continued presence in the Ireland into which he had been born. At one point in his earlier life he declared, as part of his passion for Maud Gonne MacBride, an intention to construct a Castle of the Heroes for Ireland. The Stone of Destiny at Tara, to which they had paid a visit at the time, would constitute the altar, other symbolic components would include the Cauldron of the Daghda, the *Claidhimh Soluis*, the Sword of Light, Lugh's Golden Spear of Victory and the Four Great Jewels of the Tuatha De Danaan – he even contemplated, improbable prospect, a statue of heroic Ireland.

In his poems he interrogated the mythologies too – he was only twenty-four when he wrote 'The Wanderings of Oisin', a long narrative poem in which the aged Oisin, the son of Finn McCool, meets Saint Patrick and tells him of how Niamh of the Golden Hair lured him away from Finn and the Fianna to the Land of Eternal Youth.

> And there I will give you a hundred hounds;
> No mightier creatures bay at the moon;
> And a hundred robes of murmuring silk,
> And a hundred calves and a hundred sheep
> Whose long wool whiter than sea-froth flows,
> And a hundred spears and a hundred bows,
> And oil and wine and honey and milk,
> And always never-anxious sleep;
> While a hundred youths, mighty of limb,
> But knowing nor tumult nor hate nor strife,
> And a hundred ladies, merry as birds,
> Who when they dance to a fitful measure
> Have a speed like the speed of the salmon herds,
> Shall follow your horn and obey your whim,
> And you shall know the Danaan leisure;
> And Niamh be with you for a wife.

Elsewhere across the range of Yeats's work, Celtic influences proliferate and titles lean out – 'Cuchulainn's Fight With the Sea'; 'In Tara's Halls'; 'The Old Age of Queen Maeve'. Themes, too – and in this respect, though open in early poems such as *Oisin* to the charge of poet-as-archaeologist, he operates in the same way as any poet drawing upon the classical references of Greece and Rome: Yeats merely gives the Celtic gods their own importance.

Outstanding though his poems are, and true in so many respects to the mythological idiom which inspired them, Yeats cannot be called a Celtic writer. Neither may his great contemporaries nor his successors: Synge reported, made drama from, patterns of speech among people who had transferred from Celtic language into English. Sir Samuel Ferguson, George Russell ('Æ'), James Stephens and others whose names crop up in any discussion of the Irish 'Celtic Twilight' movement wrote – with very rare exceptions – in English, and had no native working knowledge of Gaelic.

As the poets march onwards, the language question vexes considerably. Dylan Thomas, for instance, adds a wild card to the debate. Though writing in English, did his style not ring out with an individuality which at least seemed to derive from Celtic expression? All the same powers motivated him – an awareness of the natural world, the very 'force that drives the green fuse through the flower' informed some of his most renowned lines.

> And as I was green and carefree, famous among the barns
> About the happy yard and singing as the farm was home.
> In the sun that is young once only,
> Time let me play and be
> Golden in the mercy of his means,
> And green and golden I was huntsman and herdsman, the calves
> Sang to my horn, the foxes on the hills barked clear and cold.
> And the sabbath rang slowly
> In the pebbles of the holy streams.

An even greater confusion arises relating to the work of Irish poets writing in the English language. In the case of Seamus Heaney, it becomes increasingly difficult, if not impossible, to sustain the linguistic argument. Heaney, though not working in a Celtic language, comes straight from the spirit of the idiom. In a broadcast essay, 'The God in the Tree', he summarises with dynamic economy the arguments which insist upon his poetic ancestry:

Poetry of any power is always deeper than its declared meaning. The secret between the words, the binding element, is often a psychic force that is elusive, archaic and only half-apprehended by maker and audience. For example in the context of monasticism, the god of my title would be the Christian deity, the giver of life, sustainer of nature, creator father and redeemer Son. But there was another god in the tree, impalpable perhaps but still indigenous, less doctrinally defined than the god of the monasteries but more intuitively apprehended. The powers of the Celtic Otherworld hovered there.

How dare one try to summarise in one chapter – in one lifetime – the range of Celtic expression, from a face on a scabbard found in an Austrian salt foothill to a brilliantly flashing, late twentieth-century Irish vision of secrecy and human mystery? The average length of time spent by any one visitor in front of an exhibit in an art gallery or museum is, we are told, forty-five seconds. Taste and flavour do not satisfy hunger – but the occasional lingering before a beautiful or favourite piece constitutes a meal, or at least a selection from the menu. The main streams of Celtic artistic expression may have come to a halt two thousand years ago in Central Europe, later than that on the western coasts, but beautiful literary art still occurs, before which we may pause, and about which there can be no uneasy argument based on linguistics, nationality or lack of it. Poets still work in Celtic languages: they still determine beauty and pass it forward, they still take their art from the movements of the natural world beneath their feet. Somhairle MacGill-Eain, Sorley MacLean, the Scottish poet, achieves international recognition, not just because he writes in both Gaelic and English, but because his idiom has a timeless, pan-cultural dimension, hallmark of any civilisation.

> Straight trunks of the pine
> on the flexed hill-slope;
> green heraldic helmets,
> green unpressed sea;

strong, light, wind-headed,
untoiling, unseeking,
the giddy, great wood,
russet, green, two plaitings.

Floor of bracken and birch
in the high green room:
the roof and the floor
heavily coloured, serene;
tiny cups of the primrose,
yellow petal on green;
and the straight pillars of the room;
the noble restless pines.

You gave me helmets,
victorious helmets,
ecstatic helmets,
yellow and green;
bell-like helmets,
proud helmets,
sparkling helmets,
brown-red helmets.

7

THE THIRD SORROW OF STORYTELLING – THE CHILDREN OF USNA

Third, the Children of Usna, protectors of people.
Ruined by subtle and fearful strokes.
Naoise, Ardan and Ainle –
Now, my heart is broke.

Long ago in Ulster, the proudest most warlike province in all Ireland, the king, Conor MacNessa, had at his court a distinguished storyteller, Phelim, a man whose rank gave him power and riches: few among the other bards were granted stature enough to entertain the king in their own homes. During one such entertainment, news came from the woman of the house that Phelim's wife had given birth to a daughter. The king, as a gesture of congratulations, asked his own Druid, Cathbhadh, to divine the child's future, whereupon, to everybody's surprise, the Druid became much troubled. He stood up, placed his hand fretfully upon his forehead and foretold that this girl would grow so wondrous that she would give beauty a new name, that for her glance champions and chieftains would fight woeful battles, and that on account of her presence and beauty rivers of blood would flow through Ulster. The child's name – Deirdre.

When such dire presentiment descended, the throng of fine men called out for the immediate execution of the girl-child, but King Conor MacNessa forestalled them by saying that he would become the girl's guardian and see to it that she neither came to, nor caused, harm. Furthermore, when she came of age, to ensure that her great beauty would become a help rather than a hindrance to Ulster, he would marry her and make her his queen. The child was then taken away to a remote dwelling in the high woods, and placed in the trusted care of Lavarcham, who had been a nurse in the king's family when he was a child. And so Deirdre grew up secluded, knowing little of the world.

From time to time Conor MacNessa rode out on his horse to observe the growth of his future wife, upon whom Lavarcham lavished tender care. Deirdre grew in grace and innocence and one part of the Druid's prophecy seemed certain to be fulfilled – those words which referred to her great beauty. The sight of her filled the ageing king with love and desire, and he could scarcely wait until she grew old enough to be wed. Deirdre knew that she was intended to become the wife of Conor, and she never demurred: how could she, she knew no others? Until one day – and then the power of her own mind's choice took over, and she confided her views to Lavarcham.

It happened as a servant killed a calf outside the window through which Deirdre had been gazing at the falling snow. The blood of the young beast flowed against the brilliant whiteness, and at that moment a raven alighted and began to peck at the blood. Deirdre called out to Lavarcham:

See: these are the colours I adore. Much though I respect Conor, and even though I understand that I am to be his wife, I wish for a man who has those colours in his demeanour. His hair black as the raven, his cheek healthy red as that blood, his skin silver-white as the snow on the ground.

Lavarcham said she knew just such a young man: His name, she said, Naoise – a young warrior at King Conor MacNessa's court, one of the three children of Usna; his brothers, Ardan and Ainle possessed similar skills at charioteering and ball-playing and stood proudest among the Knights of the Red Branch. Lavarcham became the go-between – she loved Deirdre too much to have her committed in marriage to an old man such as the king.

She arranged for Naoise to glimpse Deirdre in the woods. The lightning touched them both. Naoise fell speechless at the beauty of Deirdre: she recognised the colours of the snow and the blood and the raven and knew her man. But both lovers reckoned upon Conor's anger, and Deirdre asked Naoise to take her away. He called out, a long and melodious call, which summoned his two brothers to his side. All four, in harmony, and excitement and love, fled Ulster and the wrath of old Conor MacNessa, and exiled themselves in Scotland.

Here the brothers distinguished themselves as mercenaries of honour in the army of the King of Scotland. The skills which had brought them renown in Ireland made them doubly legendary in their new land. Then this king also saw Deirdre and expressed his desire for her, and so the lovers came under a new threat similar to the one which had caused them to leave Ulster. This time they went to live on a remote and rocky island, but from it they established a large chieftaincy, and brought much of the west of Scotland under their command. Reputations as hunters and champions guaranteed the safety of them all: the comradeship and brotherly love of Ardan and Ainle protected Naoise and Deirdre.

Through all of these years King Conor MacNessa had brooded upon the beauty of his robbed bride-to-be. A proud man, and a desirous one, he never forgot the slight: he knew that many of the young warriors must have laughed behind their hands and behind his back at the fact that his prize had been stolen away by one of his own courtiers. A cunning man, too, and his hatching laid a plot which would achieve two objects – revenge, and the regaining of Deirdre. At a feast he announced that messengers daily brought him news of how the children of Usna, those three fine warriors, had so distinguished themselves in Scotland. He therefore intended, he said, to grant them a full and free pardon. But whom should he send in order that the sons of Usna would be convinced? His messenger must already have their respect, so that they could permit themselves to be convinced of the truth of the pardon.

Some of their dear friends among the Red Branch Knights sat at the table that night – none volunteered, an unspoken doubt hung over Conor MacNessa's statement. Finally he turned to a group which included Cuchulainn and Conall Cearnach and asked the third warrior among them, Fergus MacRoy, to bring his offer to the children of Usna and to Deirdre. Fergus's word would assure them of safe return, Fergus of the sincere tongue, the faithful heart, Fergus who took his vows, whatever they be, more seriously than any other knight in the Red Branch.

One of Fergus's bonds meant that he could not, honour-bound, refuse any offered hospitality. Accordingly, Conor MacNessa, in his cunning, approached another chieftain whose lands lay across the shore upon which the returning sons of Usna would land, and asked this man to offer a feast for Fergus alone. In effect, Fergus could not then fulfil his promise of safe introduction to Ulster for Deirdre, Naoise, Ardan and Ainle. Unaware of this treacherous arrangement, Fergus had already gone to Scotland to bring back the four exiles.

He arrived as Deirdre and Naoise played chess. During the conversation within the game Deirdre came to recognise yet again how much Naoise pined for his native Ulster, and that in this matter he also spoke for his brothers. As they murmured their way through their game they heard a cry – which Naoise identified as that of a man of Ireland. Deirdre contradicted him hastily, not because she disbelieved: rather the contrary, she had also recognised the accent of the shout and her bones cried out in dread at some unnamed fear.

As the cry rang out again the fear took shape, and she guessed that this was a messenger come from Conor MacNessa, and that some trick would result whereby all four would be pressed to return to Ulster and be killed. Fergus had been dearly loved by Naoise and they greeted each other with great emotion. Fergus then gave his undoubted and respected word that safe passage and return had been promised by Conor MacNessa, and that he would personally vouch for it.

But Deirdre, by now utterly fearful, told them of a dream she had the previous night – in which three birds appeared. They had flown from Conor's court at Eamhain Mhacha and in their beaks each held a glistening drop of honey. But when they deposited the honey upon the three sons of Usna they took away three drops of blood. The honey represented the promises of Conor MacNessa, the blood represented the fate which lay ahead. Only on the word of Fergus MacRoy could Deirdre be persuaded to return to Ireland and upon leaving Scotland she sang a famous farewell, a lament which lasts to this very day.

When the boat landed in Ulster, the chieftain whom Conor MacNessa had treacherously approached came out and greeted the travellers. He turned to Fergus MacRoy and invited him – and him alone – to a feast. Fergus refused, saying that he had a duty to discharge. But the tradition of the Red Branch Knights always prevented them from breaking a bond which they had embraced as a component of the honour, and the chieftain reminded Fergus of his bond. Fergus therefore had to break his promise to Naoise and even though he offered equivalent protection in the presence of his two fine sons, the turn of events now convinced Deirdre of Conor's impending treachery. Again she tried to warn Naoise – but the force of the men came against her and her words fell unheeded. As they approached the palace of Ulster she saw a halo of blood form above Naoise's head and she knew that her love, her beautiful man, was doomed.

A third time Deirdre tried to convince Naoise that Conor intended nothing but evil. Her premonitions had hardened into fact to such an extent that she was able to give more precise directions, She said that if the king diverted them from his court to the living-quarters of the Red Branch Knights, their deaths would surely follow soon. Again she was turned aside, this time with some irritation, by warriors confident of their own ability to defend themselves. But sure enough, when they knocked loudly on the door of Eamhain Mhacha, instead of meeting Conor, they were sent to the house of the Red Branch Knights which had been prepared for them.

The tension grew. Naoise and Deirdre refused the hospitality which the king had ordered to be laid on in the Red Branch house. Instead, they began to play chess again. The king, slightly regretful, and deliberating upon whether he ought to abandon his evil plan, sent ancient Lavarcham to report whether Deirdre had lost any of her beauty. Lavarcham, overjoyed to see her precious charges again, wept over them and warned them that it was no good – Conor intended revenge and they must flee. She went back to the king and reported that the cares and vicissitudes of exile had greatly reduced the radiance of Deirdre, but that contrariwise Naoise seemed more fine and warlike than ever.

Conor MacNessa would have changed his mind but for a man from the north called Trendhorn, whose father had been killed in combat by Naoise. Now Conor exploited the Norseman's vengeful motives. He sent Trendhorn to bring a separate report, but by then Naoise, Ardan and Ainle, finally convinced of Conor's treachery, had barricaded the house of the Red Branch Knights. Trendhorn found one tiny aperture, a skylight, through which he could observe the lovers. Deirdre glanced up from the chessboard, saw the black and baleful eyes, cried out to Naoise who threw a chess piece upwards with such force and accuracy that it destroyed one of Trendhorn's eyes. He rushed back to the king in a rage and told him that Deirdre seemed more lovely than ever and that she and Naoise sat arrogantly, as if they were the rightful rulers of Ulster.

Conor MacNessa then gathered together a bunch of bondsmen and attacked the house in which the children of Usna lodged. The Red Branch Knights stood back – they wanted no part of this treachery upon their own beloved and respected warriors. The king's mob were first repelled by the sons of Fergus, still protecting Naoise and Deirdre – who went on playing chess during the attack. But then Conor promised the sons of Fergus wide lands, and evil followed evil. As their father had been tricked into breaking his promise, they were bribed into the most heinous crime of departing from their pledge.

And still the forces of King Conor MacNessa could not conquer the house of the Red Branch. The three children of Usna routed again and again all the foes that Conor hurled against them. The numbers which Conor mustered grew and grew, until eventually a great army stood outside Eamhain Mhacha. At this point the brothers knew they must leave and find a safe place, perhaps further south with Cuchulainn. They made a shield of all their shiel's, put Deirdre safely within it and bounded clear of the walls of Eamhain Mhacha.

The king then called upon his Druids to defeat them with magic. The ground turned to wild slime beneath their feet: the four fugitives rose above it, Deirdre on Naoise's shoulders. A thick forest rose before them, so dense not a fly could pass between the branches, not a sunbeam could penetrate: the children of Usna went through without a thought. When a high roaring sea threw huge waves in their path they danced on the foam. But the Druids called upon all their magic and down from the heavens they drew a deep spiralling cloud which met the waves and froze the four in a deadly embrace. Thus, they were captured and brought to land. Conor MacNessa ordered their execution but nobody could be found to carry it out. Eventually a treacherous soldier, anxious to gain favour, came forward. The brothers could not decide upon who should die first – each offered his own head. The question was decided by Naoise who gave the executioner his own magic sword. All three lay down together and lost their heads at one mighty blow.

King Conor MacNessa had now captured the object of his long desire – but she had changed into Deirdre of the Sorrows: he had dragged her, weeping, off the dead body of Naoise. For a year and a day she lived with him in his palace at Eamhain Mhacha. As she never spoke and she never smiled, he sought to punish her even further. One day he asked her what on earth she most reviled. She replied with Conor's own name and that of his closest ally – to whom he straightaway sent her. But on the journey, the sorrow of her lot finally became too much, she uttered a last huge piteous scream to the skies and dashed herself headlong from the chariot, striking her head upon a large stone.

Where Deirdre fell the earth opened immediately and took her body, and out of her grave grew a great yew. The branches twined and spread across the wide countryside until they found the branches of another yew, which had grown from the grave of Naoise. Beneath the arch made by their marriage of leaves, lovers walk to this day, talking of Deirdre of the Sorrows and the fate of the children of Usna.

8

CREDENTIALS

By the time he walked into a BBC studio in February 1962, Saunders Lewis, spare and sharp at the age of sixty-nine, had carried his political beliefs through Wales as if bearing banners emblazoned with the word 'Truth' (in Welsh, of course). Not Welsh by birth – Liverpool in 1893 – nor eventually by religion, since he converted from Methodism to Roman Catholicism, he nonetheless had become the standard by which Welsh identity could be judged. Such credentials: man of letters, journalist, playwright and critic, nominated (albeit by Welsh nationalist acolytes) for the Nobel Literature Prize; man of action, wounded in Flanders in the Great War; man of commitment, he and others set fire, in 1936, to the construction works of a protested aerodrome in north-west Wales, for which crime he spent – while losing his University job – a year in jail: 'We are in this dock of our own will, not only for the sake of Wales, but also for the sake of peaceful and unviolent, charitable relations now and in the future between Wales and England.'

A man of spiritual fervour, too, uttered religiously – and poetically, as in 'Mary Magdalen':

> In the hollow night of the senses, in the cauldron of smoke;
> The great hair that had wiped his feet turned white,
> All the flowers of memory withered except the rain of blood;

Saunders Lewis's belief in political commitment comprised zeal and intellect and made him a formative influence on *Plaid Genedlaethol Cymru*, the National party of Wales, popularly called *Plaid Cymru*. And a man of great patriotic passion, derived from his love of his own culture, which he believed reposed in the old Celtic language and to which he wished Wales would – believed Wales should – return in full. He called the 1962 annual BBC Wales Radio Lecture 'The Fate of the Language'.

I am obliged to start and complete the writing of this lecture before the statistics of last year's census of Welsh-speaking Welshmen in Wales are published. I predict that the figures published in the near future will shock and disappoint those of us who consider that Wales will not be Welsh without the Welsh language. I also predict that if the present trend continues, Welsh will cease to exist as a living language towards the beginning of the twenty-first century, granting that Britain will still be inhabited by human beings at that time. Thus, at long last, the policy set out in the measure called the Act of Union of Wales and England in 1536 as an aim for the English government in Wales, will have succeeded.

The power now fully turned on, he traced the official and social erosion of the language through four centuries.

Let us therefore turn to the present state of affairs, the language crisis in the second half of the twentieth century. It is a precarious situation. There was a time, during the national awakening between 1860 and 1890, when it would have been practical to establish Welsh as the language of education and the University, the language of the new County Councils, the language of industry. No such thought occurred to the Welsh. I believed that such a thing was not impossible, given time and by adhering to a regular policy for a generation or two, between the two World Wars. Today that is not possible. There have been immense social changes in Wales during the last quarter century. By now Welsh is a language in retreat in Wales, the language of a minority, and a minority still diminishing.

He went on to trace the moral rigour needed to fight for Welsh and concluded with an exhortation.

Go to it in earnest and without wavering, to make it impossible to conduct local authority or central government business without the Welsh language. Insist on the rate demand being in either Welsh or bi-lingual. Give notice to the Postmaster General that annual licences will not be paid unless they are available in Welsh. Demand that all summonses to appear in court be in Welsh. This is not a haphazard policy for isolated individuals. It would be essential to organise it and to proceed step by step, giving notice of intent and allowing time for the changes to be made. It is a policy for a movement, and that movement should be active in those areas where Welsh is the everyday spoken language, demanding that all election papers and every official form relating to local or parliamentary elections in Wales be in Welsh, raising the Welsh language to be the main administrative medium of district and county.

Dynamic and ordered, Saunders Lewis's discourse shouted a fundamental cultural principle, echoed with equal power in the phrase of the Irish Gaels: *gan teanga, gan tir* – paraphrased as 'without a native tongue, therefore without a nation'.

In what used to be Merionethshire, on the wooded road between Frongoch and Bala, lies a long lake. At one end stands a series of concrete installations, visible from the highway. Invisible beneath the waters, never again to be seen, even during the most oblique penetrations of shafting sunlight, stand ruined buildings. But do not receive the impression that you might glimpse legends, those gilded palaces of the old tales, the Celtic Otherworld – as the balladeer saw 'the Round Towers of other days in the waves beneath him shining'. The drowned small houses beneath this dark water, and the church and the gaping gables once focused protest, violence, death and cultural struggle upon this tradition-steeped part of north-central Wales.

Across the border in England, the city of Liverpool required a reservoir. The village of Capel Celyn blocked the opportunity to drown the Tryweryn valley – but not for long. The authorities evacuated the villagers and built the reservoir – and at the same time created a symbol, a powerful tool in the hands of any cultural movement. The fracas, current while Saunders Lewis's words hung in the air, brought together politicians, trades unionists, religious authorities, neophyte conservation groups, students, cultural bodies, in a fever of protest. The belief that Capel Celyn exemplified Wales's political impotence within the United Kingdom

Top: A small commemorative 'cult' wagon from western Spain, dated to the second century BC.
Above: Ritual vehicle from Yugoslavia dated to approximately 500 BC.
Overleaf: A funerary cart from Austria, dated to the seventh century BC.

The custom of placing small wheeled vehicles in graves, as part of the deceased person's accompaniments, echoes all across Europe, and represents another facet of the belief that the journey to the Otherworld must be made easy and pleasurable. Whether the vehicles measured no more than a few centimetres in height, whether they were chariots specially constructed to commemorate a dead warrior in his grave or whether they were enormous carts piled high with utensils — as in the tomb at Hochdorf — the idea remained one of ritualised transport.

The votive offering, the sacrifice to the gods, has led to many important Celtic finds. In the pool at the source of the Seine, near Dijon in central France, over two hundred wooden objects were found earlier this century. They included carved statues of human organs, some of entire figures, many conveying the affliction or ailment which the supplicants wished the gods to remove.

The statue of an unknown
god, dated first century AD,
wearing a torc. Found in
Bouray, France, he is
depicted sitting cross-legged,
which corresponds with
many other deities in the
arena of Celtic worship.
Their portrayal in such a
sitting posture may have
come from the natural
household posture of
primitive people who
squatted upon the ground
within their houses.

The Gundestrup Cauldron: one of the major finds in Celtic civilisation, found in Gundestrup, Denmark, dated to 100 BC, now in the National Museum in Copenhagen. The huge cauldron, which measures 69 cm in diameter, is believed to have had ritual significance and as such provided many useful pictures of Celtic society and worship.

continued overleaf

The bull reverberates across other European civilisations, earlier and later; the warriors wearing long trousers correspond with the Roman description of the Celts wearing *bracae*, a word which in the opinion of some etymologists led to the modern word, 'braces'; the long shields, the helmets, the presence of animals, all confirm the written descriptions of the Greeks and Romans. The horned god Cernunnos ruled one part of the Celtic ritual world: his influence was so powerful that in later Christian times his horns became attributed to Lucifer. Made of silver the Gundestrup Cauldron bears extensive decoration inside and outside, and the details convey many echoes of the eastern origins of the prehistoric Celts.

The cult of the head conveys as much significance within Celtic worship as the cross does among Christians. The head featured in many stone and wooden artistic representations. Ritually it provided a more sinister image. The Celts took heads as part of battle and sacrificial ritual. In Roquepertuse, France, the Romans found a shrine with heads and skulls enshrined in lintels. In some cases, heads still had hair attached to them, and the shrines included the heads of women and children. The head, according to Celtic belief, contained the soul, and one Roman writer gave an account of victorious Celtic warriors scraping the skull of a slain enemy and using it as a wine vessel.

The Book of Kells (pp. 170, 171), the Lindisfarne Gospels
(pp. 172, 173) and other illuminated Celtic texts, which
date from, at the earliest, the sixth and seventh centuries
AD, conjure the most popular resonances of Celtic art.
These masterpieces, executed by monks in the abbeys of
Scotland, England and Ireland, were often subsequently
smuggled from country to country to escape Norse – or
other – marauders. The illuminations were created in
the most painstaking and vivid detail, and close
examination yields delight after delight, such as cartoons
of irritable old men, or butterflies, birds, insects,
whimsical animals. Much speculation has been enjoyed
as to how such detailed work was achieved: implements
included fine hairs taken from wild animals, such as fox
or badger: devices included the use of a drop of water
as a magnifying glass.

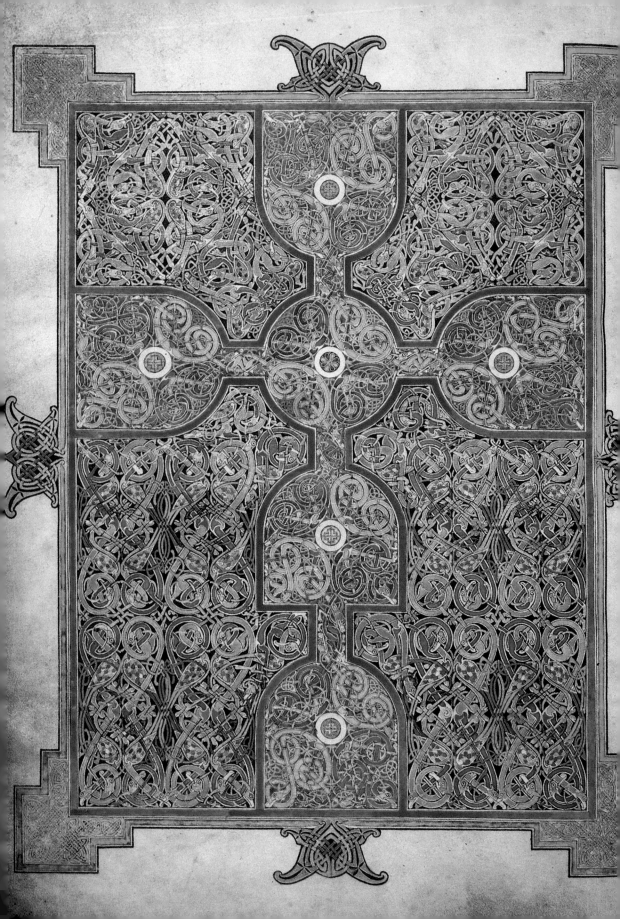

The crozier of the Abbot at Clonmacnoise, twelfth century AD: 98 cm high, now in the National Museum of Ireland. The power of Celtic Christianity appears most vividly in the richness of monastic and ecclesiastical possessions. The legendary and traditional gifts of the Celtic craftsman, descended from the glories of La Tene Culture, finally bring interlaced Celtic metalworking to a high peak, with much other European influence, including Scandinavian: the bronze crozier was made a century after the Viking defeat in Dublin and altered two centuries later.

The Ardagh Chalice, eighth century AD: 15 cm
high, now in the National Museum of Ireland.
In County Limerick in the last century a boy
digging potatoes uncovered a silver chalice, a
bronze chalice and four brooches. The main find,
the Ardagh Chalice, is made of silver, bronze and
gold, with rock crystal and glass added within the
decorations. The chalice, which must have
formed an important part of a great monastic
collection, is decorated lavishly with 'ultimate La
Tene scrolls, plain interlace, animal interlace,
plaits and frets ...' and is further described by its
custodians as 'the finest piece of eighth-century
metalwork that has ever come to light.'

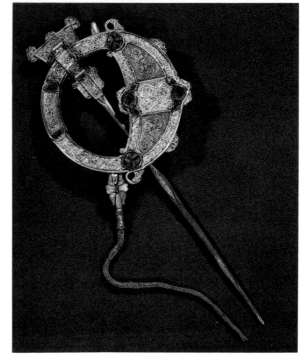

The Tara Brooch: called after the great regal site of the Irish Celts, but actually discovered several miles away on the seashore, the brooch remains the most copied and popular of all later Celtic artefacts. With human faces illuminated within purple glass, and animal heads used as grips and chain fasteners, the Tara Brooch is one of the greatest of all treasures included in the definition 'Celtic'.

of Great Britain and Northern Ireland led to other ramifications of protest. Militant nationalism began to use explosives. The Free Wales Army formed, drilled and patrolled in the hills. Two Welsh activists died on their bombs – 'own goals' as they call it in the bitter-black humour of Northern Ireland.

The combination of Saunders Lewis's rhetoric and the campaign against the submerging of Capel Celyn came at a time when postwar Britain had begun to relax. In London, new waves of frivolity and excess affirmed that the war was truly over. Now the society which had fought so hard and rebuilt so zealously could reward itself; in time the fun and games would become pop culture. The Capel Celyn campaign and Saunders Lewis's broadcast ideals comprehensively filled the postwar cultural vacuum in Welsh Wales. In the generation since the 'Fate of the Language' broadcast, not a day has gone by – according to Welsh language enthusiasts – without somebody, somewhere, serving a gaol sentence for an offence committed in the cause of the Welsh language. Other measures of success include extensive radio schedules in Welsh, a satisfying increase in the number of children who begin to know, even speak, Welsh independently of their parents. In this they have been encouraged by a duck, Will Cwac Cwac, and a flying bear, SuperTed – two Welsh-speaking cartoon characters on the purpose-built Welsh-speaking television channel, S4C.

But how may a duck and a bear become relevant to the spirit of the ancient Celts? The answer must be 'Definitively' – if we accept the linguistic definition of a Celt as 'somebody who speaks a Celtic language'. The Welsh – at least those who fought to encourage the revival of their tongue – retained, (and in some less authentic ways, even re-invented) their powerful Celtic identity. Their letters of Celtic credentials are written in a language whose roots once identified and distinguished the Keltoi.

Irish, Scots, Manx; Welsh, Breton, Cornish; no matter how peripheral now to the ancient European civilisation called 'Celtic', these six words define the dominant popular understanding of the word 'Celt'. In each case the language has influenced the definition. The Irish and the Scots still speak, to greater and lesser degrees, Gaelic, identified as a Celtic language. The Welsh have fought the most successful battle to restore their native Celtic tongue. The Bretons still battle on, diminishing as a national or even regional linguistic entity since the French Revolution. The last Cornish and Manx monoglots died long enough ago to add the romantic – but useless – patina of time to their tongues. On Man, the last native speaker of Manx Gaelic – bi-lingual with English – died in 1974. In Cornwall, though the date remains in dispute, nobody argues that the last true Cornish native speaker died in the late eighteenth century, although monoglots had disappeared by the middle of the seventeenth century.

The Celtic languages form a branch of the Indo-European family tree, with sounds and soundings from other European and Eastern language groups, the languages of Greece and Rome, Germanic and Slavonic tongues, as well as language families in the Middle East. The remaining Celtic languages fall into two significant divisions: the Gaels of Ireland, Man and Scotland and the speakers of

Welsh, Cornish and Breton. The Gaels occupy the Goidelic category called 'Q-Celtic': the Welsh and Bretons, Brythonic, 'P-Celtic'. The categorisations of P and Q arise from Celtic words meaning 'head' – which, among the Irish and Scots emerges as *ceann* or *kin* – and *pen* in the P-Celtic grouping: Kintyre in Scotland, derived from *ceann tire* – literally 'the head of the land' emerges as Pentire in Cornwall. Hazards proliferate: should Ben, originally Beann, Nevis – in Scotland, after all – be Kin or Ceann Nevis? Thus, and in innumerable other ways, minding the Ps and the Qs becomes an awkward, even humorous business, unless the researches of the linguists prevail. For instance, how would anatomical research support one theory I came across that P-Celts and Q-Celts – a phonetic as well as linguistic division – have been thus divided because the Welsh and the Bretons have differently-shaped heads from the Scots and the Irish? And therefore that their differently-shaped tongues and palates pronounced 'P' where the others click towards 'Q'?

Despite strenuous revival attempts – but by too few people – Cornish remains substantively dead. It has no official status of any power, no currency except among enthusiasts, no popular support. In 1951, a political movement with additional cultural imperatives, *Mebyon Kernow*, the Sons of Cornwall, was founded in Truro, 'to preserve and maintain the character and interests of Cornwall as a Celtic nation, to promote the constitutional advancement of Cornwall towards self-government in domestic affairs, and to foster Cornish studies and cultures'. The Sons of Cornwall have had paltry success, the organisation rarely peaks on the national scale of the United Kingdom, and any showing at a General Election has only produced risibly low polling results. The language fares little better, unless you count the souvenir element, Cornish words on dishcloths and bumper-stickers. Elsewhere the overwhelming tide of distasteful 'Celtic' replication sullies the Arthurian legends (whatever their true Celtic credentials): the village of Tintagel has set new low standards in the exploitation of the Round Table – with neon signs reading 'Excali-bar', or holiday flatlets called 'Camelot' and 'Avalon'.

Some linguists report, some enthusiasts claim, ripples of resurgence: a folk-singer who records Cornish songs, a poet who writes in Cornish, classes adminstered by the Cornish Language Board, published educational texts. The Foreword to one of these begins hopefully:

The increasing number of students of Cornish and the growing interest in Cornish as a spoken language, has necessitated a modern approach to the study of the language ... Cornish is one of the six modern Celtic languages; it is closely related to Welsh and, more particularly, to Breton.

The glossary lists over three hundred words and expressions from common English usage with their Cornish counterparts:

arghanty bank: (Latin *Argentum* – silver).
avon river: (In Irish Gaelic, *abha*, *abhann*, as in the English town of Stratford-upon-Avon: one derivation for Danube has been suggested as *Donn Abha* – the brown river).
eglos church (as in the Irish Gaelic *eaglais*, or the Latinate 'ecclesiastical').
fenester window – again a Latinate correspondence.
pyscajor fisherman (as in the Latin *piscator*, or *pisces*).

In other words, a Tolkienistic, futuristic imagery is born: *lemmyn* – meaning 'now': *tek* – 'beautiful': *drok* – 'bad': *clavyjores* – 'nurse'.

Although early cross-fertilisation must have occurred through trading contacts, the Latin content springs substantially from the Roman conquest of Britain and the consequent evolution of Romano-Celts. The question recurs whether Cornish became Breton or vice-versa, or whether Welsh and Breton became intertwined with Cornish. Debate extends far beyond the historical fact of the huge migration of the Welsh and Cornish to Brittany. Trade, abetted by culture and familial relationships, continued and maintained Cornwall's strong links with the Celts of mainland Europe rather than with the new post-Roman Britain.

The preservation of the Cornish identity may most of all be perceived in the proliferation of Cornish place-names, in words which begin with the renowned root *Pen* – or with *Tre* – meaning 'house'. Were Cornish to experience a popular revival it would have to become a standard factor in broadcasting, in the publishing of newspapers, books and magazines, on signposts and public amenities, in religious worship. To date, this shows no signs of happening except in limited ways. The dedicated, however attentive, number too few: the political axe which might resound in the grinding carries not enough edge. Regretfully the conclusion reaches through that Cornish has utterly lost the struggle for survival. Already doomed, its fate was clinched when the railways brought the English to holiday on the Cornish Riviera, further Anglicising the population.

The funeral of the Manx language tolls a much more bitter bell – because in its case all the apparatus existed whereby it could have remained alive. If circumstances had combined to create the cultural will, Manx might even have become the official language of the island's administration. The geography and the constitution already offered the means of at least a pretended political and cultural autonomy. As a further contribution, worship had established a bridgehead – the first book in the Manx language, a translation of the Book of Common Prayer appeared in 1611. Other Celtic languages – notably Welsh – were assisted in their survival or re-birth by prayer books, but the patriots of Man never capitalised upon their religion as a preserver of their culture. Furthermore, in proportion to the overall population, Manx had more widespread currency than Cornish, and lasted longer: a dictionary appeared in the nineteenth century, when the rural population of Man still spoke largely in Manx. Bibles, hymn-books and a Catechism had been published earlier – although the *arriviste* Nonconformists disparaged the dialect extensively and thoroughly: Wesleyans who prayed together stayed together.

The Manx language originated mainly from the relationship with Ireland and Scotland; some confusion arrived with the Vikings. The island's location guaranteed a turbulent history, from the days when Cuchulainn and Finn McCool and Mananaan MacLir, the god of the sea after whom the Isle is named, trod the legends and the mountaintops. For a vital period, beginning in the late fifteenth century, Man became separate from all Celtic relatives, as the Isle's English rulers imposed stringent isolation. Few arrivals or departures were permitted, and the old language – when deprived of the traditional Irish and Scottish cross-fertilisation – shrank. Consistent Anglicisation polluted the language thereafter.

In 1899 The Manx Gaelic Society was founded – with a motto which, though spelt differently, possessed the same phonetics as that Irish Gaelic note of ideological regret. In Manx, the expression 'without a native tongue, therefore without a nation' appears as *Gyn chengey, gyn cheer*. But in his 1976 survey, *Linguistic Minorities in Western Europe*, the Welsh writer, Meic Stephens traced succinctly the path of decline.

By 1874 there were still 12,000 speakers of Manx, but by 1901 it was spoken by only 4,419 people (8.1%) out of a total population of 54,752. Ten years later the number of Manx-speakers was halved and by the 1920s the language was hardly to be heard anywhere. At the Census of 1961 only 160 speakers of the language remained, and few of those were native-speakers. The last person for whom Manx was a mother-tongue was Ned Maddrell, a fisherman-crofter of Cregneash, the language's final stronghold in the south of the Island: he died, aged ninety-seven in 1974.

The most devout enthusiasts cannot claim any real hope for the resuscitation of Manx. Irritatingly for Celtic enthusiasts, lip service is paid ceremonially in the Tynwald, the Manx Parliament. The dependence upon the outside world, which brings tourists and tax refugees, has contributed further to the decline, to the point where Manx – whatever the availability of language classes – will eventually amount to no more than pretty names on bungalow gateposts.

In their death and their dying, Manx and Cornish have been reduced to the status of sad curiosity and antiquarian linguistic study. The inevitable, accompanying destruction of cultural and political identity hammers home the point of 'without a tongue, without a nation'. The tiny geographies of Man and Cornwall, their total absorption into the Britain of the Anglo-Saxons, facilitated the easy victory of English – and produced yet another fading whisper of the once-resonant Celtic group of tongues. In the thousand years following the heights of La Tene Culture, Celtic occupied a significant place in the language map of Europe – the continent was shared with, largely, the Italic languages to the south and the Germanic languages to the north. Celtic variations were spoken along the hinterlands of the Seine, Loire and Rhone rivers, of Danube, Main and Rhine.

When the Western Empire of the Romans overran France, corruption of the language followed ineluctably. The marauders from the North of Germany infiltrated the rest of Gaul and Southern Germany. Vikings and Vandals and Goths – and in Britain the Anglo-Saxons – contributed partially or wholly to the linguistic destruction of the Celts. By the seventh century AD, the major Celtic languages on mainland Europe had all but disappeared: only pockets remained. Concurrently, when the Anglo-Saxon domination of England had been completed, Celtic tongues could be heard only, albeit extensively, in the western extremities – in Wales, Cornwall, Scotland, the Isle of Man. And Gaelic continued to be the dominant tongue in Ireland for another thousand years – until the sixteenth and seventeenth century, when the departure of the chieftains dispossessed in the Plantations of Queen Elizabeth I and Cromwell created a political and cultural winter.

The interaction of conquest and language becomes even more obvious when one country attempts to struggle against the tide. The possibilities that Man and Cornwall could have retained their Celtic identities, even within the United Kingdom, tantalise and sadden when compared with the persistent struggle of the Welsh activists. If the case of *gan teanga, gan tir* (the permutation of meaning also permits 'without language, without nationhood') ever needs to be proven, the Welsh possess the title deeds to the evidence.

The principal witness, and outstanding torch-bearer of Saunders Lewis's dictum that 'Wales will not be Welsh without the Welsh language' was born in Barry, Glamorganshire, in 1912 – and might have died by his own hand in 1980. In 1979, Dr Gwynfor Evans stated that unless the newly-elected Conservative government of the United Kingdom implemented the policy of the outgoing Labour government and established a Welsh-speaking television channel, he would fast unto death. The Conservative Party had promised the same vote-catching measure in all Welsh pre-Election publicity and, when elected, confirmed it as policy. Effectively this created bipartisan agreement on the issue, since the Labour government had already voted nearly twenty million pounds for the initial engineering and development work. Then the Conservatives changed their minds and the Home Secretary, William Whitelaw, announced that, after all, a Welsh-language television channel did not seem advisable.

Gwynfor Evans became President of *Plaid Cymru* in 1945, a post he retained until 1981. In 1966, he successfully contested the constituency of Carmarthen, and went to Westminster as the party's first Member of Parliament – then he lost the seat in 1970, regained it in 1974 until 1979. His Welshness derives from instinct and emotion rather than birth: he acquired Welsh as a second language and travelled along it as his conduit into Welsh culture. His choice of fasting as a weapon came from the example of Gandhi's success in India – pragmatic choice, too, in that during the time it takes for a hunger-striker to die, room is created for negotiation. In support of this proposed hunger strike, a campaign had begun in which over two thousand Welsh citizens, of all classes and ages, refused to pay the statutory annual television licence by which the British Broadcasting Corporation is funded. Further, they had no intention of paying the resultant fines; therefore the obligatory prison sentences would have attracted widespread attention by adding untypical people – septuagenarians, for instance, and bank managers – to the prison population. The government gave way quickly and the Channel, S4C, opened in 1982, transmitting over twenty hours per week. The results gratify Dr Evans's firmness of purpose – and in curious, novel ways. Welsh language enthusiasts could never have expected Will Cwac Cwac, the exasperating duck, or SuperTed, the naïve bear, to introduce thousands of enthusiasts. The Welsh language cause has been further boosted by the growth in demand for Welsh-speaking schools, and by the actual and curious creation of a separate Welsh accent in the city of Cardiff among people who are learning the language for the first time.

Dr Evans's threatened hunger strike updated the long, painful survival of the Welsh identity. In the days immediately after the Roman withdrawal from Britain,

Above: Saunders Lewis, 1893–1985. His radio broadcast of 1962, which raised wide fears for the future of the Welsh language, further assisted the cause of such cultural and political activists as (*left*) Gwynfor Evans: his threatened hunger strike 'unto death if necessary' forced the British Government to establish an all-Welsh independent television channel.

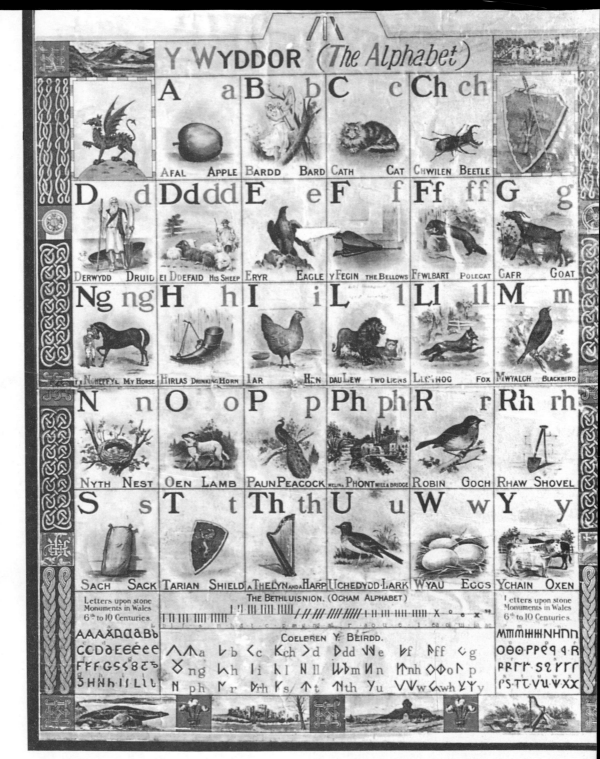

Y WYDDOR (The Alphabet)

A a	B b	C c	Ch ch
AFAL APPLE	BARDD BARD	CATH CAT	CHWILEN BEETLE

D d	Dd dd	E e	F f	Ff ff	G g
DERWYDD DRUID	EI DDEFAID HIS SHEEP	ERYR EAGLE	Y FEGIN THE BELLOWS	FFWLBART POLECAT	GAFR GOAT

Ng ng	H h	I i	L l	Ll ll	M m
FY NGHEFFYL MY HORSE	HIRLAS DRINKING HORN	IAR HEN	DAU LEW TWO LIONS	LLWYNOG FOX	MWYALCH BLACKBIRD

N n	O o	P p	Ph ph	R r	Rh rh
NYTH NEST	OEN LAMB	PAUN PEACOCK	PONT MILL & BRIDGE	ROBIN GOCH	RHAW SHOVEL

S s	T t	Th th	U u	W w	Y y
SACH SACK	TARIAN SHIELD	A THELYN AND A HARP	UCHEDYDD LARK	WYAU EGGS	YCHAIN OXEN

Letters upon stone Monuments in Wales 6th to 10 Centuries.

THE BETHLUISNION. (OGHAM ALPHABET)

Letters upon stone Monuments in Wales 6th to 10 Centuries.

COELBREN Y BEIRDD.

In the nineteenth century, the Welsh language and any remaining traces of Welsh Celtic culture came under great pressure from deliberate official denigration and from the industrialisation of Wales, with its inevitable influx of English speech. Some of the Welsh responses to such threats took a folksy elementary form – as in this alphabet wall-chart designed for the illumination of Sunday-school pupils by two Welsh schoolteachers, father and son.

tribes in the territory conforming roughly to modern Wales joined other post-Roman Celtic groupings along the west coast of the island of Britain, up through Cumbria into Scotland. Out of such unity – against the Anglo-Saxons – the two names of Wales emerged: *Cymry*, meaning 'fellow-countrymen', and *Wealas*, the plural form of *wealh*, or *walh*. This Germanic, and later Anglo-Saxon word for 'stranger', then 'Briton', derived, according to some philological sources, from a large Pyrenean Celtic tribe, the Volcae. All the Celts in this confederation shared, to varying degrees, the Celtic style of life. And all enjoyed the same continuum of Celtic expression in artistic and oral traditions – and the beginnings of literary expression – which flowered before the Viking raids in those areas which had survived Rome and defended against, or were uninvaded by the Anglo-Saxons. The Cornish succumbed to the Anglo-Saxons in the sixth century: the Welsh had more success – and even then recognised in themselves the glory accruing in the defence of their identity.

> Warriors rose together, formed ranks.
> With a single mind they assaulted.
> Short their lives, long their kinsmen long for them.
> Seven times their sum of English they slew:
> Their fighting turned wives into widows;
> Many a mother with tear-filled eyelids.
>
> From *Y Gododdin* of Aneirin, trans. Ifor Williams

The epic character of *Y Gododdin* reflects the Celtic warrior spirit outside of Wales, too. The Gododdin tribe occupied Edinburgh (*Dun Aedynn* or *Oddin*) and drew their Three Hundred champions from Celts all over Britain. But the poem's attribution to Aneirin 'of the flowing verse, prince of poets' shows how Wales claimed the old Celtic identity. Present-day Wales reflects the geographical shrinkage to which the Celts were reduced, but in Aneirin's day their federation took in many other Britons to the north, and as far as the River Humber on the east coast. Yet, the mood for survival, for a renewal of ancient identity, came to be associated almost exclusively with the Welsh – the only Celts on the island of Britain who, even then, made strenuous and continuing efforts to remain Celtic. The political aspect of this survival continued until the Welsh were eventually conquered and assimilated, first in their treaties with Anglo-Saxon rulers, then during the Norman conquests, and finally under the Tudors on the English throne.

And such irony: the Tudors, originally 'Tudur', came from estates in North Wales and Anglesey, and many a Welsh heart filled with joy when Henry Tudor defeated Richard III on Bosworth Field in 1485. But instead of celebrating a new fostering of their interests, the Welsh were further reduced. The Tudors, forgetful of all the military assistance rendered by Welsh fighting men, proceeded to rout the remnants of Celtic culture. All Welsh noblemen who aspired to the court in London sent their sons to schools in England, where their Welsh tongue was made redundant. The Reformation added thrust to the process: bardic schools, and other centres of education and culture disappeared when Henry VIII eradicated the monastic system. 'The history of the Welsh language,' murmred the commentators down through the ages, 'is the history of Wales.'

Two further hammer blows came with the Statutes of Wales in 1536 and 1542. In these Acts of Union, the *Cymry* became formally incorporated, united and annexed. Uncompromisingly, England stated the law's intention 'utterly to extirpe alle and singular the sinister usages and customes' of the Welsh. Although Wales was distant, still a remote region of small closely-knit communities, viewed from London as an outpost, no person could hold public office in Wales unless able to 'use and exercise the speche or language of Englishe'. But this was imposed upon a people who, for the obvious historic, geographic, social and cultural reasons, still remained monoglot Welsh. Consequently they remained largely unaffected by these new English machinations – until it came to the practice of law. Here the strictures became mortally dangerous. In 1634, Sir Timothy Tourner, Deputy Chief Justice of North Wales, complained that only three of the jury in a murder trial at the Anglesey Great Sessions could speak English.

An unexpected source – the Reformation's slow progress in Wales – provided succour. The people, comfortable in the traditional Latin, chose to continue with Rôman Catholicism, which – a further advantageous familiarity – used Welsh for the purposes of instruction. In Scotland and Cornwall the Reformers insisted upon English, and effectively reduced further the status of the vernacular. But the people of Wales would not accept a religion in a language they could not understand. And so, contrary to general statute, Queen Elizabeth permitted Welsh translations of the Bible and the Book of Common Prayer, and unwittingly with this, 'the Tudor blunder', she laid the foundations for the survival of the Welsh language.

The most important direct response appeared in 1588 – Bishop Morgan's Bible. William Morgan, from Caernarvonshire, had studied Greek, Latin and Hebrew at Cambridge. In his translation he achieved far more than the mere service of his faith. His gifts encompassed the poetic as well as the pious: his Bible became a cornerstone of Welsh literature, eventually constituting the single greatest aid to the survival of the language. As the language of religion, it thereby ensured widespread continued common usage of Welsh – but, more beautifully, it renewed contemporary native poets in the pursuit of their traditional expression. Morgan's exquisite grasp of the Welsh language meant that writers and students interrogated the Bible for reasons far beyond the Reformation's original intention. In the absence of Welsh in education, Bishop Morgan's Bible proved a most powerful tool, and under the Reforming English monarchy, religious matter occupied nine out of every ten books printed in Welsh. A standard had been set – however unwittingly – for the survival of a Celtic language.

The irony did not escape the English legislators and the Welsh language continued to come under constant secular attack. The insistence upon English as the language of the law led to courtroom experiences ranging from hilarity to tragedy – and possible miscarriages of justice. Beaumaris Court, on the island of Anglesey, observed in the early 1860s that 'eleven of the jurors were unable to understand the language' – and this two hundred years after Timothy Tourner's complaint of only three jurors' acquaintance with the official language. Welsh cunning had an occasional field day. In the trial of John Elias Griffith, accused of horse-stealing, the prosecutor, speaking in English, regretted 'having to address the jury in a language which they imperfectly understood': one juryman piped up, 'We do not understand a word you say.'

Less laughter attended the case of Richard Rowlands in the same court in 1862. Rowlands was accused, on circumstantial evidence, of murdering his father-in-law. The interpreter (each court had one, such as the local auctioneer, who frequently serviced Beaumaris) told the uncomprehending monoglot Rowlands that he was condemned to death, and Rowlands in Welsh said, 'O, remember these my last words to you. I am not guilty of the crime of which I am condemned.' Any chance he might have had of persuading the judge and jury of his innocence disappeared into the gulf between the languages – an injustice, whatever his guilt, which puts a chill between the lines in the local newspaper reports of the public execution.

When the church-bell commenced at ten minutes before eight to toll the death's knell, every eye was fixed on the small aperture in the gaol wall leading to the scaffold. At eight o'clock precisely to a minute, the culprit unassisted walked onto the drop with a firm step, followed by the gaol chaplain reading the solemn service appointed for such occasions ... The culprit was at once placed under the fatal beam and after fixing the noose the executioner shook hands with him and then withdrew the bolt and in an instant all was over. The majority of the women in the crowd sobbed loudly as the culprit was turned off ... We have only to add that Richard Rowlands dissimulated to the last, dying by the hands of the common hangman an unconfessed murderer.

The battle for the Welsh language raged throughout the nineteenth century. Official belief in London held vehemently that Welsh had no place in any dealings of any kind, that English and only English should be employed in all currency and activity within the region. According to *The Times*:

The Welsh language is the curse of Wales. Its prevalence, and the ignorance of English, have excluded, and even now exclude, the Welsh people from the civilisation of their English neighbours ... if it is desirable that the Welsh should talk English, it is monstrous folly to encourage them in a loving fondness for their old language ... The sooner all Welsh specialities disappear from the face of the earth the better.

Westminster continued, by way of commentary, criticism, legislation, to attack Welsh. In 1846, a commission of three monoglot Englishmen was sent to the region to investigate the application of the law in the educational system. Their report, published a year later, recommended that all education in Wales should be through the medium of English. The Education Act of 1870 introduced the infamous 'Welsh Not'. A board bearing the words 'Welsh Not' hung around the neck of any child caught speaking Welsh in classroom or playground. At the end of the day, the child bearing the board around its neck was beaten, or sent home in humiliation through the village, still wearing it. A child could only get rid of the board by passing it on: children were therefore encouraged to spy and eavesdrop on their classmates.

But where the spirit of 'without a language, without a nation' survived in Wales it possessed indomitable character. In the see-saw struggle, the Welsh fought back by contributing to the popular culture with songs and hymns in Welsh. In 1856 a weaver and his son, Evan and James James from Pontypridd, wrote a National Anthem, 'Land of My Fathers'. Local associations formed to espouse the old Welsh traditions. The establishment of the University of Wales in Aberystwyth in 1872, seemed to launch the language on a new lease of life. Welsh culture and self-conscious nationalism surged ahead, a literal renaissance, which took a further step forward in the foundation of the National Museum of Wales in Cardiff in 1907. Opposing, almost overwhelming pressures developed logically out of the Industrial Revolution – numerous English employers and workers cascaded into Wales. As a counter, Welsh national consciousness began to flourish in the industrial towns of the south and the expanding towns of the rural north and east. Welsh-language enthusiasts founded societies and newspapers to prevent the spread of English, while encouraging the love of Welsh. A Society for the Utilisation of the Welsh Language, founded in 1885, promoted the use of the composition, grammar and translation of Welsh in schools, and sought that Welsh be adopted as a recognised school subject. This – and other similar bodies – soon succeeded in attributing the beginnings of a cachet to the learning of Welsh. The principle of using Welsh in worship, established by Bishop Morgan's Bible, had long become the norm in Nonconformist worship too. Welsh-speaking evangelists, whose power of rhetoric rang like bells pealing poetry, attracted huge crowds in revivalist movements. Contests for verse in strict-metre focused attention upon the literature and culture of ancient Wales in the revived Eisteddfod – which became a fashionable and social event in the 1880s.

The social records of the time display a Wales without the equivalent of the substantial English middle-class. The culture, now with the added community power of the Nonconformist chapel, still bore the peasant traces of the old Celts. It derived from the people of Wales, was created by them. The sense of identity rose to the strongest heights where the Welsh language and bardic tradition had the widest currency. Welsh affairs, from the last quarter of the nineteenth century onwards, defined the connection between language and national identity.

Some English sympathisers, largely middle-class, cultural romantics, observed the vividness of the fight for Welsh, and apprehended – albeit ambivalently – the values of Welsh, the cultural, poetic and emotional properties, the literary potential. In 1865, two years before he descended from his ten-year occupancy of the Chair of Poetry at Oxford, Matthew Arnold delivered four lectures on 'The Study of Celtic Literature' – even though he could speak no Celtic language (and indeed drew heavily upon controversial 'Celtic' literary forgeries). However well-meaning the lectures, Arnold's ignorance and lack of a genuine Celtic cultural root become inescapably evident. The sentiments he expressed now sound offensive and imperial.

I must say I quite share the opinion of my brother Saxons as to the practical inconvenience of perpetuating the speaking of Welsh. It may cause a moment's distress to one's imagination when one hears that the last Cornish peasant who spoke the old tongue of Cornwall is dead; but, no doubt, Cornwall is the better for adopting English, for becoming more thoroughly one with the rest of the country. The fusion of all the inhabitants of these islands into one homogeneous, English-speaking whole, the breaking down of barriers between us, the swallowing up of separate provincial nationalities, is a consummation to which the natural course of things irresistibly tends; it is a necessity of what is called modern civilisation, and modern civilisation is a real, legitimate force; the change must come and its accomplishment is a mere affair of time. The sooner the Welsh language disappears as an instrument of the practical, political social life of Wales, the better; the better for England, the better for Wales itself. Traders and tourists do excellent service by pushing the English wedge farther and farther into the heart of the principality; Ministers of Education, by hammering it harder and harder into the elementary schools ... The language of a Welshman is and must be English ...

With such enemies, and without political power of any description, the Welsh nonetheless developed a pattern of protection for their language, one which ensured inspiration whenever (and frequently) necessary – and of a fearless kind, as exemplified by Saunders Lewis and Gwynfor Evans.

To lose your native tongue, and learn that of an alien, is the worst badge of conquest – it is the chain on the soul. To have lost entirely the national language is death; the fetter has worn through ... A people without a language of its own is only half a nation ... A people should guard its language more than its territories ...

But the man who wrote those phrases could never master the language to which he referred – the Gaelic of Ireland. In 1842, Thomas Davis co-founded *The Nation*, a weekly publication in Dublin, devoted entirely to the cause of Irish national freedom. Davis and his colleagues had a romantic idealism, named by others 'Young Ireland'. This movement, uttered Davis, 'must contain and represent all the races of Ireland. It must not be Celtic; it must not be Saxon; it must not be Irish.' And he expressly wished that it contain 'the Brehon law and the maxims of Westminster – the cloudy and lightning genius of the Gael, the placid strength of the Sasanach, the marshalling insight of the Norman ...'

Davis's romanticism bore fruit not in his own idealised state, to be founded on European, even Utopian, principles – but in eventual bloody revolution. The census of 1841 put the population of Ireland at 8,175,124, largely impoverished, with rampant disease, ragged tenantry. Famine ravaged the land in 1846 and 1847. Davis, aged thirty-one, and disillusioned at the political inertness of his own ideals, died a year before the Famine, but his principles remained carved into the Irish national psyche. Subsequent generations of nationalists regarded him as their inspiration. In 1922, Arthur Griffith defended the Anglo-Irish Treaty – which went some of the way to accomplishing Davis's objectives – by summoning the positive spectre of *The Nation*. He quoted Davis:

Peace with England, alliance with England and to some extent and under certain circumstances, confederation with England; but an Irish ambition, Irish hopes, strength, virtue and rewards for the Irish.

This seemed the perfect formula for the continued identity of a Celtic nation, a set of credentials which would satisfy all sides. But even when Davis forged such words in the middle of the nineteenth century, the frustrated Irish had begun to grow tired of negotiations towards Home Rule. The new credentials – blood-red, arms-carrying Irish nationalism – would carry the day. Within them Republican societies built a full range of symbolism, from the most ancient Irish to the sacrificial martyrdom implicit in Christianity.

In 1966, when the Irish government wished to commemorate the fiftieth anniversary of the Easter Rebellion (whose reverberations and mismanagement by Britain eventually led to the Anglo-Irish Treaty), a Garden of Remembrance was commissioned in Parnell Square, near the centre of Dublin. All the credentials are presented. At one end stands a wild and inspiring bronze group, of people straining under burdens, surmounted by the reaching figures of swans yearning to be free – the Children of Lir. The symbolism comprehensively summarises the emotion. When freed from the bonds of malevolent despotism a people regains human form. Ireland, implies the motif, had served many centuries fettered, impoverished and cast out by a conqueror – and the Easter Rebellion had set it free.

A cruciform pool dominates the length and centre of the Garden of Remembrance. Through the waters mosaics appear of Celtic spears, shields, broken lances and swords. This uninhibited mixture of Celtic and Christian symbol distinguishes and defines the nationalistic spirit of one man centrally associated with the Easter Rebellion – Patrick Henry Pearse, a barrister, teacher, romantic revolutionary, eventual soldier, devout Catholic, espouser of the Gaelic tongue. His mystical reputation pervaded the view in which the Rebellion continued to be held for half a century – and reflects the design of the Garden of Remembrance. Pearse sprinkled his expressions of nationalism with heavy Catholic analogies: the passion and death of Jesus Christ became a metaphor for the suffering of the Irish. 'The people who wept in Gethsemane,' he preached to his pupils, 'who trod the sorrowful way, who died naked on a cross ... will rise again, glorious and immortal, will sit on the right hand of God and will come in the end to give judgment.'

On the morning of Easter Monday, April 24th, 1916, Pearse, accompanied by several other revolutionary activists and thinkers, led a small body of armed men and women into the General Post Office in O'Connell Street, Dublin's principal and busiest public building. Along the way to their rebellion they received scant attention in the streets, a little jeering, some curiosity. On the steps of the Post Office Pearse proclaimed the Provisional Government of the Irish Republic:

Irishmen and Irishwomen: In the name of God and of the dead generations from which she receives her old tradition of nationhood, Ireland, through us, summons her children to her flag and strikes for her freedom.

The Proclamation declared the right of the people 'to the ownership of Ireland, and to the unfettered control of Irish destinies, to be sovereign and indefeasible'. Inevitably it placed 'the cause of the Irish Republic under the protection of the Most High God'.

The battle began: fire broke out inside the Post Office: casualties and their nurses, soldiers with the slouched hats of the Volunteers, others whose nationalistic aspirations had drawn them to Pearse's cause, were fired upon by the heavier concentration of military in the streets outside. Elsewhere across Dublin, sporadic fighting occurred, as urban guerrillas took over factories and public buildings, and commanded strategic positions on river and canal bridges. A British gunboat sailed up the River Liffey and opened fire: another did likewise in the bay. Within a

The Irish Frankenstein

The historical independence of Celtic Ireland continually recurred to the dismay and fear of Anglo-Saxon Britain. A nineteenth century cartoon from *Punch* portrays the Irish in much the same fearsome light as the Roman writers once saw the Scots of the far north and the Celtic tribes of unconquered parts of Wales – savage, terrifying and utterly alien.

Top: The Easter Rising of 1916 in Dublin, which left the streets of the city shattered, bombed and looted, marked the beginning of the last miles on the road to Irish independence. The symbolism of the rebels, many of whom were poets, drew upon Celtic origin and myths. In the General Post Office (*below*) from whose steps the rebels issued their Proclamation, they are now commemorated by a heroic statue of the great Celtic warrior-god, Cuchulainn.

week the rebels' action had been contained and the leaders surrendered. Pearse, symbolically motivated as ever, handed his sword to a British general – Vercingetorix at the tent of Caesar.

Thereafter one of the most potent forces in all the paradox of Celtic tradition came to the aid of the revolutionaries – death. After their courts-martial, fourteen of the leaders, including the seven signatories of the Proclamation, were sentenced to death. They included Pearse and his younger brother, William – thereby evoking the poem, 'The Mother,' which Pearse had written earlier in obvious anticipation:

> I do not grudge them; Lord I do not grudge
> My two strong sons that I have seen go out
> To break their strength and die, they and a few,
> In bloody protest for a glorious thing;
> They shall be spoken of among their people.
> And generations shall remember them,
> And call them blessed.

The executions possessed qualities both lurid and appalling, thereby guaranteeing widespread dissemination of their knowledge. William Pearse, who occupied an adjoining cell in Kilmainham Gaol, heard the shots of the firing-squad executing his brother in tne stone-breaker's yard. Joseph Plunkett, another poet, married Grace Gifford in his cell the day before his death. Most poignant of all – and in the long term, most effective in their ultimate cause – the death of James Connolly, Commandant of the Citizen Army: he had received serious leg wounds in the Post Office, had become seriously ill from loss of blood and gangrene. When the morning of his execution dawned, the authorities even feared he might not survive the short journey from Dublin Castle where he was held. Taken from the ambulance on a stretcher, he was strapped to a chair, semi-conscious, to face the firing squad, the last of the leaders to die, on Friday, May 12th, 1916.

The principle of Celtic martyrdom took over. Another commemoration symbolises it – the statue of Cuchulainn in the Post Office, depicted in his legendary death-throes, strapped to a pillar, the raven, goddess of war – and of death – perched on his shoulder. Pearse had taught his pupils to re-create and perpetuate in Ireland the knightly tradition of Cuchulainn: 'better a short life with honour than long life with dishonour. I care not though I were to live but one day and one night, if only my fame and my deeds live after me'.

For those nationalists to whom the Celtic traditions could provide rallying-points – especially in the absence of a vigorous, nationally-spoken language – the death of the 1916 Leaders offered the perfect opportunity. Death glorified them – and it also had the practical aspect of drawing worldwide sympathy from a public shocked by the barbarity of the executions, especially that of James Connolly, and touched further by the presence of poets among the dead, by the drama of Plunkett's marriage.

Heroes all, and how deeply they have reposed within the national popular consciousness, at the level of political and folk myth. Yeats encased them in the glorious accolade of his poetry, where oxymoron moans like a Greek chorus:

> Was it needless death after all?
> For England may keep faith
> For all that is done and said.
> We know their dream; enough
> To know they dreamed and are dead;
> And what if excess of love
> Bewildered them till they died?
> I write it out in a verse –
> MacDonagh and MacBride
> And Connolly and Pearse
> Now and in time to be,
> Wherever green is worn,
> All changed, changed utterly:
> A terrible beauty is born.

From 'Easter 1916'

The Celtic resonances, even if not naturally evident, were constructed to suit the occasion. Ancient heroes were invoked, and the glory of patriotic death dominated. A poor and ill-equipped thing the Rebellion may have been, and foolhardy – and in the eyes of some commentators, ungentlemanly, with England utterly preoccupied with the Great War. But it created instant mythology. Subsequent Republican activities and events reached into the trove of 1916 for nourishment and magic. Pearse and Connolly come to the lips of speechmakers with facility. (Connolly emerges with greater strength based on his own socialism: genuine political ideals have been wrought as much from his life as from his death.) The Provisional Republic's Celtic credentials developed from the new legend – envisioned in the blood-spattered flagstones of Kilmainham Gaol.

The Insurrection died: if the leaders had been hoping to foment national turmoil, little immediate sign of it appeared. But in the months and years immediately after 1916, arming and drilling had either continued with renewed passion, or began afresh in previously uninvolved areas. From 1918 onwards, and especially in the years 1919 to 1921, intensive guerrilla campaigns spread across all provinces. Flying columns of the IRA lived in the hills attacking convoys of military, and striking at their installations. Quick, sudden raids, based on local information, hammered the morale of many a British garrison commander, and no matter how frequent or bloody the reprisals, military casualties remained high and horrific enough to pressurise the political leaders. The myth-making worked in tandem, creating enough balladry and lore to fuel freedom's spirit, and, more important, to create international sympathy. No revolution within the British Empire had ever resorted to the international press as the Irish War of Independence did. Thus tweaked, public opinion – especially in valuably sentimental America and sympathetic Germany – proved as effective a weapon as the Winchester rifles of the guerrillas.

Quick raids on the flanks of a convoy, or a headlong rush upon a camp, then an equally swift retreat into the woods – these tactics characterised the Irish guerrilla campaigns, just as Julius Caesar experienced in Gaul. Admittedly few other strategic means offer themselves to a poor rural population, which has neither the strength nor the resources to found a formal army. But other characteristics of the ancient Celts seem oddly congruent. For instance, just as the Three Hundred were chosen in Britain at the time of the Gododdin to defend the federated Celtic tribes of Wales and Cumbria, and just as the Celtic champions of old were single combatants, the flying columns of the IRA comprised villagers and men from the fields – who in turn became local heroes. Each man had a legend – or several – attached to him, and this tale clung, tied on with threads of gold wherever he went afterwards. Those heroes who survived became politicians: those who died attained even more glorious stature. Michael Collins, most golden of them all, barely in his thirties when he died in the Civil War, stood – still stands – at the centre of the myth. Tall, good-looking, clean-living, agreeably boisterous, enigmatic, powerful and commanding, his very persona created a necessary legend and one which persists. Part of the aura came from his extraordinary work as an Intelligence Officer for the IRA, cat-burgling military dormitories and offices at night and reading documents taken from desk drawers and soldiers' tunics. The names given to him – notably 'The Big Fellow' – and the hero-worship, still attaching over sixty years after his death, make him a Cuchulainn-like figure.

I was born twenty years after the Anglo-Irish Treaty had been signed, the first full generation's space of Independence. The credentials which this new Ireland manifested as part of our Celtic heritage included the ancient mythologies of Cuchulainn and Finn McCool, of the Red Branch Knights and the Children of Lir – as well as Saint Patrick, Saint Brigid, the Book of Kells, the limestone abbeys in the middle of the fields, the ruined castles and the glorious days of the Isle of Saints and Scholars and its sacral kingship. The continuum of Irish nationhood came to us via these Republican lessons of forceful glory rather than the passive but more authentic residue of language. Even though it could be proven that Gaelic descended directly from Goidelic, the original Celtic language and its attached dialect spoken on the island of Ireland, and even though it could be seen plainly that such Irish-language organisations as the nineteenth century's Gaelic League led directly to the foundation of the Irish Republican Movement, the language never came close to equalling the power of the martyrdom. Successive generations of politicians betrayed it by never mastering it: contrariwise, those who made it their preserve created an élitism. And, bitter paradox, the people who spoke it by birthright evaporated, deprived by economic neglect, winnowed by migration to urban centres in Ireland, or emigration to Britain or America.

On the curriculum, subjects studied 'through the medium' (of Gaelic) carried an extra ten per cent in terms of examination marks – positing the ludicrous potential of a brilliant student achieving more than one hundred per cent, and the even more ridiculous fact of having subjects such as Latin and Greek, and in one (alleged) instance, English grammar, taught in Gaelic to gain that extra ten per cent. But against such largesse sat the dreaded compulsory aspect. Gaelic had to be taken, and unless the minimum statutory mark – the equivalent of a pass – had been achieved, all other subjects, no matter how brilliantly understood, were rendered null. Without Gaelic the entire examination stood at naught.

For the majority of the people no active consciousness of the language existed in daily life. Gaeltacht areas, principally along the western seaboard, in which native speakers continued to use the Gaelic vernacular, received special funding. But Gaelic continues to decline. Now that the myths of 1916 and previous political generations have faded too, the Celtic credentials of Ireland, which politically, culturally and linguistically remained vivid up to the seventeenth century, have been eroded, surviving only in the fabric, in the collective unconscious – and emerging unselfconsciously in the music, the speech, the imagination.

But how could the Celtic identity in all the richness of, say, the ninth or tenth centuries, ever have been preserved? Ireland had experienced centuries of the worst kind of oppression. After the genocide intended by Elizabeth I, and the unbridled murderousness of Oliver Comwell, and the life-denying, vastly unjust Plantations of the sixteenth and seventeenth centuries, which threw long-incumbent families out, and installed lesser British citizens, Celtic Ireland lay ragged. The great Irish families dissolved, dismantled, and their leaders fled to fight in foreign armies: the society which had shone since the times of La Tene dwindled into poverty and depopulation. Penal laws, introduced in 1704, restricted religious expression, ownership, education. Those people who remained Catholic were denied succession rights to their own land, access to all but rudimentary education, and freedom of Catholic worship. Facilities for educating priests were withdrawn – forcing scholastic candidates to seek seminaries in France, Belgium, Spain.

Eventually, after long and vociferous political campaigns, the government in London, which since the 1800 Act of Union governed Ireland utterly, was forced to restore Catholic rights, in the 1829 Emancipation. The refuge and inspiration now afforded to the peasant classes by their newly-freed religion became an inspiration. The church gate proved a powerful rallying-point. Politicians and orators who addressed the crowds after Mass on a Sunday morning harked back to a glorious past, the Golden Age, the Island of Saints and Scholars. Thus, the confluence of ancient mythology and imagistic Catholicism formed the new Irish identity – but diluted the true Celtic spirit.

Near Penhors, on the Bay of Audierne in Brittany, every September the smoke (according to one memoir) rises in clouds across the fields leading down to the sea. The people are baking the sea bread, in long, rectangular, compartmentalised ditches, open-air ovens, divided by rows of stone slabs. All winter long the women have harvested the seaweed off the beach, and when the tide goes far out they follow – the crop lies thicker on the far reefs. They haul the seaweed ashore, arrange it to dry through the spring and summer, and when the autumn comes, they burn it so that the ash from the burning of the seaweed falls down into the ovens. When packed into loaves of sodium by the men, the lorries take it away to the pharmaceutical factories. Some of the old women who look on, no longer able for the heavy work, wear the tall Breton coif, high and stiff with lace – unbending sails which add dignity, but little pace, to the progress of the ship.

Opposite: Workers in a sardine canning factory in Brittany. Many Breton women still wear the traditional *coif*, which varies among different regions. Apart from the music, and some spirited but sporadic attempts to maintain the Breton language, few other realistic traces of old Celtic Brittany remain.

Top: Grinding the corn in Skye. When the last of the clans settled in the Highlands and Western Isles of Scotland, to form a major part of the Celtic fringe, even then their troubles had not ended.

Above: Committed to a poor and hard existence of crofting and small fishing, many families became dispossessed at the hands of Anglicised landlords who evicted their tenants when they discovered that sheep yielded more income than rents.

The making of the sea bread granted the community a ritual, common in all peasant populations, and no different in practice or intention in Brittany. And a metaphor: old values have been processed. Just as the seaweed was destined for the pharmaceutical factories, Brittany's old ways have become subject to extra-territorial processes, but nonetheless something clear and identifiable still distinguishes the activity. Herein lies the danger – that Brittany and Bretons may only be identified by quaintness. Is this the same curse on any minority whose identity has clung, despite the overbearing presence of a host country or powerful near-neighbour – or, as in Brittany's case, both? The trap has been sprung on the region more than once, and in many different ways. Each way remains unacceptable to those natives who wish to believe – romantically or otherwise – in an old Breton identity descended from the region's redoubled Celtic past.

Nothing is left of my early civilization but wreckage. There are still some trees, but no more forests. To speak only of its objects – as soon as they were dispersed, they lost almost all their meaning. Museums have been built for them; and sometimes with touching care, the large room of some farmhouse has been reconstructed down to the last detail. But that room doesn't live any more, doesn't work any more. Unfortunately, some people got the bright idea of putting dummies in them to represent the inhabitants. Heartbreaking. All things considered, the objects are better off in glass cases. That at least is honest archaeology, and it interests everyone except those who see their own lives reflected in that archaeology. For it isn't the peasants who have a taste for old things; it's the bourgeoisie. A taste for old things is one of the obsessions of our time. Due to nostalgia for a period during which the simplest objects were made by hand? Or because they compensate for a way of life that urges change upon us season after season? A reaction against synthetic materials, which are doubtless very convenient but to which we are unable to become attached, as we are to sculpted wood, wrought iron, carved stone, and woven wicker? ... Or is it an admission on our part that our predecessors, however wretchedly underdeveloped compared to us, had a certain feeling for beauty on a human scale?

Pierre-Jakez Helias published *The Horse of Pride*, memoirs of his Breton childhood, in 1975: 'Since I am too poor to buy any other horse, at least the Horse of Pride will always have a stall in my stable,' said his peasant forebears. The book, later filmed by Claud Chabrol, focused attention and French guilt upon Brittany – and sparked off many a spurious search for roots among the haute-bourgeoisie. The brilliant coast of Brittany, with place-names singing in the charming 'z's' of the ancient Brythonic, offered a fertile breeding-ground for a new psychological fashion. This also had political possibilities: during the Election campaigns of the late 1970s, the French President, M. Giscard d'Estaing, 'looked into the Breton soul' and – hoping to find votes there – announced a cultural charter for the region to prove that 'Brittany is no longer isolated from France: there is no contradiction in being entirely French and living your own culture'. A politician's promise: Brittany, independent-spirited love-child of the ancient Celtic peoples, plump food for the slow buzzard of centralised bureaucracy, remains a sin upon the French conscience.

Pierre-Jakez Helias slept his earliest days in a box-bed: the metaphor will transfer usually in the contemplation of Brittany. A box-bed folded out from the wall, a separate domestic compartment and utensil, which only came into consideration when night fell. Made of durable, dark, fine timber, well crafted, sturdy, an inbuilt security reinforced with strong local linens and cottons, a box-bed offered a comfortable self-contained darkness and a place to dream. And in time the box-bed became a museum piece, viewed with mild wonder. Here in this old and restoring culture, the way of life possessed secure values. But now the quaint box-bed had outlived its time.

In Brittany the land looks and feels like Wales, Connemara, Cornwall. Two vast forces command the life – the Atlantic Ocean and the green rural hinterland. The waves break in their great whiteness all along rocky coasts, whose villages, one by one, must yield to tourism, to holiday homes for the Parisians or others from greater France, to British in their ferried caravans disgorged at Le Havre and Cherbourg. Souvenir power abounds: the striped Breton sweater of the *matelot*, and the bicycle of the onion-seller, such stock figures once in London and the south coast of England, come to life in the cobbled lanes of Brest and St Malo. The houses and white cottages, small and clustered, or sparse on headlands, like sheep on far hills, echo the Celtic cliché elsewhere, on the fringes of Northern Spain in Galicia, out by Clew Bay in County Mayo, deep in the heather land beneath the Twelve Pins of Connemara, the northern Highlands of Scotland. Fishing festivals at high summer, with the squeezed and lively *bombard* pipe, draw together groups of self-nationalised – as well as genuine authenticated Bretons and other Celts – in deliberate celebrations of the spirit.

The religion, the presence of the church in the village, and the personality of the priest play a part unmatched in any of the other Celtic fringe countries except Ireland. At festivals they lead the people in their great localised ritual, the *pardon*, sometimes in crowds several thousand strong as if demonstrating some powerful, non-political solidarity. The names of the saints who enchant these occasions, and their sudden feast-day egregiousness call back to mind the worship of their ancestors, the ancient Celts, twenty centuries ago.

On June 23rd at St Jean-Du-Doigt, the Pardon of the Fire;
On the third Sunday in July at Douarnenez, the Seagulls festival and the Blessing of the Sea;
On the first Sunday of August (Lughnasa in the Celtic calendar) the Festival of the Golden Gorse;
On the last Sunday but one in August, at Concarneau, the Festival of the Blue Nets.

Further within the souvenir culture, the word *pardon* calls up the picture of the inevitable Breton Calvary, the instantly recognisable group of religious sculptures in a village or by a church, made of limestone or granite and unique to Brittany. Many calvaries date from the late sixteenth century – the villagers built them to keep away the Great Plague, or to give thanks for having avoided it, and each one depicted, or referred to, the Passion of Christ. Encrusted with detail and embellishments, they hallmark each village and commemorate local saints.

The calvaries recall a tradition for monumental commemoration peculiar to Brittany since prehistory. Standing stones at Carnac – more than three thousand of them – reflect a power and engineering among the pre-Celtic occupants of Brittany. At Carnac, and numerously elsewhere, each stone, each menhir, whether singly or part of a group, marked a sacred intent or place. Each sacred place also suggested practical uses, so that a menhir often indicated a spring or the source of a stream. Other prehistoric resonances connect with similar sites elsewhere: Newgrange in Ireland and Stonehenge, where several of the menhirs are believed to have been erected with astronomical intent, in the way that the solstice plays such an important part at Newgrange. Did the pre-Celtic tribes of Gaul and the West already share a distinctive common root and ancient prehistoric culture? And the saints suggest the same continuation of the work of the gods. Saint Michael, the patron of high places, belongs to Mont St Michel, to St Michael's Mount in Cornwall and to Skellig Michael, the anchorite settlement off the south-west coast of Ireland.

Other legends, which transfer between pagan and Christian, upholster the national and pan-Celtic fabric. To Brittany, King Arthur and his knights journeyed in search of the Holy Grail, a cup out of which Christ drank at the Last Supper. By then it contained some drops of divine blood – and was brought to Celtic lands, Brittany or Britain, by Joseph of Arimathea. On the fringes of Arthuriana, Tristan, Prince of Lyonesse, drank with Iseult the potion which bound them for ever to each other, and when he died in his castle, she, though promised to another, followed him to his grave.

Intensifying the fate of Celtic nations, Brittany's credentials lie therefore in her psyche – notwithstanding a proud and independent history. The Venetii, who inhabited the Armorican Peninsula overlapping from Brittany into Normandy, gave the Romans one of the most difficult battles in the advance of the Western Empire. The re-migrations of the Welsh and the Cornish, and their benign settlement of Brittany reinforced the Celtic character deeply: the peninsular geography which made Brittany virtually an island, defined it. But time, and the unavoidable oppression of France have emphasised the 'folk' aspect of Breton credentials. The region has not survived the centralisation which Paris introduced within a few years of the French Revolution. In the two intervening centuries, Breton nationalists have had to struggle energetically to retain any cultural heritage, to keep Brittany out of the museums – a process which both initiates and confirms the embalming of a culture. The political annihilation of Brittany by Paris drew everything into line behind it – language, economy, separation of expression. The official denigration crushed every rising bubble of Breton independence, hung clogs around the necks of children who spoke Breton in school (shades of the 'Welsh Not'), allowed politicians to renege on every campaign promise of support for the Breton culture. Academics have fought battles for decades to raise the Breton language to the level of a degree subject. Small local radio stations broadcast exclusively in Breton and play music chosen from a wide selection of Breton and other Celtic recordings. Clubs and societies and theatre movements and publishers, all individual and without any concerted official support, maintain, according to their own lights, a vigorous effort to keep Breton expression alive.

In a population of approximately two and a half million people, it becomes more and more difficult to assess how many speak Breton. Decline seems certain, even though between a third and a half of the population possess awareness of the language in varying degrees, from an elementary knowledge to full daily speech. Where it strikes hardest the vigour of the campaign astonishes. Cells of semi-official activity, such as the faculties of Celtic studies in Rennes, purvey the language in living power and glory, running a forceful counter to the utter lack of Breton in the nationwide media of France: Breton-language broadcasts may be measured in minutes rather than hours.

Elsewhere, more lethal activity has reminded France of the Bretons' capacity to fight. In 1977, a banned Breton nationalist group claimed responsibility for the bombing of ten rooms in the Palace of Versailles. In the previous year the bombers' activities included over two hundred explosions, in which they destroyed tax offices, crucial radio transmitters, military establishments. (Breton activists even have their own patron saint – Saint Barbara, whose father died in a lightning flash.) Several nationalists were sent to prison after protracted and emotional trials. 'What inspired our acts,' proclaimed one, 'was a desire to live our lives as Bretons.' And from another, 'I honestly think that if wanting to speak one's language, desiring more freedom and justice for one's people, is to be called "a backward youth", as the prosecution has called us, then I am a backward youth and proud of it.'

The prosecution's terminology sums up the Breton grievance – being regarded as 'country cousins' by Paris and the rest of France (of whose population Brittany forms seven per cent). And in a deadly way, Brittany suffers the direct brunt of being regarded as remote, rural, unimportant. In 1978, a huge oil tanker, the *Amoco Cadiz*, foundered off the beaches of Brittany. A quarter of a million tons of thick fuel oil polluted the shoreline. Paris did relatively little, claim the Bretons – certainly the government, they insist, did not display an urgency comparable with what might have been expected had the accident happened on, say, the Riviera, or along coasts with more powerful national lobbies, Normandy, Picardy.

Within two years the protestors came out in force again. Over the rocks of the ancient coastal kingdom of Cornouaille the threat of radiation hung. Paris planned to build a 5,200 megawatt nuclear power station on the Pointe du Raz near Plogoff. Embarking upon the theme 'Brittany is not a dustbin', the people hung rats upon the telephone poles, emptied quantities of refuse in the streets, blocked the roads and lanes with tractors and protest marches. They confronted the military who fired teargas grenades, they marched up against the lines of riot police, they sang the '*Marseillaise*' to demonstrate that their protest was not uniquely for Brittany, but for all of France. On a hill nearby they built a large sheep-pen – without planning permission – to make the point that they wished to preserve life, and if necessary would go to unofficial lengths to do so. The official enquiry heard much emotional evidence to the effect that Plogoff stood at a sufficient distance from Paris for government not to be worried. The issue reflected the deeper principle, though – that in terms of the overall administration of France Brittany, Breton language and culture, notwithstanding old, proud traditions, now conforms to French identity: Breton credentials have no autonomous currency.

Poignantly, it was a Breton scholar who coined the phrase 'façade Atlantique' – to describe the once-uncharted vastness of the Atlantic Ocean, at whose edge all advancing culture had to halt and stay, remain suspended or turn back into itself.

Behind, and on three sides of the peninsula called Brittany, the 'façade Francais' effected, in real terms, much more damage – which will eventually prove terminal. If interrogated along the lines of Saunders Lewis's roasting clarion to the Welsh, and if measured further along the latitude and longitude of ancient tradition, every Celtic territory, therefore, has failed. Classes in the Cornish tongue may bravely raise a voice here and there: Manx affords interesting linguistic study and academic discourse. Welsh language still represents some power: the Gaelic of Ireland holds at least a position of respect in education, in some corners of society and in the verses of young poets. In Scotland only the Western Isles and parts of the Highlands can offer anything like a Celtic credential.

Every Celtic culture seems, therefore, doomed to eventual extinction. It may take several centuries, but the huge territorial imperative of the neighbouring dominant states, and the overwhelming force of other cultures cannot be resisted: newspapers, television, are no less imperial than actual military invasion. The rediscovery or attempted revival of Celtic cultures will dwindle inevitably – as in France, where Celtic languages in varying dialects of Gaulish, remained on the national tongue until approximately the fifth century AD, then disappeared with seemingly inexplicable speed.

Reach into the histories of the Celts for the cultural metaphors. On Skye, where the Gaelic of Western Scotland still lingers with a little vigour, you may reach Boreraig by road, but only if you abandon your car and walk some miles through rough ground, thick with ankle-trapping heather. Easier and more beautiful to go by sea, take a boat from Elgol, Loch Slapin, Loch Eishort: on the beige shore at Boreraig, several huddles of stones, the remains of walls, the outlined rooms of long-devastated cottages. In April 1853, the families living along the shores of the loch and a quarter of a mile up on the higher ground, received notice that they would be evicted by the trustees of their landlord, Lord Macdonald. He wanted the land for sheep – wool fetched a good price these days. The families were called Macrae and MacInnes and their forefathers had served in the soldiery of their landowner. The people grew barley, did some fishing in the loch, light grazing on the hillside. *The Highland Clearances* by John Prebble describes the scene on that 'golden day in September' when Macdonald's representatives came to Boreraig:

Most of the men of the townships were away, working in Glasgow or on the railways that were crawling like vines across the Lowlands, but some were in the hills with their cattle. They heard the crying of women, the barking of dogs, and a hammering as the officers nailed up the doors of the cottages. They came down in haste, and there was a short brutal struggle on the shore by Boreraig. When it was over, Alexander MacInnes, John and Duncan Macrae were in irons. They were dragged thirty miles to Portree and their families followed them, weeping. ... The doors were nailed up and the people were told to go. When the officers left at dusk the women and children crawled into byres and sheep-cots. And waited.

After some (untypically successful) legal representations in Inverness, at which a jury upheld the right of the people of Boreraig to remain on their holdings, the two Macraes and MacInnes returned to the shores of Loch Eishort, managed to reopen some of the dwellings.

'Five days after Christmas [wrote John Prebble] in a bitter wind and drifting snow, the factor Macdonald came again with his men.' This time the houses were rendered entirely unsuitable for habitation. For months some of the people clung stubbornly to their homes, living in the open, in the lee of a wall or the relics of a shed or covered with ferns, in rain, snow, frost.

By the first warm days of summer the townships were at last empty, and in time Lord Macdonald's Trustees found a tenant for the land. The market for wool and mutton was uneasy that year, owing to the war in the Crimea. Fleeces that would have fetched 21s. 6d. a stone in 1853 were being sold for less than 15s. but the newly published *Wool Market Circular* in Inverness said that prices for ewes and wedders were still high and this promised an early return of stability.

Due south of Boreraig, across a fat tongue of Skye, at Armadale, the Clan Donald Centre, organised and glossy, was set up by expatriate Macdonalds, Americans mostly, to commemorate and perpetuate the glorious and powerful name of the Clan Macdonald. They have much to remember – Lordship of the Isles, the massacre of their clan at Glencoe, the support and safety of Bonnie Prince Charlie. The publicity for the Clan Donald Centre even includes mention of the clan member who wrote the refrain for the song which became 'Loch Lomond' – but I searched and searched, without success, for any mention of the clearance of Boreraig.

9

THE LOVE OF ETAIN

Once upon a time in Ireland there lived a proud young king called Midir. In his fairy palace in County Longford he arrayed himself in splendour, for Midir possessed great beauty. His hair reached down to his shoulders and shone with the lustre of gold, his eyes clear, grey, truthful. He wore a tunic of fine purple cloth; in one hand he bore a great spear of pointed bronze, in the other a large round shield whose gem-encrusted surface gleamed in the sunlight.

Now, at that time too, there lived a princess called Etain, of gracious birth, whose radiant beauty, whose incomparable grace made her the fairest maiden in all of Ireland.

> Shapely are all until compared with Etain
> And dear are all until compared with Etain.

Eyes blue as flowers, eyebrows blue-black and shining bright as the shell of a beetle, teeth small and even, as pearls in her mouth: Etain's abundant golden hair was woven into two tresses and each tress woven into strands, the point of each strand completed by a little golden ball. Each cheek glowed rosy as the blushing foxglove, lips gleamed red as the berries of the rowan, each slender arm white as the snow of night, her shoulders soft, high and white, wrists tender and polished and white, nails pink and delicate. Her neck arched as long as a swan's and smooth as silk and white as the foam of a wave, her thighs smooth and white, her knees round and firm and white; her ankles as straight as a carpenter's measure; her feet slim and dainty and white.

> I do not know who it is
> That fair Etain will go to bed with,
> But I know that it is true
> The fair Etain won't sleep alone.

sang the poets.

Midir, the proud and beautiful young king, fell in love with the fair Etain and took her to wife. But Midir already had a wife, the fierce and jealous Fuamnach.

With her magic cunning, Fuamnach, jealous wife of Midir, banished the fair Etain. First she struck her with a rod and turned her into a pool of water. Then the pool gathered up into a great worm and the worm into a butterfly of purple hues who filled the air with perfume and sweet music. In this form Midir recognised his beloved Etain and she attended him constantly, lulling him to sleep with her humming and waking him at the approach of a hostile person.

But Fuamnach perceived this relationship, and in her anger and jealousy raised a storm which for seven years blew Etain the butterfly hither and thither, over and hence, across the land of Ireland. Her cruel fortunes changed when a stray gust of the tempest blew her through the casements of the fairy palace of Angus, in the valley of the River Boyne not far from the Hill of Tara of the Kings. Angus recognised the butterfly Etain as one of his own kind, an immortal, but he was unable to release her wholly from the spell of the jealous Fuamnach. Instead, he made a sun-filled garden for her, full of flowers rich in honey. In this glade she spent days of peace and light. At night Angus changed her back to her womanly form and enjoyed the beauty of her embraces.

The secret, though, was not kept; Fuamnach, still obsessed with jealousy, discovered Etain's hiding-place and again caused a storm to expel her. This time, in the palace of Etar, a hero of Ulster, the butterfly was blown into the golden cup of mead which the wife of Etar was raising to her lips. She swallowed the butterfly, who then entered her womb and Etain, in all her lissom grace, was born as a mortal's child, a thousand and twelve years after her first birth.

The High King of Ireland at that time was called Eochy, who had no wife and whose people wished him to marry. So he set forth to find Etain – his wife-seeking messengers had brought back descriptions of her famous beauty – and he found her by a clear spring, attended by her handmaidens who were assisting in the washing of her hair. In one hand the fair Etain held a comb of bright silver ornamented with gold: the silver basin which held her washing-water was adorned with four birds, and round the rim were jewelled clusters. In the other hand she raised a large oval mirror in which she perceived a face even more beautiful than her own – even though she knew that it was the face of herself, Etain, that she viewed.

She was draped in a vivid purple mantle, beneath which she wore another gown fringed with silver: the outer cloak was fastened at her breast with a gold brooch. Over these garments she wore a tunic with a long hood, a glossy tunic of stiff cloth, green silk under red and gold embroidery: it was fastened at her bosom with exquisite clasps of gold and silver and the bright gold and the green silk rivalled each other for the light of the sun and for the eyes of the men who sought Etain's hand in marriage. King Eochy was smitten by her great beauty, and thought her hair like the colour of the iris in the summertime, or red gold after its burnishing. He paid court to Etain, won her love and her hand in marriage, and made her his queen at Tara.

But the king had a brother, Ailill, who fell in love with Etain at first sight. So greviously did the malady strike him that he wasted away and made as if to die. During the king's absence on a tour of his kingdom of Ireland, Ailill was left in the care of Queen Etain. She questioned him regarding the truth of his mysterious ailment, and at first he hid behind much riddle and metaphor, until finally his obsession exploded in a torrent of words. He told her that his love for her was closer than a skin to him, overwhelming like a flood: loving her was akin to doing battle with a ghostly spirit, a spectre.

Etain, upon witnessing this surging tide of passion for her, and rather than have a man die unnecessarily, decided – although she was not in love with Ailill – to commit for his sake a glorious crime, and a tryst was made, far away from the royal palace. On the eve of the appointment, however, Ailill was stricken by a deep slumber from which he did not wake in time. In his stead, his shape visited Etain – but the shape's attitude towards her seemed chilly and saddened.

But – Ailill had been put to sleep by the fairy king, Midir, who then assumed Ailill's shape in order to tell Etain that Ailill no longer loved her. In truth, Midir had worked magic to oust a rival: now Midir appeared to Etain, not as Ailill but in his real shape, and implored her to fly with him to the Land of Youth, to eternal safety.

Fair woman, will you travel by my side to a wondrous country where music plays? In that land the hair becomes as the petal of the primrose, and the body assumes the colour of snow ... Sweet gentle streams flow through the countryside, there is honey-mead and flowing wine; the people are incomparable and unblemished, love has no sin, no guilt ... Woman, if you will come with me to meet my fine people, you shall have a crown of gold upon your head, and honey, wines, ales, sweet new milk, beers, shall all be yours there, lovely woman.

All this came as a surprise to Etain, who thought herself no more than a mortal, albeit beautiful, princess, and she expressed considerable reluctance to depart her palace and forsake her king: this stranger had neither name nor pedigree. Midir then told Etain the old story of their earlier love and of her butterfly origins over one thousand years earlier. Slowly she agreed to return with him to their old home in the Land of Youth – but on condition that her husband, King Eochy, agreed to her departure.

Shortly after this, Midir appeared before King Eochy, bearing with him a silver gameboard: the pieces were made of gold and jewels. The games began; time after time Eochy won, and as payment Midir performed great tasks – he hewed down huge forests, he made tracts of marshland arable, he built roadways through the bogland and everything he did improved the kingdom of Eochy. One last game was played and Midir asked that the stake be at the pleasure of the winner. This is the game that Midir won and the forfeit fell to Eochy. Midir asked for his heart's desire – to hold the fair Etain in his arms and be granted by her a kiss. After much painful thought, the High King told Midir that a month hence his wish would be granted.

But when the appointed day arrived, Midir found that Eochy had sealed off the Hill of Tara against his arrival. A feast was in progress, where Etain served the wine. By his own magic Midir appeared in the middle of this banquet, brilliant, shining, armed. Transferring his spears to his left hand, he clasped Etain round the waist with his right hand, held her under his shoulder, they rose softly from the ground and flew through the window in the roof of the palace. When the king and his warriors rushed out to apprehend them, all they saw was a pair of swans flying together through the air high above Tara. To this day it is well-known that swans, once they mate, remain lovers and partners for life. Midir and Etain, the magic swans, circled for a time, then they flew off to Slievenamon in County Tipperary, far to the south, and through this fairy mountain they were to enter the Land of Youth.

Eochy brooded, consulted a Druid, who soothsaid, with the aid of three wands of yew, that Midir and Etain were to be found in Midir's palace – which Eochy and his men then attacked, began to dig up. Nine years they besieged Midir's realm, with the fairy host repairing each piece of damage as fast as Eochy and his soldiers had caused it. Finally, Midir appeared again and promised Eochy that he would return his queen to him. Suddenly fifty women appeared, all identical to Etain. Eochy chose one – without knowing that she was his daughter. She went with him back to Tara as his wife and from their marriage-bed, father and daughter, mortal and immortal, gave incestuous life to Conaire Mor, one of the great legendary kings of Ireland, a hero for all men and for all time.

10

BEQUESTS

The descriptions of James Macpherson do not always suggest the most attractive of men. 'Perverse and unamiable', according to one source, he kept only 'tavern company, the prey of toad-eaters and designing housekeepers': other epithets employed to describe him include proud, coarse, sullen, lecherous, intriguing, bullying. An account of Macpherson as a young man found him 'a plain-looking lad, dressed like a preacher. What he said was sensible, but his manner was starch and reserved.' He stood six feet three inches tall, had 'a fair and florid complexion, the countenance full and somewhat inclining to the voluptuous in expression, but marked by sensibility and acuteness'. Dr Johnson had – unsurprisingly – an opinion, too, relayed, of course, to Mr Boswell.

I described to him an impudent fellow from Scotland who affected to be a savage, and rallied at all established systems.
JOHNSON: 'There is nothing surprizing in this, Sir. He wants to make himself conspicuous. He would tumble in a hogstye, as long as you looked at him and called to him to come out. But let him alone, never mind and he'll soon give it over.'
I added, that the same person maintained that there was no distinction between virtue and vice.
JOHNSON: 'Why, Sir, if the fellow does not think as he speaks he is lying; and I see not what honour he can propose to himself from having the character of a lyar. But if he does really think that there is no distinction between virtue and vice, why, Sir, when he leaves our houses, let us count our spoons.'

Johnson knew what he was talking about, but – alas! for them – many eminent literati of the day did not. James Macpherson perpetrated a series of 'Celtic' forgeries with brilliance and clumsy daring, and in the process he created a kind of bequest which dogs the name 'Celt' to this day. In 1759, at the age of twenty-three, Macpherson remarked to a Scottish playwright, John Home, that he had collected from old people in remote areas, largely the west of Scotland, several pieces of ancient poetry, all in the Gaelic, by a legendary Ancient called Ossian. Since Home did not understand Gaelic he asked that Macpherson should translate some verses in order to enable an opinion. When Macpherson did so and showed them to Home, the playwright became very excited, began to spread the word on the literary grapevine and took the verses to a publisher. What happened then generated great and wide blushes. Many glowing opinions issued forth as to the startlingly fine quality of these epics. One critic breathed:

The two great characteristics of Ossian's poetry are tenderness and sublimity. It breathes nothing of the gay and cheerful kind; an air of solemnity and seriousness is diffused over the whole. Ossian is

The Gorsedd, a Welsh bardic and druidic ritual conducted in association with the Eisteddfod, had its origins in a spurious eighteenth century ceremony initiated by an imaginative stonemason. Unchallenged, the rites, which were originally conducted within a ring composed of a handful of stones, have no direct relevance to any significant or spiritually important part of Celtic rite.

James Macpherson, 1736–96. His 'Ossian' forgeries hoaxed many eminent literati, but led to a huge revival *of* interest in the Celts and their civilisation.

perhaps the only poet who never relaxes, or lets himself down into the light and amusing strain; which I readily admit to be no small disadvantage to him with the bulk of readers ... The extended heath by the seashore; the mountain shaded with mist; the torrents rushing through a solitary valley; the scattered oaks; and the tomb of warriors overgrown with moss; all produce a solemn attention in the mind, and prepare it for great and extraordinary events.

Even such luminaries as Thomas Gray and David Hume, despite some caution, found much to praise, and abroad Goethe commenced a translation, while various European composers used the poems as inspiration for odes and scores. Artists such as Ingres and Angelica Kauffmann painted Ossianic themes. Napoleon read Ossian on his way to exile. Fashionable people named their children after the Fenian heroes: the King of Sweden named his son 'Oscar' – with an interesting reverberation; an eventual court physician, Dr William Wilde from Dublin, also called his son 'Oscar' and threw in for good measure 'Fingal', the title of Macpherson's most enjoyed piece.

All had been duped – or had they? The controversy over the authenticity of 'Ossian's' work lit up the literary world uniquely. Opinions raged back and forth. Dr Johnson again showed his superiority. Came the enquiry from a Macpherson supporter: but could a man of modern age have written poems of such evident antiquity? 'Yes, Sir, many men, many women, many children.' On the other hand, those who had supported Macpherson ardently and publicly felt obliged to stick to their opinions rather than admit their gullibility.

Part of the difficulty lay in the nature of Macpherson's work and the encouragement he had received. To begin with, he genuinely seems to have collected some Gaelic antiquarian material. In his own educational processes he may have become fired with the notion that the Celtic mythologies must have bred their own Homer, and this figure, if discovered and properly annotated, could make a man's scholarly reputation. As a result of that first enthusiasm generated out of his meeting with the playwright Home, Macpherson set off, sponsored by various learned authorities, on a tour of the Highlands and islands of the west to find this Homeric Celt. The days of the wandering scholar had not long since passed, and within living memory the strolling, cadging Bard, descended from the greater tradition, had been heard reciting in Latin and Gaelic. Some manuscripts of such scribblings, taken down by schoolmasters, or recalled by blacksmiths, even passed into Macpherson's hands. But clearly he fell into a gulf – between his own expectations (and those of the sponsors whom he had excited) and the lack of material sufficient to satisfy those hopes. Therefore he depended upon his imagination, and invented a substantial corpus of imaginary Gaelic epic poetry, attributed to a character called Ossian, who else? This great figure had descended (as Macpherson then encouraged people to presume) directly from the most ancient Bards of the Celtic courts in the west of Scotland. When he returned to Edinburgh to report his findings to his eager sponsors, he showed them scraps of papers and manuscripts – 'much stained with smoke and daubed with Scotch snuff' – and the beauty of Macpherson lay thereafter in the eyes of his beholders.

The suspicions began to ignite when he was asked to put his findings on public display. He rejected the implicit allegation scornfully, and over the next decades the 'manuscripts' – or rather, Macpherson's 'translations' of them – appeared. By the time he died, in 1796, after a varied life which included political positions of doubtful integrity, he had been thoroughly discredited, even though the myth seemed to be achieving perpetuity. 'Originals' of Ossian's work – to be more precise, the 'manuscripts' of them which Macpherson had 'collected' on his westerly travels – continued to appear.

In academic Scotland, in literary London, the Macpherson forgery scandal rattled on for decades: long, exhaustive *apologiae* appeared from both sides. But Europe still embraced Ossian: *Fingal, an Epic Poem, in Six Books* which appeared in 1762, and *Temora, an Epic Poem, in Eight Books*, published in 1763, remained as required reading among important people for many generations. The final verdict, to the extent that anybody has bothered to issue one, seems to suggest that although Macpherson undoubtedly exercised considerable imagination, especially in the Ossianic poems, there may have resided a grain of authenticity in their origination. But because Macpherson had promised to his sponsors – much more than he could ever deliver, he simply forged the lines to make up the difference. The wry observation arises that if he could have found some way of advancing his own literary case and had published the Ossian poems as his own work, he might have been accepted on their (sometimes not inconsiderable) merits: and the poems he collected could have been granted their status and descent as part of the oral tradition.

Their acceptance, initially in Scotland, and with much less doubt in Europe, makes a point central to any consideration of the legacy of the Celtic civilisation. When Macpherson created Ossian, Gaelic Scotland and what was left of its political aspirations had been finally subdued at Culloden. The Gaels, and those other Scots who embraced the romance of the Gaelic cultural image, had now been denied – for ever, it seemed – the last remaining glow of Celtic gold. Ossian gave it back to them, and in full: the romance, the pace and the pulse of the descriptions, the honour, the landscapes, the warrior spirit, the beauty. In effect a Bard had been re-born (born had they but known) and whatever the miserable political realities, Celtic song rang out again, the glorious past had come to life. The willing welcome for Macpherson's Ossian reflected a deep desire to cling, almost at any cost, to that – or to any – ancient pride: such seemed the force of the Celtic heritage. Without the prospect of a legacy, after the muck of Culloden, any bequest would do.

No civilisation which burnt so deeply into Europe could be totally eroded in less than two thousand years. But two categories of Celts must be acknowledged – the ancient breed, whose brilliance and lethal, migrating presence earned them the title 'Fathers of Europe' – and the 'Celtic Fringe' who now occupy the politically-created ghettoes along the Atlantic coasts of North-Western Europe. Undoubtedly the former fertilise the latter – clear bequests appear in the imagination, in the thought processes, even in the stereotyping first applied by the Greek and Roman writers. To identify the Celtic legacy up to the point of complete scholarly satisfaction simply may not be possible, especially as the Celts did not write down their own European history. Much of our impression, out of which we form the shape of any desirable inheritance, must come from the imagination – theirs as well as ours.

The warriors of the Fianna, who served under the mighty Finn McCool, were obliged to undergo several tests before they could be admitted to this extraordinary elite. Each aspirant had to stand in a pit up to the height of his own forehead and defend himself against the spears of the Fianna, though armed only with a small shield. He had to be able to run helter-skelter through a wood, yet not disturb a leaf or a twig. While running at top speed he should pluck a thorn from his foot, even though being pursued by the other warriors, and yet not halt his gait for a second. And he must jump a lath set to the height of his forehead. Unless all the tasks were completed, entry to the Fianna remained impossible – but above and beyond the accomplishment of them, the style in which they were achieved also contributed to the assessment of the applicant. Grace and individualism and panache were expected, and these, as much as the necessary technical, physical abilities, counted towards success.

A party of Celtic delegates met Alexander the Great, who had been much impressed with their fearlessness. He asked them whether there had ever been anything which they dreaded – and they told him they feared that the sky would fall on them.

Over the waters sailed a boat, whose mariner one day flung out his anchor and swam down the anchor rope into the deep. Just then, the people emerging from the monastery chapel at Clonmacnoise looked up in astonishment to see, in the sky, a man – the mariner – struggling downwards towards them holding on to a rope, and so they seized him. They thought he had come from the clouds – whereas he had the impression he was entering an underwater world. In the Celtic imagination, time and space mean all, and the same point may be reached from more than one direction.

At Lyonesse, 'among the mountains by the winter sea', the dying King Arthur addressed Sir Bedivere:

> I think we
> Shall never more, at any future time,
> Delight our souls with talk of knightly deeds,
> Walking about the gardens and the halls
> Of Camelot, as in the days that were.
> I perish by this people which I made –

When Sir Bedivere, having succumbed twice to his own greed, finally executed the king's request and hurled Excalibur out into the water,

> The great brand
> Made lightnings in the splendour of the moon,
> And flashing round and round, and whirl'd in an arch,
> Shot like a streamer of the northern morn,

Seen where the moving isles of winter shock
By night, with noises of the northern sea.
So flash'd and fell the brand Excalibur:
But ere he dipt the surface, rose an arm
Clothed in white samite, mystic, wonderful,
And caught him by the hilt, and brandish'd him
Three times and drew him under in the mere.

The difficulty in assessing the Celtic legacy begins with their renowned imagery, their imagination, their inclusion among, influence upon, later romantic European literature – even up to the comics and science fiction of the twentieth century. Macpherson, descending from, and corrupting, the Celtic and quasi-Celtic spirit, the pre-Raphaelites with their sickly heroines of long streaming tresses, have taken these qualities and used them to interfere with, romanticise further, the word 'Celtic'. That immediate view of the romantic Celt – though founded on the basis that at least part of the civilisation embraced a warrior cult and therefore a chivalric element – has too often led to the part being taken for the whole. Unfortunately their paradox attacks too, and on the wrong side: although the archaeology deserves all the sober study it receives, when finally put on display the artefacts encourage further the reputation for grandeur and golden power. Hochdorf's prince has become a case in point: when the proceeds of that burial were filmed for the first time, the television news bulletin called the event the discovery of 'a Celtic Tutankhamun'.

More practical considerations must be taken into account in order to ameliorate matters, and to balance the impression of a purely romantic bequest. For example, the Celts' abilities as a farming people – in which they contributed hugely to the development of Europe. The methods of agriculture which they employed created economies (and led to their downfall: the Roman army's continual dynamic depended upon maintaining supplies of food, and Celtic territories became granaries). Their advanced farming of livestock, in which they developed strains of cattle for particular draught purposes, their constitution and development of new grain cultures, their sophisticated herbal cultivation, and their all-round exploitation of this practical culture, laid down a stability in the countries in which they developed.

When this agriculturally-based economy led to a wealth, which generated a style – as opulent as the Prince of Hochdorf – other foundations of Europe, more imaginable than tangible, were also put down. France, where nationally the Celts reigned deepest, maintains a worldwide reputation for the good and stylish life. From time to time, the legendary Celtic descriptions of the apparel of kings and warriors and princesses have informed fashion. The style that was Gaul led, initially – however remotely – to the *chic* that is France.

In more cerebral areas, the legacy embraces artistic expression. In *Celtic Art – an Introduction* (1973), Ian Finlay wrote:

Romantic art did not begin with the nineteenth century. It is one of the problems of trying to clarify the study of Celtic art for the general reader that the subject attracts large numbers of sentimentalists and finds itself linked with causes from Jacobitism to Art Nouveau. The Ossianic mists will never disperse. But Celtic art is Romantic with a capital R, a major element in that great stream of anti-classical art which has contributed so much to European culture, and which later produced the phenomenon of Gothic art and – later still – such artists of genius as Byron and Beethoven, Turner and Delacroix. Without this surging stream Europe might have been a barren desert fringing the ruins of Mediterranean civilisations. Even classical revivals were to be inspired by Romantic visionaries. The strange, precarious tensions and balances that support the web of Romantic art are clearly present in the art of the Celts.

More than that, in the line of European art, no abstract expression took hold for a long time after the Celts. Assuming that we agree their decline at, roughly, AD 100, during the height of the Western Empire, not until the Cubists and Picasso, nineteen centuries later, did European art display the same abstractness. Within the entire range of Celtic art, the presence of representation, as in classical or Renaissance art, constitutes a tiny and late percentage, and registers a minimal importance.

The consideration of a legacy becomes in itself a quest for identity. The requirement to have roots, to come from some traceable collective unconscious, generates powerful impulses. These can contribute to some explanation for the survivals – such as they are – of the Celtic languages, especially in Wales. Some years ago, referenda in Britain failed to produce the necessary quota of majority in the issue of devolution for Scotland and Wales. Significantly, although the voters turned out in favour, too few of them did so to reach the minimum electoral requirement – apathy, not antipathy, carried the day. Thereafter, debate proceeded along lines of whether devolution would have 'improved' – that is to say intensified – the Scottish or Welsh identities. Those in favour said 'aye': those against said nothing, not their issue. According to disconsolate nationalists, the campaign was marked by a cynicism, not least among some of the elected representatives who sat at Westminster on behalf of Welsh and Scottish constituencies. They belonged to a tradition which had been eroded since the time of Henry Tudor (even before that in Scotland) and in the eyes of their opponents, their behaviour matched that of the Welsh courtiers who had looked to Henry's London rather than Wales.

In any discussion of Celtic identity, the stereotyping, which began with the Romans, arises. The word 'Celt', in most popular connotations, never reaches into Austria or Bohemia or back to Scythia, never countenances Hallstatt or La Tene, or the Urnfielders or the Beaker People. Straightaway, 'Celt' conjures an argumentative, possibly drunken Scot, an equally drunken but vaguely charming Irishman: both will have reddish-blonde hair and feckless airs. Hard on their heels comes an intense Welshman, small and dark and aggressive, or a Breton with an injured air of langour and a reputation for laziness. So entrenched are the impressions – especially the reputations for drunkenness – that it seems pointless to try to correct the impression, to remark, for example, how far down on the European league table of drinkers the Irish remain, or that many Scots, in dour religious observance, practise temperance.

They are exceedingly fond of wine and sate themselves with the unmixed wine imported by merchants; their desire makes them drink it greedily and when they become drunk they fall into a stupor or maniacal disposition reported an historian from the first century BC, Diodorus Siculus – and the stereotype persists.

Push the term further, and we create our own archetypal 'Celts' – Americans, wearing wide tartans and bearing a craze for photographing their roots. But those very Celtic origins, however vague or culturally vulgarised, have been powerful enough to create important political lobbies in the United States, where the Kennedys emulated the old system of the Celtic *tuath*, and used the extended family as a dynastic power base. And the Clan Donald Centre on Skye derives its funds from a Celtic bequest – the name Macdonald.

The legacy becomes further confused with such deliberate creation – or invention – of a Celtic inheritance. The National Eisteddfod of Wales offers a legitimate forum for the display of poetry, song, music: but the very word Eisteddfod also calls up – especially outside the Principality – images of the Druid and the Bard. Quite right that it should, in the sense that these two figures, along with the king, the silversmith and the warrior, once represented and guarded the cultural core of Celtic civilisation. Less pure and easy, in terms of a Celtic or, indeed, traditional bequest to Wales, rests the Gorsedd.

Gorsedd Beirdd Ynys Prydain – the Throne (or Assembly) of Bards of the Isle of Britain, meets on significant Welsh cultural or historical occasions. The members comprise the Order of Ovate, who wear green robes and who are regarded as having contributed to Welsh (and, in some cases, other Celtic) culture; the Order of Poet, Author and Musician, whose members wear blue, have been specifically examined upon their proficiency in letters and music and verse; and the Order of Druid, in white gowns, comprises invited people, all acknowledged to have made substantial contributions to Welsh culture, notably the language. A programme note from a recent Gorsedd summarises:

The Gorsedd is an association of bards, writers, musicians and artists along with men and women noted for their service to the Welsh nation, the Welsh language and its culture. The members acknowledge their allegiance to Wales and its culture by joining together in pageantry five times a year. They hold what is called a Gorsedd, and when an Archdruid is installed he vows to preside justly over the service of the Gorsedd to Wales ... One of the offices of the Gorsedd of the Bards of the Isle of Britain, therefore, is to remind the nation of its cultural roots, of its Welshness, and of the devotion of the Welsh people to the arts, especially the art of poetry, and all things created in word, form and sound which adorn the life of the nation with beauty and dignity.

For a non-Welsh observer, the Gorsedd creates a dilemma. Few doubts can be cast upon the laudable principles and cultural sincerity of the organisation and its members and events. But in origin and practice it belongs dangerously close to the bogus works of James Macpherson, or the soft Gothic rumblings of Tennyson, the drawing-room conceits of the pre-Raphaelites, or the salon-Celtic dabblings of Napoleon III. Rubrics of the Gorsedd bear names such as the Horn of Plenty, the Flower Dance and the Great Sword. Even allowing for the role which ceremonial may play within any culture or its expression, the contribution to Welsh values – much less to any Celtic heritage – of these dances and gestures and postures becomes doubtful upon closer inspection. Such rites, and the accompanying robed parades in green, blue and white, have fuelled many a lampoon, kindled many a spark of scorn.

The Gorsedd boasts precarious origins. In 1792, Edward Williams, a middle-aged stonemason and amateur antiquary from Glamorganshire, belonged to a group of London Welsh cultural activists. He made himself egregious among them by insisting that the Glamorganshire tradition, from which he claimed to have derived – which he did, geographically at least – descended without interruption from the Druids of pre-Roman, i.e., Celtic, Britain. He took the name of Iolo Morganwg, called himself 'The Bard of Liberty' (he had been addicted to laudanum as a young man) and set out to provide those marvellous necessities of arcane carry-on, a ritual, and some documentation.

The ritual occurred on September 23, 1792, the autumn equinox, in the unprepossessing environment (in terms of Welshness) of Primrose Hill, an inoffensive North London suburb. Iolo Morganwg and other 'Bards' made a stone circle on Primrose Hill, in the middle of which they placed a *Maen Gorsedd*, an altar: on this they placed a sword which the Bards gathered together, heads bent, to sheathe.

The necessary aged credential of documentary scholarship for this Gorsedd had about as much credibility as the spontaneous ring of stones on Primrose Hill. Iolo produced manuscripts from his own hobby of antiquarian collection: not enough authentication was called up to challenge him vigorously in sufficient time. His finest hour came in 1819 in the garden of the Ivy Bush Hotel in Carmarthen during the Eisteddfod. Iolo took a handful of stones from his pockets, made a circle with them and repeated the ceremony of Primrose Hill. The principle of the right man in the right place comes into play at this time – or rather the right ritual for the right moment. The Eisteddfod, as a national institution, genuinely provenanced and motivated, attracted in those days no more than lukewarm commitment.

We might not have heard of the Gorsedd again [wrote the distinguished archaeologist, Stuart Pigott] had not Iolo seen an opportunity for furthering his nonsense – for it can be called nothing else – by getting it attached to the genuine if moribund Eisteddfod ... The Gorsedd, which Iolo originally had hoped might supersede the Eisteddfod, was now assured of a future as an integral part of it, nicely calculated to appeal to nationalists and romantics, the credulous and the pompous.

Iolo and his Gorsedd caused damage in one fundamental way: accurate scholarship (which either did not exist, or refused to come forward) would have proven the cultural dishonesty – the forgery – of the Gorsedd rituals. But a popular and feebly romantic view of Bards and Druids was allowed to gain currency – the Celtica of the pre-Raphaelite drawing-room. Iolo and his pocketfuls of stones confirmed the popular images outside Wales of what the Celtic inheritance might be – men in long robes saying or chanting weird sounds and doing odd things within stone circles, and to what end? In Scotland Macpherson had forged a great Celtic poet-figure, and he gave those non-Gaels who desired fashionable association with the antiquity of the Celts, what they were looking for. Iolo did the same in Wales, albeit for marginally more genuine, if eccentric, reasons – and became a godsend to those who wished to see Welsh culture diminish. Remember Matthew

Arnold's attack on the Welsh language? A Gorsedd at Llandudno gave him ample opportunity to patronise the Welsh even further.

The Gorsedd was held in the open air, at the windy corner of a street, and the morning was not favourable to open-air solemnities. The Welsh, too, share, it seems to me, with their Saxon invaders, an inaptitude for show and spectacle. Show and spectacle are better managed by the Latin race, and those whom it has moulded; the Welsh, like us, are a little awkward and resourceless in the organisation of a festival. The presiding genius of the mystic circle, in our hideous nineteenth-century costume, relieved only by a green scarf, the wind drowning his voice and the dust powdering his whiskers, looked thoroughly wretched; so did the aspirants for bardic honours; and I believe after an hour of it, we all of us, as we stood shivering round the sacred stones, began half to wish for the Druid's sacrificial knife to end our sufferings.

The hidden agenda of Matthew Arnold's jokey and pompous patronage asked – and still asks – an awkward question. How can the genuine causes of Welsh language, poetry, music, identity, be pursued unselfconsciously – the key word in the preservation of any culture – with the continuing presence of such unnecessary counterfeit? Do the principles of Saunders Lewis and Gwynfor Evans need daft and shaky inventions?

The presence of the Gorsedd illustrates the dilemma of the Celtic bequest. In a number of territories the word 'Celtic' and all the attendant legacies has meant a pleasingly egregious identity. Being 'Celtic' guarantees a right to the possession of romance and colour. 'Celts' – with long memories – may still distinguish themselves haughtily from those who once colonised them. The modern Celt can create a kind of ethnic élite, satisfy the hunger for roots – hunger which increases under the pressure of monolithic cultures.

The old Celtic world stood for freedom on all fronts – imagination, movement, belief – as witnessed by the brilliant and curvilinear art forms, the great migrations, the multifarious deities. Celtic art, within its own form of expression, had no beginning, no middle, no end: of itself unto itself, it invited more than participation, it insisted upon total involvement, it became its own inner world. The right to interpret remained the guiding principle. Even when representational art makes an appearance, particularly under the influence of the Romans, who imposed the finite upon the Celtic artist in the same way as they had done upon the Celtic worshipper, the representation still appears reluctant. The Celts' great and ceaseless migrations predicated and epitomised physically their political posture: the freedom of all movement, intellectual, social, environmental, artistic, had always been much too important to accept any ordered enclosures such as the bureaucractic processes of the Roman Empire. The military reverberation of this posture gave them no protection: if the Western Empire had to be opposed, then it ought to be fought as much for the honour and glory of the warrior, and for the preservation of the familial society as for any national or political reasons. Vercingetorix, remember, could not raise an army against Caesar in Gaul without widespread coercion of his fellow-Celts.

In modern terms, and allowing for pretentiousness, the cultural revivals of th 'Celtic Fringe' represent this refusal to participate with the conqueror – a real

The warrior cult of the Celtic legends, given romantic emphasis by Arthurian legends and the idylls of the Round Table (*above*) continues to inform contemporary aggression. Republican activists in Ireland (*opposite*) frequently call down the names of the old mythological heroes in their rhetoric and in the names of their societies and clubs.

unrealistic bequest. The Bretons in France fight for independence, speak the language, wheedle, force or cajole grants-in-aid out of the central government in Paris. And all in order to distinguish themselves from France and the French by holding on to their intensively Celtic traditions. Although the political facts weigh overwhelmingly – ludicrously so – against them, stubbornly they make the language live on, in ever-shrinking pockets, and where spoken it creates the most immediate of frontiers.

The Welsh have perfected this device: their language is frequently operated, manipulated, as a true border – the speaking of Welsh in a public place accumulates and takes on a greater significance if 'strangers' are present. The Scots display more sense and realism: language and poetry, as spoken and practised particularly in the western islands, keep the sound alive, and some of the spirit intact. But they have long since accepted what happened. Two thousand years ago, the Celts of Europe, from which they are – or may be – descended went into a decline. History did the rest: the only real lingering defiance came, and still comes, from a scattering, in numerical terms, of Gaelic-speakers. And generations ago, Glasgow and Boston took the cream of those.

Being 'Celtic' today means old memories dying hard. Ireland, as it capitalised culturally upon the Romans' failure to invade, continues to plead a special case. Argument may rage: should Northern Ireland be seen as a Celtic legacy or a Celtic fringe issue? Magnificent rhetoric may be derived from the old Celtic imageries, of this brave and élite warrior corps defending the culture of their people against the erosion, and the final destructions of the invader. The polarisation between the communities underlines a cultural cliché – and the natives, aka Catholics, aka nationalists, aka Republicans, aka Celts have all the bright music, the native culture, the deepest traditions. And that the Planters, aka the Protestants, aka the Unionists, aka the invaders, aka the Romans/Anglo-Saxons, aka the English, have no indigenous culture. Where is their music? Who are their poets? What is their language? Back comes the cry – how many centuries do you have to live in one place to create a civilisation? To see it in terms of a Celtic bequest is not entirely or satisfyingly accurate except among devils who cite scripture for their own purposes. (In reality many of the original Planters of Ulster came from Scotland: out of what tribal or genetic pool did they swim? Some of the Picts, after all, spoke a Celtic language.)

The real Celtic bequest in Ireland lies elsewhere – in the words, and the way in which they illuminate the imagination. In this respect, as with Wales, the term 'literature' broadens to include the oral tradition. This body of deep and brilliant material, timeless and varied, has unique characteristics.

The first Irish poet, Amheirgin, a man of, and with, the Milesians, came to Ireland in 1268 BC, and bequeathed for all time 'The Song of Amheirgin'. In a reconstruction within his book *The White Goddess*, the poet Robert Graves, himself a curious mixture of Celtic bloods, interrogated the poem in detail and found many correspondences within it, which reached not merely into Wales, Ireland's nearest Celtic neighbour, and into the work of the Welsh Bard, Taliesin, but across pre-classical Europe.

I am a stag: *of seven tines,*
I am a flood: *across a plain,*
I am a wind: *on a deep lake,*
I am a tear: *the Sun lets fall,*
I am a hawk: *above the cliff,*
I am a thorn: *beneath the nail,*
I am a wonder: *among flowers*
I am a wizard: *who but I*
Sets the cool head aflame with smoke?

I am a spear: *that rears for blood,*
I am a salmon: *in a pool,*
I am a lure: *from paradise,*
I am a hill: *where poets walk,*
I am a boar: *ruthless and red,*
I am a breaker: *threatening doom,*
I am a tide: *that drags to death,*
I am an infant: *who but I*
Peeps from the unknown dolmen arch?

I am the womb: *of every holt,*
I am the blaze: *on every hill.*
I am the queen: *of every hive,*
I am the shield: *for every head,*
I am the grave: *of every hope.*

In an elaborate interpretation, in which he aligns himself with others who have attached the same significance to the 'Song of Amheirgin' – as widespread a currency, they claim, as the Koran – Graves relates the poem to calendars, to ancient pre-Celtic alphabets, and he argues both actual and mythological relevance, not just for the Celts and their predecessors, but for other early European civilisations – for instance, *a propos* that first line, 'I am a stag: *of seven tines:*

The antlers found in the burial at New Grange [the big pre-Celtic cemetery on the banks of the River Boyne, in eastern Ireland] suggest that the stag was the royal beast of the Irish Danaans, and the stag figures prominently in Irish myth: an incident in *The Cattle Raid of Cuailgne*, part of the Cuchulainn saga, shows that a guild of deer-priests called 'The Fair Lucky Harps' had their headquarters at Assaroe in Donegal. Oisin was born of the deer-goddess Sadb, and at the end of his life, when mounted on the fairy-steed of Niamh of the Golden Hair, and sped by the wailing of the Fenians to her island paradise, he was shown a vision: a hornless fawn pursued over the waters of the sea by the red-eared hounds of Hell. The fawn was himself. There is a parallel to this in the *Romance of Pwyll Prince of Dyfed*: Pwyll goes out hunting and meets Arawn King of Annwn mounted on a pale horse hunting a stag with his white red-eared hounds. In recognition of Pwyll's courtesy, Arawn, though sending him down to Annwm – for the stag is Pwyll's soul – permits him to reign there in his stead ... The fate of the antlered king – of whom Cernunnos, 'the horned one' of Gaul, is a familiar example – is expressed in the early Greek myth of Actaeon, whom Artemis metamorphosed into a stag and hunted to death with her dogs.

'The Song of Amheirgin' was handed down orally. (Julius Caesar had no illusions as to why the ancient Celts wrote nothing down – as long as knowledge, rite, wisdom, rune, did not become common property, those holding such knowledge in their heads exercised power: they retained exclusivity, and in the case of arcane practices, generated fear.) The literature began in the telling of the land's story by the Bard. The note in the voice of a rural Irish storyteller, a lingering *seanchai* of the last century, rang straight and true from those storytellers at the king's table during a banquet of the Red Branch Knights or within the palace of King Eochy. Such a narrator of tales arrived in his village in County Kerry or Dyfed or Benbecula via the ninth century, largely monastic, lyric and nature poets, and via the flourishing (despite – or because of – great odds) of the seventeenth, eighteenth and nineteenth-century poets in Celtic, who came out of the bardic schools and went among the people. The metalworker of La Tene tried to recapture the essence of his world in the making of a pot or a cloak-fastener. This basic impulse, artistic and frequently romantic, persisted within the literary expression. Daniel Corkery, in his book *The Hidden Ireland*, introduced the chapter 'The Court of Poetry':

Now again, we are in the eighteenth century ... I raise my eyes, I peer into the shimmering distance. Along the skyline of the far-off hills, I look for a clump of trees, gapped in the middle. A hundred motley fields of roots, of pasture and corn, lead up to it; and set haphazard among these fields, clutching them together, grouping them, are thriving farmsteads with trees and hay-barns – a homely landscape, its slope, its thoughts, its heart, one would surely think, set always upon this neighbouring city of Cork, its natural centre; centre too, for many other places, larger and much farther away. Hidden in that far-off clump of trees are the white walls of a tiny hamlet, Whitechurch by name. To the left, as I look, lies Blarney, and nearby runs the road to Dublin ... For me to gaze thus into that trembling distance, where the little wind-swept hamlet, trees and all, fades into the light of the sky, is to sink softly, and with perhaps some gathering wistfulness, into the Gaelic world of the eighteenth century.

So seductive are the images and idioms of the Celtic past – waylaying even a writer of Daniel Corkery's intellect – and so seductively have they been carried forward that the issue fudges between the ancient European civilisation and whether the Celtic fringe has descended from it. The most accurate discussion of the Celtic legacy requires commonsense.

The sensible summary of the word 'Celt' and what it means must proceed through a number of phases. It must regard the basic fact that on the western seaboard of Europe, before the Celts drifted over, there had dwelt strong indigenous peoples. Although perhaps not as sophisticated as the inhabitants of what is now Germany or Bohemia or Scythia, they nonetheless had their own culture and identity. They had not perhaps penetrated or populated fully the interiors of their countries or developed the tools to exploit the land: largely a Stone Age people, reaching into Bronze. Scattered, still instinctively nomadic, too few in number yet to have developed any power of migration or conquest – the nearest they came to political activity arose through internecine strife, over cattle or land or a woman or a husband or a possession. When the Celts came, migrants, colourful strangers, with superior weapons and utensils, they had to be feared, but also admired. They already had a name – perhaps even called themselves by it – 'Keltoi', the outsiders, the strangers. They had been developing for some centuries deep within Europe, and had kept on pushing outward for reasons of economics, or the sense of freedom, or the desire to flee invaders. These Celts took with ease to the lands in which they now found themselves, developing their agriculture and refining it. Much of this summary picture derives from telescoped hypothesis, based on a combination of imagination and material goods found in their graves and fields. The rest is, literally, history – and what the modern Celts have done with it.

But it cannot be argued that a modern person living in a Celtic land ought be regarded as a Celt any more than the invention of tartan may be accredited to the Celts, simply because pieces of plaid have been found in their graves. The idea of plaid derives from any primitive tribal pattern-making.

In the last, hard analysis, the Celts, therefore, must be defined as an ancient European people who spread across the world and who created a civilisation, with cultural and even genetic considerations. They had a grand mythology and they created exciting and profound art: these facts made them a most suitable case for heritage.

From the descriptions of the earliest writers we have established clear impressions of their warlike and hospitable behaviour, their mysterious and powerful Druids, their entertaining and clever Bards, their laws and their studies and the equal rights of men and women. We know how all that civilisation subsequently disappeared into the maw of history, overrun, swamped, by fiercer, greater tides.

But can we really reach out and say whether any of the true characteristics of the ancient Celts exist today – that there is a specific kind of Celtic imagination, and that the people of the 'Celtic Fringe' countries inherit it? Those vital clues to a culture, the materials of archaeology, especially the grave goods and lavish burials, have wilted in the face of Christianity's stark burial rites: the kind of funeral given to the prince at Hochdorf could never be endured within a religious framework that preaches

> Remember man thou art but dust
> And back to dust thou shalt return.

Some traces of the warlike behaviour persist, and may still be seen: more than one British general retained his Scots, Welsh and Irish regiments for particular types of bitter, brutal combat. In the armies of France after the fall of the chieftains in Ireland, the cry 'Bring on the Irish' rang out at Fontenoy – they had been kept in reserve until the worst. And always the music – no notation, no formal structure, just rampant imagination, embellishment, individual ornamentation.

The Irish and the Welsh literature stands as the latest, the last Celtic monument. The same kind of romance acted out between Midir and Etain, or the quest of the sons of Turenn, which flowed over into such works as Malory's Arthurian tales, still influences today's bestsellers lists, has contributed to the eternal triangle of Hollywood. But by now, any pure descent from the Celts of Central Europe has been so diffused, buried so deep, that any culture, fringe or otherwise which quarries – or forges – it defeats itself.

Civilisations prove most proud and wondrous when they are dead. Their former glory allows a genetically legitimate escapism which possesses creative value and provides that most valuable of personal commodities – a personal well, a pool from which to draw belief and survival and identity, proof of the need to belong to something ancient, wonderful, individual.

The word 'quark' is used by scientists to describe the smallest measurable particles of matter, so infinitesimal they make atoms look bulky. Quarks have four names: 'up, down, strangeness and charm'. The South American writer, Jorge Luis Borges, once wrote a story about a man who found he had inherited Shakespeare's memory. Yeats belonged, he believed, to an ancient tradition and excavated it for treasures of mythology and rune. He wrote:

Ireland has written in her Gaelic literature, in her old love tales and battles, the forms in which the imagination of Europe uttered itself before Greece shaped a tumult of legend into the music of her arts; and she can discover from the beliefs and emotions of her common people, the habit of mind that created the religion of the muses. The legends of other European countries are less numerous and not so full of the energies from which the arts and our understanding of their sanctity arose, and the best of them have already been shaped into plays and poems.

Yeats also reported a conversation in which he asked an old man in County Sligo whether he had ever seen a fairy or the like, and the man replied, 'Amn't I annoyed with them?'

The Celtic legacy is a local problem – if seen on the scale of the map of the world. The spread of the Celtic civilisation, no matter how glorious or grand in itself, when measured in the context of world culture remains tiny, an insignificant group of admittedly vivid people, who happened to sophisticate themselves early-ish in the history of the world, due largely to matters of temperate climate and willing mobility. They are now preserved – somewhat – in the language of those people who still speak, however diminishingly, a Celtic tongue. But principally they reside in the notebooks of archaeologists and in the glass cases of Europe's museums. In 'What is a Welshman', the Welsh poet R. S. Thomas, wrote

> The paintings are under glass,
> or in dry rooms it is difficult
> to breathe in; they are tired
> of returning the hard stare
> of eyes: The sculptures are smooth
> from familiarity. There is a smell
> of dust, the precipitation
> of culture from dead skies.

The romanticism which has permeated the worst aspects of the Celtic Fringe suffered early corruption at the hands of charlatans like Macpherson and Iolo Morganwg. Extraordinary configurations with hieroglyphics and mathematics have frequently accompanied the endless – but sillier – quests for a Celtic identity, and for a restoration of the Celtic Golden Age. The more relaxed aspects of Celtic civilisation accept that the subject has long become largely academic. In this frame of mind, excellent and absorbing archaeological, historic, linguistic and cultural results emerge, all of them valuable to the layman in halting, arresting or at least warning of the tides of imperial cultures. Admitted and agreed other characteristics f personality, of the imagination and even of behaviour may still be detected –

no matter how diluted the people of the Celtic Fringe have become. And the feeling in the bones, less reliable than, say, the language in place-names, at least assists the imagination towards a collective Celtic unconscious.

As a native of a Celtic Fringe country, in whose archaeology and whose history, powerful trails offer connections between the people of Ireland and the Celts of Europe, I have to face myself on the issue of whether it is valid still to seek a Celtic heritage. I am bound to answer that it seems more imaginative than real. I admit that I detect an undeniable quickening of my spirit when I stand in front of the bier on which they laid the chieftain of Hochdorf, and touch the gold in which they wrapped him. But there is an equal quickening of the blood on the lower floors of the Louvre among the Egyptology. If I grasp at the beauty of some of the passages in the *Tain* or the vigour of Bryan Merriman or the wonder of Amheirgin, then why do I equally quicken at the Greeks, Homer, Euripides, Sappho?

The difficulty arises when reaching dangerously towards Macpherson's or Iolo's nonsense. Unless placed firmly within the framework of the – admittedly dry – scholarship, the search for a Celtic heritage is spurious. Safe within that haven explanations follow and may be examined while losing none of the enjoyment or ebullience of the Celtic romance: the evidence, collected and annotated actually assists the imagination.

In their book *Celtic Heritage – Ancient Tradition in Ireland and Wales*, Alwyn and Brinley Rees made the following point:

In diverse ways, myth and ritual loosen the grip of the temporal world upon the human. Under the spell of the storyteller's art the range of what is possible in this world is transcended: the world of magic becomes a present reality and the world of everyday is deprived of its uniqueness and universality. The storyteller, like the juggler and the illusionist, by convincingly actualising the impossible, renders the actual world less real. When the spell is over the hearer comes 'back to earth' but the earth now is not quite so solid as it was before, the cadence of its time is less oppressive and its laws have only a relative validity … as myth and ritual are realised, the present world becomes a stage and ordinary life a play.

So it is with the Celts, and with any pursuit of them – the real Celts, the fathers of Europe. And yet, they offer the most tantalising glimpses. They believed in the suspension of reality. And they feared that the sky might fall.

BIBLIOGRAPHY

The books listed below have all proved useful, whether for consultation, quotation or background. This list represents a selection of essentials and (some) favourites. I have not chosen to enter the titles of all the books referred to, or otherwise used. Nor have I listed all the many journals, proceedings and other publications to which I made reference. I wish to thank especially the staff at the London Library, the National Library of Ireland and the British Museum.

Abercromby, John, *The Bronze Age Pottery of Great Britain and Ireland.* Clarendon Press, Oxford, 1912.

Annals of the Four Masters of the Kingdom of Ireland. Hodges & Smith, Dublin, 1851.

Ashe, Geoffrey, *King Arthur's Avalon.* Fontana, London, 1973.

Barber, Richard, *The Arthurian Legends.* The Boydell Press, London, 1979.

Barber, Richard, *A Companion to World Mythology.* Kestrel Books, London, 1979.

Beckett, J.C., *The Making of Modern Ireland, 1603–1923.* Faber & Faber, London 1969.

Bettelheim, Bruno, *The Uses of Enchantment.* Thames & Hudson, London, 1976.

Bieler, Ludwig, *Ireland. Harbinger of the Middle Ages.* Oxford University Press, 1963.

Bingham, Caroline, *James I of England.* Weidenfeld & Nicolson, London, 1981.

Borlase, William, *Dolmens of Ireland.* Chapman & Hall, London, 1879.

Boswell, James, *The Life of Johnson.* Penguin, London, 1979.

Brailsford, John, *Early Celtic Masterpieces from Britain.* British Museum Publications, London, 1975.

Briggs, Katherine, *Abbeylubbers, Banshees & Boggarts.* Kestrel Books, London, 1979.

Brown, Peter, *The Book of Kells.* Thames & Hudson, London, 1980.

Caesar, Julius, *The Conquest of Gaul* (Trans. S.A. Handford). Penguin, London, 1951.

de Camp, L. Sprague and Catherine C., *Citadels of Mystery.* Fontana, London, 1972.

Campbell, Joseph, *The Masks of God.* Viking Press. USA, 1968.

Carney, James, *Early Irish Poetry.* Mercier Press, Dublin, 1965.

Carney, James and Green, David, *Celtic Studies.* Routledge & Kegan Paul, London, 1968.

Cavendish, Richard, *King Arthur and the Grail.* Granada, London, 1980.

Chadwick, Nora, *The Celts.* Penguin, London, 1970.

Chapman, Malcolm, *The Gaelic Vision in Scottish Culture*. Croom Helm, London, 1978.

Childe, V. Gordon, *The Dawn of European Civilisation*. Routledge & Kegan Paul, London, 1957.

Chippindale, Christopher, *Stonehenge Complete*. Thames & Hudson, London, 1978.

Clark, Grahame and Piggott, Stuart, *Prehistoric Studies*. Hutchinson, London, 1965.

Coles, J.M. and Harding, A.F., *The Bronze Age in Europe*. Methuen, London, 1979.

Collis, John, *European Iron Age*. Batsford, London, 1984.

Cowe, P. (ed.), *Treasures of Early Irish Art, 1500 BC–AD 1500*. Metropolitan Museum of Art, New York, 1977.

Cruise O'Brien, Conor and Maire, *A Concise History of Ireland*. Thames & Hudson, Ireland, 1972.

Cunliffe, Barry, *The Celtic World*. The Bodley Head, London, 1979.

Dillon, Myles, *Early Irish Society*. Colm O'Lochlainn, Dublin, 1954.

Ellmann, Richard, *James Joyce*. Oxford University Press, 1959.

Filip, Jan, *Celtic Civilisation and its Heritage*. Collett's, Wellingborough UK, in association with Academia, Prague, Czechoslovakia, 1977.

Finlay, Ian, *Celtic Art: An Introduction*. Faber & Faber, London 1973.

Flower, Robin, *The Irish Tradition*. Oxford University Press, 1947.

Fox, Cyril, *Pattern & Purpose – A Survey of Early Celtic Art in Britain*. National Museum of Wales, 1958.

Fox, Cyril, *A Find of the Early Iron Age from Llyn Cerrig Bach, Anglesey*. National Museum of Wales, 1946.

Fox, Cyril, *The Personality of Britain*. National Museum of Wales, Cardiff, 1952.

Gantz, Jeffrey (trans.), *Early Irish Myths and Sagas*. Penguin, London, 1981.

Gibbon, Edward, *Decline and Fall of the Roman Empire*. Oxford University Press, 1929.

Giot, P.R., *Brittany*. Oxford University Press, 1960.

Giraldus Cambrensis, *Topography of Ireland*. Dun Dealgan Press, Dundalk, 1951.

Glover, Janet R., *The Story of Scotland*. Faber & Faber, London, 1960.

Grant, Michael, *History of Rome*. Faber & Faber, London, 1979.

Graves, Robert (Introduction), *Larousse Encyclopaedia of Mythology*. Hamlyn, London, 1959.

Graves, Robert, *The White Goddess*. Faber & Faber, London, 1961.

Guest, Charlotte (ed.), *The Mabinogion*. Folio Society, London, 1980.

Gwilym, Dafydd ap, *Selected Poems*: (trans. Rachel Bromwich). Penguin, London, 1985.

Healy, James N., *Second Book of Irish Ballads*. Mercier Press, Ireland, 1962.

Helias, Pierre-Jakez. *The Horse of Pride*. Yale University Press, London, 1978.

Henry, Francoise, *Irish Art in the Early Christian Period to AD 800*. Methuen, London, 1965.

Herity, Michael and Eogan, George, *Ireland in Prehistory*. Routledge & Kegan Paul, London, 1977.

Hughs, Robert, *The Shock of the New*. B.B.C., London, 1982.

Humble, Richard, *The Saxon Kings*. Weidenfeld & Nicolson, London, 1980.

Humphreys, Emyr, *The Taliesin Tradition*. Black Raven Press, London, 1983.

Hyde, Douglas, *Literary History of Ireland*. T. Fisher Unwin, London, 1889.

Jackson, Kenneth H., *A Celtic Miscellany*. Routledge & Kegan Paul, London, 1951.

Jeffares, A. Norman, *W.B. Yeats: Man and Poet*. Routledge & Kegan Paul, London, 1949.

Jones, Gwyn (ed.), *The Oxford Book of Welsh Verse in English*. Oxford University Press, 1983.

Joyce, James, *Finnegans Wake*. Faber & Faber, London, 1975.

Jung, C.G., *The Undiscovered Self*. Routledge & Kegan Paul, London, 1958.

Jung, C.G., *Four Archetypes*. Routledge & Kegan Paul, London, 1972.

Kearney, Richard (ed.), *The Irish Mind*. Wolfhound Press, Dublin, 1985.

Kennelly, Brendan (ed.), *The Penguin Book of Irish Verse*, Penguin, London, 1970.

Kilbride-Jones, H.E., *Celtic Craftsmanship in Bronze*. Croom Helm, London, 1980.

Kinsella, Thomas (trans.), *The Tain*. Dolmen Press, Dublin/Oxford University Press, 1969.

Kinsella, Thomas (ed.), *The New Oxford Book of Irish Verse*. Oxford University Press, London, 1986.

Kruta, V. & Forman, W., *The Celts of the West*. Orbis, London, 1985.

Laing, Lloyd, *The Archaeology of late Celtic Britain & Scotland*. Methuen, London, 1975.

Laing, Lloyd, *Celtic Britain*. Routledge & Kegan Paul, London, 1979.

Lavelle, Des, *Skellig – Island Outpost of Europe*. The O'Brien Press, Dublin, 1976.

Lehane, Brendan, *The Quest of Three Abbots*. John Murray, London, 1968.

MacCana, Proinsias, *Literature in Irish*. Department of Foreign Affairs, Dublin, 1980.

MacCana, Proinsias, *Celtic Mythology*. Newnes Books, London, 1968.

MacGregor, Morna, *Early Celtic Art in North Britain*. Leicester University Press, London, 1976.

Maclean, Fitzroy, *A Concise History of Scotland*. Thames & Hudson, London, 1970.

MacLean, Sorley, *Springtime and Neaptide – Selected Poems, 1932–1972*. Canongate, Edinburgh, 1981.

MacNeill, Maire, *The Festival of Lughnasa*. Oxford University Press, 1962.

MacReamoinn, Sean, *The Pleasures of Gaelic Poetry*. Allen Lane, London, 1982.

Malory, Thomas, *The Chronicles of King Arthur*. Oxford University Press, 1977.

MacHugh, Roland, *Annotations to Finnegans Wake*. Routledge & Kegan Paul, London, 1980.

Megaw, J.S., *Art of the European Iron Age*. Adams & Dart, London, 1970.

Montague, John (ed.), *Faber Book of Irish Verse*. Faber & Faber, London, 1974.

Neill, Kenneth, *An Illustrated History of the Irish People*. Gill & Macmillan, Dublin. 1979.

Norton-Taylor, Duncan, *The Celts*. Time-Life Books, USA, 1975.

O'Curry, Eoghan, *On the manners & Customs of the Ancient Irish*. William & Norgate, London, 1873.

O'Kelly, Claire, *Illustrated Guide to Newgrange*. John English, Wexford, 1967.

O'hOgain, Daithi, *The Hero in Irish Folk History*. Gill & Macmillan, Dublin, 1985.

Paor, Liam & Maire de, *Early Christian Ireland*. Thames & Hudson, London, 1958.

Piggott, Stuart, *Ancient Europe*. Edinburgh University Press, 1965.

Piggott, Stuart, *The Druids*. Thames & Hudson, London, 1968.

Powell, T.G.E., *The Celts*. Thames & Hudson, London, 1958.

Prebble, John, *Culloden*. Penguin, London, 1967.

Prebble, John, *The Highland Clearances*. Penguin, London, 1969.

Raftery, Barry, *La Tene in Ireland*. Available through the School of Celtic Studies in Dublin.

Rees, Alwyn and Brinley, *Celtic Heritage – Ancient Tradition in Ireland and Wales*. Thames & Hudson, London, 1961.

Richmond, I.A., *Roman Britain*, Penguin, London, 1963.

Ritchie, Graham and Anna, *Scotland, Archaeology & Early History*. Thames & Hudson, London, 1981.

Ross, Anne, *Everyday Life of the Pagan Celts*. Batsford, London, 1970.

Rowan, J. Eric, *Art in Wales 200 BC–AD 1850*. Welsh Arts Council/University of Wales Press, Cardiff, UK, 1978.

Scullard, H.H., *From the Gracchi to Nero — a History of Rome from 133 BC to AD 68*. Methuen, London, 1959.

Sharkey, John, *Celtic Mysteries – The Ancient Religion*. Crossroads Publishing, New York, 1975.

Stead, I.M., *The Battersea Shield*. British Museum Publications, London, 1985.

Stephens, Meic, *Linguistic Minorities in Western Europe*. Gomer Press, UK, 1976.

Taylor, B. and Brewer, E., *The Return of King Arthur*. Boydell & Brewer, London, 1983.

Taylor, Roger, *The Death and Resurrection Show*. Anthony Blond, London, 1985.

Tennyson, Alfred, *Poems and Plays*. Oxford University Press, 1971.

Thomas, Gwyn, *Living a Life – Selected Poems, 1962–'82*. Scott Rollins/Selected Books, Amsterdam, 1982.

Thompson, E.A., *Who Was Saint Patrick?* The Boydell Press, London, 1985.

Thuente, Mary, *W.B. Yeats and Irish Folklore*. Gill & Macmillan, Dublin, 1980.

Tolstoy, Nikolai, *The Quest for Merlin*. Hamish Hamilton, London, 1985.

Wacher, John, *The Coming of Rome*. Routledge & Kegan Paul, London, 1979.

Waddell, Helen, *The Wandering Scholars*. Constable, London, 1954.

Whitehouse, David and Ruth, *Archaeological Atlas of the World*. Thames & Hudson, London, 1975.

Williamson, Duncan, *Fireside Tales of the Traveller Children*. Canongate, Edinburgh, 1983.

Wilson, David, *The Anglo-Saxons*. Thames & Hudson, London, 1960.

Yeats, W.B., *Collected Poems*. Macmillan, London, 1973.

Yeats, W.B., *A Vision*. Macmillan, London, 1981.

Yeats, W.B., *Fairy and Folk Tales of Ireland*. Colin Smythe, UK, 1973.

INDEX

Page numbers in italics refer to illustrations